ICE 'N' GO

ICE 'N' GO

Score in Sports and Life

Jenny Moshak with Debby Schriver

The University of Tennessee Press • Knoxville

Copyright © 2013 by The University of Tennessee Press / Knoxville.
All Rights Reserved. Manufactured in the United States of America.
First Edition.

Unless otherwise noted, the photographs have been created by
or are the property of Jenny Moshak.

The paper in this book meets the requirements of American National
Standards Institute / National Information Standards Organization specification
Z39.48–1992 (Permanence of Paper). It contains 30 percent post-consumer waste
and is certified by the Forest Stewardship Council.

Library of Congress Cataloging-in-Publication Data

Moshak, Jenny.
Ice 'n' go: a perspective on sports and life / Jenny Moshak with Debby Schriver.
— First Edition.
pages cm
Includes bibliographical references and index.
ISBN-13: 978-1-57233-871-5 (hardcover: alk. paper)
ISBN-10: 1-57233-871-7 (hardcover: alk. paper)
1. University of Tennessee, Knoxville—Sports.
2. Physical education and training—United States.
3. Sports for women—United States.
I. Schriver, Debby. II. Title.
III. Title: Ice 'n' go

GV691.U58M67 2013
796.04'30976885—dc23
2013001540

To my family who keeps steering me in the right direction;
to all my great friends who fuel me, it's all about the positive energy;
to Mike, Barb, Karen, and Jim, the best ride leaders ever,
I would ride with you anywhere;
and to Chris, my partner, through every journey in life,
because this is no guided tour.

Life is like riding a bicycle. To keep your balance you must keep moving.
—Albert Einstein

Contents

Figures

Tables

Foreword

When I began coaching the University of Tennessee Lady Volunteer basket-ball team in 1974, it was just two years after Title IX federal legislation was passed. At the time, I'm not sure I realized the impact it would genuinely have on women in sports. Looking back now, I am amazed how different our world is today. I am thrilled to see the shift from limited opportunities for women to endless possibilities. I am thankful for the visionary leaders who pressed the question of equity, and the courage of their convictions which created a wider world for all of us.

A beneficiary of one of those endless possibilities is Jenny Moshak, who broke through her own glass ceiling by joining the ranks of the certified athletic trainers and certified strength and conditioning specialists—a field which had been predominately male-oriented for so many generations in collegiate sports.

For twenty-five years, I have seen Jenny excel as absolutely one of the best in the sports medicine business. Now you can read about her compre-hensive examination of the role of sport in life in this book. During her career, Jenny has always been an advocate of enjoying the journey in sports. In addition to her great expertise in the field, she has always surrounded herself with outstanding people and put into practice the sound advice from physicians, researchers, psychologists, sociologists, coaches, and pro-fessional athletes. I have always said, "You win in life with great people." Jenny is definitely one of those, and her spirit comes through on every page of this work.

Ice 'n' Go is a culmination of the breadth of knowledge and insights from her career in sports medicine. In this book, she covers a broad spec-trum of preoccupations related to sport and well being: social issues, medi-cal concerns, motivational techniques, gender roles and expectations, the impact of youth sports on our children, and how the body works, heals, and recovers. Jenny offers a holistic model for athletes of all ages and abilities to balance the mind, body, and spirit as a way to enjoy the journey. An out-standing athlete herself, she also shares lessons she learned during her own demanding cycling ride from coast-to-coast of the United States.

As a parent of an athlete, I recommend this as a must-read for all families with children involved in the sport experience. Our youth are now suffering significant injuries at earlier ages. Obesity is at an all-time high. Sound nutritional diets have fallen prey to the lure of convenience and false promises of instant energy. Battled and bruised, our youngest athletes are showing signs of burnout and suffering emotionally, physically, and spiritually.

Balance in our lives is off; we are compromising our health, often missing sports' most significant rewards. Jenny's relevant stories, timely information, and positive advice lead her readers down a healthy path to a rich and long life in sport.

The impact of Title IX legislation cannot be overstated. It changed women's lives . . . and certainly mine. It afforded me the opportunity of thirty-eight wonderful years of coaching and empowering young women. Besides an incredible number of victories and eight NCAA Championships, I am most proud of the 100 percent graduation rate we achieved. Our success came from a combination of my own personal determination, education and experience, but most importantly, a support system that found credence in Title IX.

As we embrace each and every day, we carry the lessons of history. The most challenging moments provide the greatest possibilities for transformation. I am grateful for the many opportunities I have had that inspired those who possess a similar passion and love of basketball.

Embrace the journey that awaits you in *Ice 'n' Go* as Jenny shows you how to score in sports and life.

Enjoy!

Pat Summitt

Preface

Sports coverage is a constant 24/7 in our world. For many folks sports offer a relief from their daily routine and often bring sundry people together, producing common ground for fans and athletes alike who would not otherwise be interacting because they are separated by ethnicity, age, geography, class, politics, or religion. Frequently that disconnect disappears when we celebrate together team's triumphs or commiserate over athlete's injuries.

As never before we are amazed when athletes are able to perform unimaginable feats due to such game changers as innovative training techniques; sports psychology; the emphasis on good nutrition; continuing, in-depth media coverage; the scope of medical advancements; and a new understanding of the importance of intense rehabilitation.

Some of the pertinent issues I cover include the ways that children participate in organized sports, often at the expense of both their physical well-being and the joy they would experience in "unorganized" play.

As an athletic trainer of elite athletes who perform at the highest level, I know the pressures their sport and our culture place on them, pressures that may also create impossibly high expectations for youth and recreational athletes as they too strive for excellence. In a modern, big-time university program, I think that what is of considerable interest are how conflicted some student-athletes become and how they deal with education, burnout, injury, and unrealistic expectations.

I applaud sport's many benefits. As athletes are maturing, they develop such values as dedication, loyalty, sportsmanship, leadership, team concepts, commitment, and a strong work ethic. Then again, I believe we ought to recognize the detriments—the fact that too many times sport emphasizes winning at all costs, and is fertile ground for homophobia and our culture's deep insecurities over body image, shape, and size.

Another topic worth examining is the evolutionary history of Title IX, the legislation pivotal to providing new opportunities to women and girls and placing gender equity in sport at the center of every educational institution. Sadly, we still fall far short of the goals. As important as sport is to so many of us, the role it plays is often out of balance. In this book my aims are both descriptive and prescriptive. Based on my years of working with highly successful sports programs and remarkable athletes, I see how great the players' achievements are and unfortunately how skewed our views can become in a sports-obsessed culture.

I prescribe antidotes to the ills that sport can cause to help every athlete who seeks balance, health, play, and fun in their lives. My own struggles to take the right road to achieve a healthy balance were instrumental in my developing the model SCORE, which I introduce in chapter one.

After many years of rarely taking a break from the demands of being a full-time athletic trainer, I embarked on a twenty-seven-day odyssey pedaling my bicycle across America with twenty-four other cyclists. To our credit, we mostly didn't compete with each other, and we weren't trying to win anything. Surviving each day was victory enough! We did connect with this incredible country of ours, and while the trip was often grueling, my engagement in this "sport" gave me great joy. Every chapter contains excerpts from a journal that I kept during the ride, an experience that was the inspiration for this book. I hope that by reading it you will be motivated as I was to find the capable athlete, as well as the whole person within.

A Note on Interviews

The authors have been privileged to interview administrators, government officials, healthcare professionals, athletes, parents of athletes, and a number of other contributors to this story. We have tried to identify clearly whom we are quoting, and a thorough listing of interviewees can be found at the back of the book. In the interest of readability, we have elected not to provide formal citations for these quotations.

Acknowledgments

We are indebted to many individuals for the production of this book.

Early in the "exploration" stage, Dr. Priscilla Blanton, professor of child and family studies at the University of Tennessee, provided a valuable sounding board to find our direction. P. Kay Coleman painted the picture of the early impact of Title IX in education and business.

Dee Kantner, a trailblazer in her own right, guided us to women's early triumphs in sports.

Along the way friends and colleagues encouraged me to "write it down." Helen Moshak read, responded, and read again every word of the manuscript. She gave countless hours and energy offering her expertise and support throughout the entire project. Mom, you never missed a beat!

And Dad, John Moshak, your detailed eye and timely opinions kept us on course.

I have the amazing good fortune to have Chris Hofmann's unwavering support and belief in me.

Jana Hunter's reading gave us an objective athlete's and writer's third eye to fine tune subject matter and organization. Thanks to Jana and additional readers, Ice 'n' Go is enjoyable, inspiring, and pertinent to a broad audience.

A number of Lady Volunteer colleagues gave much of their time and support to our efforts. Julie Hallums always responded willingly to our frequent needs to find numbers, statistics, and sources to study significant trends in sport. Without her detective work our conclusions would be conjectures. Long-time colleague and friend Debby Jennings gave insight and research assistance.

We extend deep gratitude to Pat Summitt who inspires everyone she comes in contact with, including this author, and for what she has done to advance women and girls in sport and careers.

I appreciate America by Bicycle for rolling me across this beautiful country.

Thank you Joe Whitney for helping me train my mind.

Assistance with illustrations, statistical figures, and content clarification came from Dr. Russ Betcher, Marti McClard, Dr. Marisa Colston, and Casi Dailey.

We are especially grateful to Scot Danforth, director of the University of Tennessee Press, whose guidance and faith in our work have made all the difference. At every step of production — editing, design, and promotion — the press gave our passion form.

Finally, we extend our sincere thanks to every individual who talked with us. Your stories, candor, insights, experiences, and wisdom furnished the power points for our message.

Chapter 1

On Ice

Ice 'n' Go is my mantra. It serves me well in my work, and it serves the injured athletes I treat. As an athletic trainer at the University of Tennessee, I have the latest and greatest rehabilitation resources at my fingertips. It might be surprising, then, when I tell you that ice is the single most important item in my toolbox. Applying it is often the first step to healing. Athletes who come to me so sore from pushing toward perfection, hoping for a magic cure for their aches and pains, are sometimes taken aback when I hand them a bag of ice. What they soon appreciate is that ice provides pain relief, reduces inflammation, eases spasms, and saves the life of cells. Calling it a miracle product may be an overstatement, but it is amazingly effective, readily available, and inexpensive.

Does my mantra work? You be the judge. During the first game of the 1997 NCAA women's basketball tournament in Knoxville, Tennessee, starting point guard Kellie Jolly sprained her ankle. In obvious pain, she limped off the court, leaning on my arm. Our team physicians evaluated her and took X-rays. Diagnosis: lateral ankle sprain. Playing status: questionable for the rest of the tournament. We won the game that day; however, Coach Pat Summitt and the team were anxious about our chances of winning the championship without Kellie, our leader, captain, and playmaker.

We set up a makeshift athletic training room in the locker room. For the next 36+ hours I administered nonstop treatment and rehabilitation on her ankle: electrical stimulation, compression, exercises, and massage, but ice was the main modality. Two days later Kellie was reevaluated by the doctors, and they were amazed at her recovery. Cleared to play that night, Kellie ran onto the court to a standing ovation during team introductions. We went on to win the game and subsequently the national championship.

Ice is nice and often will suffice!

My mantra's last word is Go. Here's a good example of how that part works. One of our players fell off a loft bed in her dorm room, scraping her hamstring on the corner of a desk. By the time she came into the training room her leg was badly swollen and black and blue from below the back of her knee up to her buttock. She had the worst bruising I had ever seen. Our doctors and I all thought she would be out of commission for a long time. We got right to work. Ice again was the main modality; however, I also incorporated motion—stretching, riding a bike, kicking in the pool—to keep the muscles moving. Go, go, go! She ended up practicing the next day and played in our basketball game two days later. Although the leg was not pretty, she was fully functional and never missed a beat.

Motion is the lotion!

Although ice and motion are critical when treating an injury, balance is the key to healing and a healthy life thereafter. Our body is acutely interrelated with our mind and spirit. Early in my professional career, I was training for a marathon when my body stopped running. I became so sick that even a short walk left me winded and weak. I needed to listen to what my body was telling me. It was a defining moment both personally and professionally. From that point on I became an even more determined competitor with a passion to achieve my goals, while having learned the lessons of a reality check. This eye-opening experience brought new insight to my educational and clinical skills and generated a professional model of nurturing and growing the athlete who is in each one of us.

Balance is the talent!

Ice 'n' Go: Score in Sport and Life began to germinate somewhere along my 27-day coast-to-coast cycling trek across America in the spring of 2006. Starting out, the original goal of my journey was simply to reach the eastern shore. To my surprise, though, by the time I dipped my front bicycle wheel into the Atlantic Ocean, I had found my true self. The expedition ignited revolutionary insights that led me to the true meaning of balance, joy, and satisfaction. My experiences have shown me the way to set meaningful goals—goals that each of us can achieve in our own fashion to make our lives better, even if we are never praised or rewarded for reaching them. Overcoming the obstacles, unexpected twists, and unforeseen outcomes in our life's journey requires effort, stamina, and fortitude. I have excerpted my journal from that great trip at the ends of the chapters of this book: I hope this will help readers stay inspired and share part of my joy in life's journey.

So together let's examine the barriers and discover a way to strike and maintain balance. Get your playbooks. The final SCORE is not about winning or losing. It is about your SELF as the player, using CONFIDENCE as fuel, embracing each event as an OPPORTUNITY, with REWARD being the true satisfaction and EXCITEMENT the motivation that propels the spirit. Let's go!

SCORE Model

S—SELF

Discovering your inner resource, developing self-esteem, creating motivation to become a valued member of the team.

C—CONFIDENCE

Building faith in your own abilities by understanding and trusting yourself. This is the route to trusting others.

O—OPPORTUNITY

A growing sense of self and confidence leads to clarity in recognizing, embracing, and taking advantage of the things that life brings.

R—REWARD

Sport provides tangible rewards, but some of the greatest are intangible, and so it is in life.

E—EXCITEMENT

Celebrating rewards sparks excitement and further energizes the next endeavor.

Day 1: Costa Mesa, CA, to Thousand Palms, CA, 122 miles

Hello Everyone,

I have completed my first day of 122 miles, and it is THRILLING! I dipped my rear wheel into the Pacific Ocean and followed a mellow eight-mile bike path that got us out of busy California. Two climbs sixteen miles and eight miles long. Tail winds that flew us at 28–30 mph into Palm Springs. So cool, if they are all like today . . . holy cow! "I believe I can fly!"

And we get to do it again tomorrow—how fun!

Jenny

Day 2: Thousand Palms, CA, to Blythe, CA, 118 miles

Hey Dudes,

The ride is going well. Day 2 is over and another successful day with 118 miles checked off. Hot through the desert—in the nineties—but not as hot as it could have been. One 24-mile climb through Box Canyon, eighty miles of interstate riding, the only way to get through the desert, but a good shoulder to ride on. Head winds for most of the day—can't have it all—thank goodness for drafting. Lots of eating and lots and lots of drinking. Waaaater!

And we get up and do it again tomorrow—how fun!

Jenny

Chapter 2

Come Play

My absolutely breathtaking bicycle journey across America through canyons and over mountains brought me the thrill of freedom. Even when I was a child, my bicycle gave me the independence to venture beyond my neighborhood into other worlds. In fact, unorganized play essentially did the same thing—unwittingly teaching me about the body, relationships, courage, and creativity.

My friends and I were always moving—running, jumping, biking, and playing games in the neighborhood, at parks and rec centers, and at school. We used to arrive at school early so we could play games on the playground—four square, jacks, tag, kickball, and hopscotch. We had gym class, recess, lunch with playtime, and then we went home and played outside until dinner. In the summers we were out playing all day, returning home briefly for meals. In our neighborhood we could join in any number of ball games—bounce or fly, 500, pitch-and-catch, kickball, pick-up softball—at the corner park and in church parking lots. Anyone could play, boys and girls together. Equipment was minimal. We shared bats, balls, and mitts. The position of captain was different for every game. To decide teams the captains tossed a bat into the air, barrel side down, caught it as it fell, and then we kids took turns wrapping our hands around the bat toward the knob. The one whose hand ended up on top of the knob chose first. We played by our own rules, and when conflicts did arise, most often we easily resolved them.

There was always a core group. We kids fell into roles, mutually determined by age, experience, skill, and how often we showed up. We played until dinnertime. I would be upset if it was my night to do the dishes, because that meant my siblings were outside playing again before I was. After dinner we played flashlight tag, hide-and-go-seek, and chased the fireflies until mom called us in. Then she would call a second time, and we knew it was not a good idea for her to have to call us a third time. I remember these days as the best of times—carefree, filled with energy and fun. Children frolicking in the pool, one of the kids mustering the courage to dive off the side for the first time, legs shaking, eyes closed, hands clenched together, and then the splash—a head pops out of the water with a look of surprise and joy. She scrambles out of the pool to do it again and again.

Today we know that free play is more than fun; it is essential to our development as a balanced and healthy person. Children begin to develop physically through play that requires hand-eye coordination, movement patterns and skills, running and changing directions, jumping and landing, getting in and out of situations. Random play is a steady stream of creativity rich in imagination. Children are observant and mimic what they see. They often won't ask how to do something—they just try to do it based on what they have seen and what works for them. They make up games, figure out rules, and many times there is no win/loss component to their activity. They combine games and come up with something totally new. They are inventing their sports, adding dimensions, and problem-solving. Using fantasy scenarios, kids imitate their heroes: "5-4-3-2-1 . . . and she scores at the buzzer for the win!"

Child development expert Dr. David Elkind describes four major types of play: mastery, innovative, kinship, and therapeutic.[1] He points out that these are not stages but rather are qualitative features of intellectual, social, and emotional learning that occur at the same time with fluid boundaries. Mastery play involves actions that construct concepts and skills. For example, when I was growing up, we played freeze tag. The idea was that when tagged by an opponent, you had to freeze in that position. When someone on your own team tagged you, you were unfrozen and free to move. The skills of the game involved running, stopping, changing direction, holding the same position over a period of time, and strategizing.

Innovative play happens when the child alters activities, as we did with kickball in the gymnasium. The traditional way to get players out was to hit them with the ball before they reached the base. We added the option of having a fielder shoot and make a basket before the runner reached base.

Kinship play begins when children play together in an unstructured way. This would happen naturally in the after-dinner hours when neighborhood kids casually joined in our games as they came outside. Kate Ryan, a former competitive swimmer and advisor for youth activities, values the rapport groups of children develop with each other. "Looking back on my own sports activities, I had the most fun when the groups were mixed ages," she recalls. "The competition factor was minimized, and we all had a good time. The younger kids looked up to the older kids, and so instead of wanting to beat each other in competition, we supported each other and wanted everyone to do as well as they could."

Therapeutic play describes the process of developing strategies to deal with stressful life events. When I was young, we played make-believe. We found our props in the basement and used real-life scenarios. Looking back on that now, what I especially notice is that we often created a different and happier ending to what was at the time a stressful event. One time, we made up a scene for one of the kids whose parents were getting a divorce. In our story, we brought them back together again with a kiss and a hug. I know this helped us process and cope with troubling situations. Good happens with play.

Looking to learn more about the significance of play, I came upon the National Institute for Play. What a dynamic organization that is. Founder Dr. Stuart Brown says that we cannot overstate the importance of play to healthy development and that the activity establishes creativity and innovation. His words resonate: "When we play, we are engaged in the purest expression of our humanity, the truest expression of our individuality. . . . The ability to play is critical not only to being happy, but also to sustaining social relationships and being a creative, innovative person."[2] He says that play is "so important to our development and survival that the impulse to play has become a biological drive. . . . Studies show that if they are well fed, safe, and rested, all mammals will play spontaneously."[3] I don't need to look very far to attest to the validity of his observation. Our two dogs, Sami and Sosa (Yes, we are Cubs fans), are constant reminders of the joy and good that comes from daily play.

The question is: have kids stopped playing? Play is no longer easy to come by. For many reasons outside the control of even the most well-meaning parent, family life has changed in the United States. Economic stresses, safety, and changing family structures present real challenges to providing children with the environments and play times they need for healthy development. In many neighborhoods, even when adults are at home with children, they do not feel safe sending them out to play, because the loss of neighborhood connections and increased crime compromise safety. Working parents need childcare; preschool and after-school care activities have become the norm. Free playtime can be, and usually is, a part of childcare programming, but the time dedicated to random play falls far short of what a growing child needs.

Sosa and Sami.

When do children begin to lose imaginative play? When adults enroll them in organized sports at too young an age, they are limiting unstructured playtime with other children. Super Soccer Stars encourages parents to enroll children as early as two years of age in their programs. Marketing messages assure them that their child will improve soccer skills, experience positive reinforcement, and have endless fun. I am appalled at this approach! At age two, children are just beginning to discover each other. They are learning to share toys, playing with shapes and sizes, developing basic coordination skills, improving verbal expression, and interacting with each other. Human development is progressive: crawl before you walk; walk before you run. Organizations like Super Soccer Stars are asking our children to run before they crawl.

The shift from random play to supervised games with boundaries, rules, and skill sets that are meant to correlate with success takes away the power from the child's imagination and gives it to the leader of the activity, a coach/teacher/parent/volunteer. In the process, the advantages of relatively aimless play are lost. Youngsters will work to please their parents and coaches and to be valued by them. If adults focus only on the critical incidents of the game (scoring, blocking, winning, missing the mark, rules, etc.) and not on the less tangible but more significant markers such as the child's own small triumphs and joy, the children will not remember having fun.

When I was working at a summer job with Parkside Sport and Fitness Center, in Des Plaines, Illinois, I supervised the aftercare portion of the camp. All through the day, children moved from one structured sport to the next. The aftercare was free play. One day the children decided to make up their own version of soccer using a combination of soccer and basketball skills. A father came to pick up his 10-year-old son and saw him dribbling the soccer ball with his hands instead of his feet. Running toward the field, he began shouting instructions to his son: "What are you doing? Get that ball out of your hands! Dribble with your feet!" I spoke to the father in private, explaining that we encouraged creative play in aftercare because the children received formal instruction all day long. He responded that if his son was going to play the sport, he was going to play it how "it was intended to be played." The next day I noticed that this little boy was quieter than usual and a little sad. Free playtime allows children flexibility and new ways to enjoy the activity other than adhering to stringent rules and the winner-take-all mindset of competitive sports. When scoring and winning become the point of organized sports, there are no do-overs.

I agree with five-time NCAA track and field champion, coach, and trainer of fifty Olympic medal winners Loren Seagrave, who laments the demise of free play: "Free play is a lost concept today. It is much easier to sit

Beyond Hope—just outside Wickenburg, Arizona.

in front of a television or video game. We used to clamor to be outside, play in the snow, and in the summer we rode our bikes and didn't come home until the streetlights came on. Can we get to free play as it used to be?"

Day 3: Blythe, CA, to Wickenburg, AZ, 117 miles

Hey Dudes,

Another day in the desert—low nineties and lots of sun. Crazy biking tan lines—the stripes on my forehead from my helmet are priceless. Head winds, cross winds, and then a steady cross wind made the day interesting. Thirty-seven miles of interstate riding resulted in two flat tires—on the rear wheel, of course! Darn those little wires from blown radial truck tires. Mild climbing today. Everyone tried to save energy because we hit the mountains tomorrow—out of the heat and up, up, up. We traveled through HOPE and SALOME, where "The Women Dance."

Gatorade is my friend and yes, I am sitting in a cold bath tub every night.

And we get to get up and do it again tomorrow—reminding myself how fun this is!

Jenny

Big wheeling.

Chapter 3

P. E. Please, ASAP

Our bodies are designed to move. Movement improves circulation, neurological function, sensory stimulation, muscle development, bone strength, cardiovascular endurance, cellular metabolism, and elimination of waste. Physical fitness is connected to mental capacity. Movement positively influences self-esteem, behavior, stress relief, and the balance of brain chemistry.

Not only is free play during free time decreasing, but physical activity is also disappearing from our schools. Changes in public education are limiting physical activity and exercise. Statistics indicate that accessibility to physical activity for youth in and out of the school setting is in danger. That is unacceptable.

In a 2009 ABC news report, Geraldine Sealey said: "Gym classes are being sacrificed across the country to save money and satisfy federal mandates stressing test scores in math and reading. Just over half of all students nationwide are enrolled in a physical education class, and by high school only a third take daily gym classes. In fact, more than 60 percent of children aged 9 to 13 do not participate in any organized physical activity after school hours, and 23 percent do not engage in any free-time physical activity at all."[4] As of 2010, only five states required physical education in every grade through high school, with only one state, Illinois, meeting the national recommendations of 150 minutes per week in elementary school and 225 minutes in middle and high school.

Dwindling dollars for education with growing demands for high test scores on core curriculum subjects (math, science, English) continue to push school districts to eliminate physical activity in the public school system. While the medical community warns of the dangers of childhood obesity and its associated diseases and conditions, the public education system is phasing out physical education. The Centers for Disease Control and Prevention (CDC) reports that, in the United States, childhood obesity has tripled from one generation ago, affecting 17 percent of children and adolescents and is continuing to rise.

Yet researchers at the California Department of Education have found evidence linking higher academic achievement with higher levels of fitness. Dr. George Ziolkowski, director of pupil personnel services at East Pennsylvania School District in Allentown and a proponent of daily physical education, points out that this is not a new concept: "This is something the Greeks knew. Let's start talking about how kids who are physically fit and feel better and have rest will do better in school."[5]

Children who are taught to be active and move when they are young are more likely to remember the lesson and continue to be active and move as adults. My discussion with Chris Hofmann, a former physical education teacher and youth coach and an athletic trainer at a Division I university, reinforces this concept. "I always tried to incorporate some fitness programs and lifetime activities in the curriculum—cycling, Frisbee golf, walking, and disco dance—because teaching people to be active when they are young will encourage them to keep moving as they age. Movement is a basic component of fitness. Ongoing participation is key."

We know that self-esteem developed through sports activity enhances academic success, reinforces lifelong activity, and that public health experts and physicians recommend daily gym class from kindergarten through high school. Yet physical education is disappearing from the list of public school responsibilities. Physical education is following the path of driver's education. Today private organizations teach children how to drive. The privatization of physical education will mean that parents have to make a conscious and financial effort to see that their children exercise. It is to our children's detriment if our educational system focuses only on the development of the mind and ignores the development of the body. Physical education must be returned to the core curriculum in all public and private schools. Add that fourth R—vigorous Recreation—to the three R's—Reading, 'Riting, and 'Rithmetic—to foster a healthy and productive future for our children.

Day 4: Wickenburg, AZ, to Cottonwood, AZ, 105 miles

Hey Cowpokes,

Temps were in the sixties and sunny. The wind was all over because of the mountains. Yes, today was a climbing day. Three big climbs:

the first up Yarnell Pass (elevation 4,850);

the second into Prescott, Arizona (elevation 5,346);

and the third to the top of Mingus Mountain (elevation 7,023), for a total of over 11,000 feet and 28 miles of climbing; the other 77 miles were not all downhill, either.

And boy, did I do something stupid today. I am blaming it on the altitude. For some reason, the ride up Mingus Mountain was very tough, and I could not figure out why until the person I was riding with said how impressed she was that I was in my front big chain ring. For those of you who are not cyclists, it means I was working far harder than I had to. So for 6.5 miles I was grinding out the mountain . . . aaaaaaarrrrrrggggggggghhhhh-hhhhh! (OK, that's the "G-rated" version.) I will probably make the "Duh of the Day" on the ride website. And other riders will probably make the quote of the day when they said to me, "Pick a gear, any gear."

Of course after all that hard work, there is a prize at the end. My top speed on the descent from Mingus Mountain was 42 mph . . . WEEEEEEEEEEEEEEEEEEEEEEEEE! More climbing is on the schedule tomorrow, and before you say it, I will be in the right gears. Can you say, "aspirin, please?"

Believe it or not, I had a veggie burger on the mountain in Jerome, Arizona—who would have thunk it in cow country?

And we get to get up and do it again tomorrow—how fun!

Jenny

Chapter 4

Caution: Youth Sports Ahead

Opportunities for children to participate in organized sports exist at every age and skill level—from pee wee to little leagues, travel teams to elite development programs, and church to city leagues. Children as young as three can be enrolled in just about any sport—karate, soccer, basketball, swimming, skating, softball, tennis, baseball, and gymnastics, among others. It is hilarious to watch a pee wee league of five-year-olds playing football. What fun! Although, one might be hard-pressed to identify what the kids are doing because they are just running around the field bumping into each other.

The advantages of physical activity through organized sports are well documented. Young people who are active in a sport develop confidence and build strong self-esteem. Participation in athletics gives feedback about physical talents and the experiences of winning, losing, and being fair. I know for a happy fact that many children are absolutely thrilled to participate. By being on a team, their spirits thrive, their bodies grow healthier, and their minds expand as they learn new skills. Friendships develop. No wonder parents are eager to enroll their children in sports programs!

The guiding philosophy of the best youth-centered sport programs is to provide exposure to the game, inspire exercise, give everyone the opportunity to play, and have fun. When they do this, such programs capture the virtues of less organized play that kids might be inclined to create on their own.

So what's the problem with a young child getting into organized sports? Several pitfalls, such as overzealous parenting, year round participation, and competing at too young an age can sabotage the benefits. Parents need to be aware of the possible consequences and how to avoid them. I would advise parents to consider these four caution areas before enrolling a child in youth sports.

First, be very clear about why you want your child to join a team. Did the child bring up the idea? Did she express interest when you brought up playing a sport? Do you feel she could benefit from the interaction with others? Does he have energy to burn?

Unfortunately, it is not unusual to see obsessive parents driving their child to run faster, swim harder, or kick higher. They may be living vicariously through their offspring. Meg McDaniel, the mother of two boys, told me that having a child participating in sports can be intoxicating. "We can get caught up in being proud of our child's accomplishments, but this pride can become egocentric. My oldest boy Chris was very talented in baseball. I loved watching him play and hearing everyone in the stands cheering for him. So, when Lee, my youngest boy, decided not to play basketball in high school, I realized I was more disappointed for me than for him because I wanted those intoxicating feelings to continue."

T-ball and flowers—the sights and smells of fun. Photo by Sherry Price. Courtesy of the McMurray and Webb families.

Caution

Four-time Olympian, Division I track athlete, and president of Joetta Sports & Beyond, Joetta Clark Diggs laments that parents are often not tuned into their children's true interests. "Parents are willing to pay just about anything to have their children play regardless of what they want. When we ask the children why they want to play, you'd be surprised at some of the answers we get. 'My parents did this sport, so they want me to do it.' 'I don't want my parents to be mad at me for saying I don't like this sport; so I keep playing even though I no longer like it.' 'I'm good at ice skating and my parents put a lot of money into my lessons, so I can't tell them I want to try something else.'" Parents need to be open to the idea of an alternate sport or activity if their child is consistently unhappy in the sport.

Parents also may view sport as a ticket to college or to the gravy train associated with being a professional athlete. The statistics don't punch this ticket or drive the train. In 2009, approximately 73.3 million children, preschool through high school, participated in youth sports. Of this number fewer than 7.7 million participate in high school athletics. As of 2011, the NCAA reports 444,077 student-athletes in Division I, II, and III sports. This means only 5.74 percent of high school athletes go on to play at the collegiate level. The NCAA also indicates that fewer than 1 percent of college athletes, male or female, go on to play professional sports, whether the sport is men's basketball, football, baseball, ice hockey, tennis, soccer, or golf, or women's basketball, softball, soccer, tennis, or golf. The evidence clearly shows that most athletes never reach the professional level. Parents need to rethink their motivation.

Yet another way parents go overboard in their drive to ensure their child's success is in utilizing genetic testing. For $100 and a swab sample from the child's mouth, a laboratory will test for ACTN3, a gene that is possibly linked with superiority in sports. This latest fad has unleashed controversy among geneticists, scientists, and psychologists. Dr. Stephen Roth, a University of Maryland genetics researcher, has studied the ACTN3 and observes that, while this gene contributes to athletic performance, it is only one of two hundred that have been associated with athletic achievement.[6] The research is still in its infancy. If parents are looking for signs of guaranteed success, currently genetic testing is not the answer.

Second, all prodigies are children but not all children are prodigies. A wise parent will understand that starting a child in sports at a very young age and following a year-round schedule of practice, competition, and travel does not turn that child into a prodigy. No matter the means, we cannot teach children to be gifted.

The philosophy of "the earlier, the better" suggests that if a child starts young enough, she will have a better chance to succeed. But this concept is a myth. For every Tiger Woods or Mia Hamm, there are thousands of Todd Marinoviches or Jennifer Capratis, whose careers flamed out very early because of physical injuries, emotional issues, or burnout. There are many examples of highly successful athletes who did not specialize in one sport—Michael Jordon, Jackie Joyner-Kersee, Charlie Ward, Babe Didrikson-Zaharias, and Jackie Robinson to name a few. Tennis champion John McEnroe did not limit his youth sports experience to tennis. Today he voices concern about this all-consuming trend in youth sports. "When I was twelve, thirteen, I was playing soccer and basketball and whatever I did to keep myself sane . . . and from not walking away from the game because I had outlets. . . . People put the kids in the middle of nowhere, isolate them, so all they can do is live and breathe tennis. . . . Never would I have made it if I had to do that. It would have been a form of torture."[7] Playing a variety of sports works. John McEnroe is the former number one player in the world, winner of seven grand slam singles tournaments, nine grand slam men's doubles, and one grand slam mixed doubles tournament.

Elite performance coach Loren Seagrave asserts from his vantage point regarding athletic development that "all studies show that an early start in sports and early specialization do not enhance chances that a child will become an elite player." He says, "Players who are really successful play different sports growing up, even in high school. Those who played one sport didn't develop the well-rounded athleticism needed to be successful in a sport."

Nikki McCray, an assistant women's basketball coach at the University of South Carolina, is unquestionably a success in women's basketball. Her accomplishments include eight WNBA seasons with three all-star appearances and two Olympic gold medals. McCray is proof that early specialization is not required for success. She didn't pick up a basketball until her freshman year in high school. She also played volleyball and ran track and field all four years. McCray believes that multiple sports participation improved her athleticism and kept her interested. "I had the skills that allow me to play all three sports which kept me in shape. I enjoyed meeting different people, learning from several coaches, and having varying experiences," says McCray. "You only have one body so be smart. Year round, single sport play wears you out."

Child development educator Dr. David Elkind finds no reliable evidence that an early start in an individual or team sport gives children a

Table 1. Long-Term Athlete Development (LTAD)[1]

Stage	Age	Objective
1—FUNdamentals	Males 6–9; Females 6–8	Build overall motor skills. Speed, power, endurance developed using FUN games. Running, jumping, and throwing techniques are taught. No more than once or twice per week participation in single sport. Participation in different sports three or four times per week.
2—Learning to Train	Males 9–12; Females 8–11	Build overall sports skills. Training-to-competition ratio 70:30.
3—Training to Train	Males 12-16; Females 11-15	Build aerobic base, build strength toward the end of the phase, and further develop sport-specific skills. Training-to-competition ratio 60:40.
4—Training to Compete	Males 16-18; Females 15-17	Optimize fitness preparation and sport, individual position-specific skills as well as performance. Training-to-competition ratio 50:50
5—Training to Win	Males 18 and older; Females 17 and older	Final phase of athletic preparation. Training-to-competition ratio 25:75.
6—Retirement/ Retention		Retain athletes for coaching, administration, officials.

[1]Developed by Dr. Istvan Balyi.

lasting advantage or talent edge, but he also sees parents struggling with the decision. "The concept of child competence, which drove much of the hurrying of childhood in previous decades, is very much alive today. Parents are under more pressure than ever to engage and over schedule their children in organized sports that may be age-inappropriate."[8] They "feel forced into it because of what other parents are doing. If parents do not enroll their children in these programs, their children are left without playmates."[9]

Parents should wait to enroll their children into organized sports until their age and skills are appropriate. Hungarian sports scientist Dr. Istvan Balyi, who works with elite athletes, recommends that a child not even enter the sports system until age six, and even then the focus should be to play and enjoy a variety of activities. Dr. Balyi has created a useful model, Long-Term Athlete Development (LTAD), which suggests five age-appropriate steps of progression for developing the champion athlete.[10]

Randy Huntington, former technical coordinator of sports science for USA Track and Field, urges parents to keep children's activities in sync with their developmental stages. "What we have in the U.S. are parents trying to get their kids into game environments as soon as possible," he warns. "We're slotting kids in the Train-to-Compete phase and largely bypassing the FUNdamentals and Train-to-Train stages."[11]

Soccer appeals to parents for a first-time sport because of the kind of action they see it requiring. Most children can run and kick. Of the 18 million Americans who play soccer, 78 percent are under the age of eighteen. In the 1990s, soccer was recognized as the fastest-growing high school and college sport in the United States. What parents don't think about when they choose soccer for their little ones is the strategy needed to be successful in the sport. Young children cannot understand the directives that parents and coaches are screaming from the sidelines. The cognitive and social abilities needed to understand complex patterns and communication in action-oriented sports only begin to develop around the age of eight. So, rather than expecting strategic decisions out of young children, focus on fun and fundamentals.

From an injury and wellness perspective, the American Academy of Pediatrics stands firmly on the opinion that children should focus on the fun of activity and not on the competition until age ten. I receive calls from parents inquiring about weight training programs for their children. I tell them that their children's activities should involve different exercises such as hanging from the jungle gym bars, climbing on playground equipment, and just plain running around. I don't recommend weight training until their muscles and nerves are fully developed, sometime between the ages of thirteen and fourteen.

I am seeing the negative results of the current trend to enroll children too soon in youth sports each time a new class of athletes arrives on campus. I may see some bodies that are eighteen years old according to the calendar but forty, fifty, or sixty years old according to their condition, because they started at a young age playing one sport competitively, year-round. When we do freshman class physicals, we are often stunned by the wear and tear we discover. To my dismay, I saw that on one of our teams every freshman had at least one significant problem—ranging from disc degeneration in the lower back, to a stress fracture, to severe tendonitis, to a recent concussion that was still symptomatic.

Parents of young children shouldn't lose sight of what sport is all about: fun first! Then there are the extras, the valuable bonuses of fitness, personal challenge, teamwork, and sportsmanship. Children deeply immersed in youth sports today are vulnerable to emotional distress and physical injury. Pee wee leagues start before kindergarten, and travel leagues begin at age eight. Children are getting hurt. They should not be playing so hard that this happens.

I talked with WNBA star Tamika Catchings, who shares my concern as she works with children through her Catch the Stars Foundation. "Children are being placed in a sports regimen at too early an age. The demands right off the bat are too high," she says. "You've got a four-year-old practicing Monday, Wednesday, and Friday for an hour. To me it is scary." She sees that there are some kids at training sessions who don't want to be there, but their parents are forcing them. "The one thing that I want children to learn is that it can be as enjoyable as you make it. I think the biggest message that we have to get out is to let the kids have fun." Tamika's foundation underscores her philosophy with its mission to "empower youth to achieve their dreams by providing goal-setting programs that promote literacy, fitness, and mentoring."

Third, refrain from letting children play one sport all year long. Even if the child fights this decision, parents who want to do what's best can comfortably set a limit, because organized youth sports are structured in seasons with beginning and ending dates.

My colleague Angie Keck, a former collegiate golfer and coach, shared with me an experience she had. "The baseball coach was organizing a summer travel team, and he asked us if our son was interested in being on the team. I said, 'Not really. He will just play in the spring.' My husband works every other weekend, and this limits our time together. It's not fair to my younger daughter or to me to spend all our summer driving places and watching baseball. I am not going to build our family time around the schedule of a 9-year-old. The coach said, 'Don't you want to ask him?' I said, 'No. I make the decisions for him at this age. When he is 16, then I will ask him.'"

Even youth leagues that stress general activity and fun in the beginning arrive at the moment when children face a dividing line according to skills. The better skilled athletes move into elite travel teams, and the children who want to play and have fun are left behind. Consecutive summer sport camps and instructional sessions weigh in with top priority over family vacations, fun at the zoo, or even a sleepover with friends.

In spite of the fact that educators, child development professionals, and medical experts present overwhelming evidence against specializing in one sport year-round, the numbers of children who do so continue to climb. I strongly recommend that kids take seasonal breaks. They can try another sport or activity, go hiking, or simply enjoy unstructured time. A break in a one-sport schedule can prevent burnout and injuries in the future.

Dr. Colleen Hacker, a Pacific Lutheran University psychology professor who has worked with the U.S. women's national soccer team, shares my concern about playing the same sport all year. "It's the question of what we lose by focusing on winning when young. Parents and kids think that in order to win, maybe you need to practice year-round. . . . Gradually their world begins to shrink so that all of their achievements, all of their self-worth, all of their confidence at a very young age is from one place. That's where the danger occurs."[12]

I see this danger when an athlete suffers a severe injury that takes her out of her sport. All of a sudden she starts questioning who she is, how will she fit in, and if she will get back the status she held before the injury. I teach athletes that there is more to them and to life than their sport. They have many qualities and talents, and being an athlete is only one aspect of who they are.

The U.S. Olympic Committee's Coaching and Sports Science division surveyed 760 athletes competing in a wide variety of sports at the Olympic Games between 1984 and 1998. Their findings underscore the significance of unorganized play, age-appropriate activities, and involvement in multiple sports.

- Olympians were most often introduced to their sport through unstructured activities.
- Once enrolled in organized sports, quality coaching was important in the acquisition of technique.
- Clubs and community-based programs, not school teams, were primarily responsible for the training of these athletes, but school physical education classes played a key role in developing fitness and skills.
- The average Olympian took three years to find competitive success at the local level as a child, and that gap was closer to five years in sports such as soccer and hockey in which players start young.
- It took twelve to thirteen years after introduction to a sport before they made their first Olympic team.
- Many played multiple sports as teenagers, dispelling the myth of early specialization.

My fourth caution is to make sure parents model a healthy view of winning and losing so that their children gain the most from the experience. My concern is that at an early age the goal is to win at all costs instead of enjoying all the benefits of participation. Focusing only on the final score at this level takes the fun out of sport. If a parent's sole emphasis is on winning, the value of the experience for the child will be based only on winning. If the parent does not handle a loss with grace and a healthy perspective, the child will be a sore loser.

Keeping a healthy perspective about winning and losing also prepares children to deal with life's successes and inevitable losses. Dr. Rebecca Morgan, a board-certified family practice physician who also holds a certificate of special qualification in sports medicine, says, "When kids feel the pressure of not being allowed to fail, they don't know how to handle it when they do fail." Failing gives children opportunities to learn how to deal with difficult feelings, to communicate their needs and frustrations, problem-solve, and learn everyday coping skills. Losing is never easy, but we need to shake hands and let it go. After all, sporting contests are simply games, with outcomes that don't, or shouldn't, affect our well-being in the long term.

How does a parent achieve such a noble, yet not always popular, goal? Rather than focusing the conversations around the team's outcome or individual's success, here are some questions to ask: Do you like your teammates? What was fun? What did you do together? What did you learn? What did you like best at practice? What did you do that you are proud of? Parents should realize they are parents and not coaches, a role that is sometimes difficult to relinquish. Their role as parents is not only to support and protect the child, but also to allow the child to learn life lessons such as respecting authority, rising above acts that may not seem fair, and competing with integrity and grace. During a game, the parent who is yelling instructions from the sideline, demanding the coach's attention during a game, and gossiping with other parents about coaching decisions and player performance is creating conflict and setting a bad example of sportsmanship, not to mention embarrassing the child.

Pushy parenting doesn't stop at youth sports. It continues right up to and through college. I have seen athletes in our program with two sets of coaches—their college coach and their parents. Inevitably these two sets are not on the same page. It is more than likely that the parent who is adamant that his or her daughter keep the ball and take more shots is in direct conflict with the coach's game plan and is affecting team chemistry. Some parents are more concerned with their daughter's individual stats—being a starter, making more points, having more playing time—for her professional resume than for her team's victories. This emphasis on developing the superstar overshadows the health and emotional benefits gained by playing on a team. I am astonished to see this happen with athletes at all levels—even to the star players of Final Four championship teams. During postgame treatments I hear the athletes on their cell phones discussing the game with their families. Sometimes when their conversations are over, they process them with me, saying that their parents don't understand, that they point out everything they think the athlete did wrong, what they should have done differently. These negative reviews can take the joy out of sport. I believe families should be supportive, care about the athlete's health, and whether she had fun and enjoyed playing the game. A coach's responsibility is to point out areas of improvement for the athlete; a parent's role is to give them unwavering support.

Lessons of sports participation affect how people tackle challenges in other aspects of their lives. Athletic performance expert Loren Seagrave has a well-established reputation with proven results among athletes from youth to professional levels based on broad sport development. His philosophy is "to make it possible for every child to obtain the success enjoyed by playing sports." He routinely hears evidence of their success from parents. "We don't need a stopwatch to know that Abbey is faster. The biggest thing we see is that she is so much more confident in the classroom and on the field," says Seagrave.

Dr. Lauren Loberg, sports psychologist and former collegiate diver, has sound advice for parents: "Don't compare your child to other athletes. Give your child the choice of whether he wants you to attend practice. Teach your child to communicate with the coach. It's as hard for a child to talk as it is for parents not to talk."

When the parent remains connected with the child throughout the sport experience, it adds to the child's enjoyment and education.

- Let the young player have fun.
- Be alert to changes in attitudes and interests.
- Keep channels of communication open. Always be open to talk, but don't force it.

Kids reap the benefits of youth sports when we emphasize play, not competition.

Day 5: Cottonwood, AZ, to Winslow, AZ, 108 miles

Hey Cowpokes,

I'm "Standing on the Corner in Winslow, Arizona." We started in the rain this morning—and I thought it did not rain in the desert. Thank goodness for Gortex. We went into the town of Sedona, where a friendly woman told me it had not rained in three months—just our luck. The good news is the wind was not blowing; the bad news is snow was in the forecast for Flagstaff, where we were headed and had lunch. So the layers went on.

Pedaling through Red Rock Canyon and Slide Rock State Park was extraordinary. The rock formations, the trees, the meadows, were simply spectacular. Has to be one of the most beautiful places in the country, and this was in the rain. Breathtaking beauty. And I am still thinking this as we climb, climb, climb over 7,000 feet. The climbing was tough and steep with switchbacks. At one point you could look over the edge and see the road wind around four times—did I just climb that?

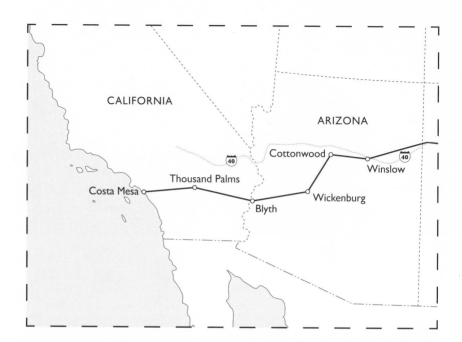

Switchbacks characteristic of Red Rock Canyon and Slide Rock State Park.

And for all of you who were wondering, I was in the right gear! The rain subsided, and when we got to Flagstaff, it was actually pleasant—high fifties with the sun trying to come out. I am glad the weather people in Flagstaff are as accurate as the forecasters in Knoxville. During lunch I was the audience to a majestic snowcapped mountain.

We biked through the Northern Arizona University campus and onto the famous Route 66 into the high desert, eventually getting onto Interstate 40 with some great tail winds pushing us along at 25 mph. Unfortunately, the shoulder of the interstate was very bumpy—aaah, the blessing of padded shorts. Rode the interstate into Winslow.

Hard to imagine that is 100+ miles—you can see rock formations out of Old West movies, forest, meadows, snowcapped mountains and high (6,000 feet) desert. Breathtaking!

And we get to do it again tomorrow—how fun!

Jenny

Chapter 5

Bad Coach, Good Coach

Coach. In the world of athletics that's an impressive title, one to be taken seriously. To athletes the coach is the single most powerful authority figure from preschool sports to the professional level. Representing a wide range of personalities, philosophies, training, experience, and knowledge, coaches are members of the circle of influence that—if they are good—provides instruction, motivation, affirmation, nurturing, and the bolstering of self-esteem to athletes of all ages. But not all coaches are created equal.

A youth coach may be a teacher from the local school, a college student who plays the sport or is interested in working with youth, or another parent whose interest has been piqued by their child's participation. In addition, there are career coaches from the youth to professional levels with full-time salaries. Accountability and supervision of a coach lie with the board of volunteer parents, parks and recreation supervisor, a school principal or superintendent, an athletic director, or an owner. Coaches carry great responsibility for a child's development, and parents often entrust the coach with their child's physical, emotional, and even spiritual growth.

"When you consider the impact both positive and negative that a youth coach can have on a child's young life," sports performance expert Loren Seagrave cautions, "it's amazing to me that all you need to coach is a clipboard, a stopwatch, and a whistle. Coaches can do permanent harm to athletes, particularly young ones, if they don't understand the mental, emotional, and physical developmental needs of children."

President and founder of Sports Management Resources, Dr. Donna Lopiano says that there should be standardized requirements for coaching in terms of technique, skills, knowledge of the game, safety, and ethics. "We seem to care little about how we coach but rather about setting records, appearing on television, and achieving championships." Dr. Lopiano advocates for the certification of coaches at all levels from youth sports to college. As an athlete, athletic director, and international business leader, she offers a perspective that is grounded in history and vision. "As long as we have big money in the system, and as long as there is reinforcement for winning and not a concomitant reinforcement for just being a good teacher/coach, the focus can be skewed," she says. "I think the answers lie in coaching certification. If you have certified coaches, chances are, even if you are out for the golden ring, you are going to be better at doing it than someone who is not certified. You are not going to kill kids along the way. This is serious. Coaches are operating in high stress and high heat conditions and can kill a kid with a word."

The privatization of sports has resulted in jobs for coaches at every level, and the more elite the program, the more lucrative the coaching opportunities may be. Josh Gray, a youth soccer coach in Knoxville, Tennessee, estimates that annual salaries for youth sports coaches start at approximately $15,000 and can go as high as $100,000 for soccer club directors or high-profile coaches. Unfortunately, an elite program does not necessarily mean that the coaches meet the highest standards.

Regrettably, mandates and certifications for coaches in all sports and on all levels are unlikely. With tighter budgets, public education program cuts, and the continuing push for privatized sports offerings, it is improbable that there will be the financial resources or the will to provide consistent training or to establish a governance body to enforce compliance. To date, track and field, weight lifting, swimming, gymnastics, and soccer are the only sports that require some level of certification. This makes a parent's responsibility to take an active role in placing their child with the best coach possible that much more critical.

A skilled and sensitive coach can make a big difference in an athlete's life. My friend Jamie Bloom is a prime example. I have had many discussions with her about her experiences coaching swimming on the youth, high school, and collegiate levels. Currently a Y (formally known as YMCA) swim coach, Jamie told me one of her favorite stories about Nicole, a high school junior who had been with the Y team for four years. Nicole was a sweet, somewhat passive athlete who was often conflicted because she was extremely anxious about racing competitively. When she told Coach Bloom she was thinking about quitting, they talked about all the pros and cons of staying. "We decided that one of her biggest stressors was the expectation of performance times," Coach Bloom said. "Together, we developed a positive motivational strategy so that we would spend the year being process oriented rather than outcome oriented. We had to get the rest of the coaching staff and her teammates on board. It was really important that we all spoke the same language with Nicole and made sure our focus was her focus. Result: she had a very successful year."

The next spring Coach Bloom talked with Nicole about the possibility of qualifying for Y's National Championships, a very scary conversation for Nicole to have because her biggest fear was failure. What if she put herself out there, really made the commitment to give it a shot, and then didn't make it? This meeting left them both in tears. Coach Bloom told her she could think about it and use the summer to concentrate her training on getting ready for the next level so that if she decided in the fall that she was going to take on this challenge, she would be ready.

In August, when all of the swimmers in the Y's National Team group gathered for the National Championship planning meeting, Nicole was there. "Her first meeting to discuss goals in September was pretty amazing!" Coach Bloom said. "She was a bit apprehensive about taking this chance and knew that she was going to be way out of her comfort zone. But she was willing to give it a try." Nicole talked about gaining tons of self-confidence, how she saw herself as someone who was setting a good example to the rest of her teammates, and how excited she was about the possibility of the year. "Oh, and by the way," Coach Bloom said, "Nicole is also going to be swimming in college next year!"

Coach Bloom recognizes the influence that coaches have on their athletes and says that respect is essential. This respect grows from the trust athletes have in themselves, in her as the coach, and among team members. She teaches her athletes to depend on themselves and their teammates. She motivates through positive reinforcement rather than through fear and punitive measures.

Parents need to be aware that a coach who is not tuned into the needs of children and instead is self-centered and focused on seeking fame and adoration can seriously harm a child. Misconduct by coaches with their athletes is the darkest side of youth sports. Instances when coaches use the power of their positions to exploit the vulnerability of youth in various ways, including verbal, mental, and sexual abuse, are traumatizing and leave deep scars and lasting devastation.

I heard a sad story about a youth swim coach and Brooke, a seven-year-old girl. Brooke swam the backstroke and was fairly fast. She really liked being on the team but had difficulty swimming distances. Her favorite event was the medley relay where she could shine doing the backstroke leg. Coach Gail had been coaching an age-eight-and-under summer swim team for five years. When anyone broke her rules, the consequences were swimming additional laps, a verbal lashing in front of others, and being taken out of events. At the second meet of the summer, Coach Gail decided to put Brooke in three events: backstroke, butterfly, and freestyle relay. Brooke was so slow swimming the second leg of the freestyle relay that when their fourth swimmer was leaving the block, all the other lanes had completed the event. Afterward, Brooke felt blamed for the loss. Coach Gail could have comforted her, given her constructive feedback and motivation, but did not.

The next morning, when Brooke's mother dropped her off at practice, Brooke watched the car drive away and ran into the bathroom. When her teammates came looking for her, she said she was feeling sick and didn't come out. After practice, she saw Coach Gail standing by her mother's car. Spotting Brooke, Coach Gail called her over and admonished her for missing practice. Coach told her mom that Brooke needed to come early to the next practice and swim four extra laps, freestyle. Feeling alone and embarrassed, Brooke just wanted to disappear. At a time like this, parents should talk about the situation with their child and assess the coach's style and attitude.

I encourage parents to be "snobs" when looking for coaches for their young athletes. Seek out the best. The coach who communicates effectively, teaches, responds to individual needs, and appreciates the appropriate developmental stages of children has a jump-start on being a positive influence, role model, and teacher. And remember that developing your young athlete is a process. Find the right coach at every level as your child gets older, stronger, smarter, and more competitive. Parents need to understand that each coach is likely to play a significant role in their young athlete's life, so it is up to them to make sure it is a positive one. Basketball coach Heidi VanDerveer says, "Parents need to find a program that creates a positive environment for their children so they can be confident and valued. Confidence equals success, and success equals confidence."

When evaluating a coach, the parent ought to consider how the coach responds to losses. Losses are an inevitable part of the sports experience, and the coach's reaction leaves lasting impressions on children. The mother of a boy on a middle school basketball team told me a disturbing story about a coach's reaction to a loss. Her son's team took third place at a tournament. In the locker room after the game the coach threw the trophy, shattering it against the wall. He barked, "Third place isn't good enough!" Hearing that, this wise mother removed her son from the team and reported the coach's action to the principal.

Collegiate diving coach Jane Wobser says, "Athletes look to see how we react. If we make losing a big, huge deal and get angry about it, then they learn that failing is a big huge deal. We try to have one or two goals coming into a competition, stressing small victories. Maybe the meet didn't turn out the way you wanted, but think about some of the good things that did come from it and think about what you learned. Losses make the wins even better." High school swim coach Jeff Wobser echoes her sentiments. "If the coach thinks it's the end of the world, then the athletes will think that too. We have to teach the process and learn from the process." Another productive approach is the one taken by youth soccer coach Josh Gray. He says, "When we lose, I try to find something to learn from the experience so that it doesn't occur again. With each loss comes a lesson, and I take that lesson and incorporate it into the next practice."

A part of coaching is giving constructive feedback. Athletes are sometimes their own worst enemies. They take to heart every criticism directed at them. Perfectionism is often a major trait of an athlete's personality along with the desire to please others, a focus on external rewards, the drive to succeed and overwork even through pain, "all or nothing" thinking, and high expectations. Given these characteristics, it is not surprising that athletes tend to focus on the negative more than on what they are doing well.

I remember the time our basketball team captains approached Coach Pat Summitt with the complaint that the coaches were constantly criticizing the players and were very negative in practice. Coach Summitt did not agree with their complaint, so she decided to test their grievance by introducing this feedback system. When a coach made a positive comment or complimented a player, the player was instructed to respond, "Two points." When a coach provided constructive criticism, the player was to say "Rebound." Coach Summitt had the managers keep track of the number of times each response was given. At the end of practice the team was surprised to learn that the "two points" responses outnumbered the "rebound" responses. The feedback system succeeded because it entailed a clean delivery of information, acknowledged that the message was received, and gave good reasons to move forward.

Matching athletes with coaches can be tricky. Sometimes even the best coach and the most talented player are not necessarily a good combination.

I knew a basketball player who vomited at the beginning of each practice. After running a battery of tests and determining that there was no medical reason for it, I took her into my office and asked if she really wanted to be at Tennessee. She began to cry and said, "No." She felt that she would be letting her father down, along with all the people who wanted her to be here. I convinced her to talk with Coach Summitt. She was surprised and pleased by the coach's response. With Coach Summitt's support and help, she transferred to another school and went on to have a successful collegiate and professional career. The moral of this story is that the coach/athlete fit is not "one size fits all."

Ultimately coaches are also responsible for the safety of their athletes; however, it is not the first thing on their minds. Because they focus on building a winning team, they can miss signs and symptoms that an athlete is in danger of injury. A coach and her thirteen-year-old basketball player with a painful swollen knee came to see me during Coach Pat Summitt's summer team camp. I evaluated the knee and didn't find any real structural damage, so I asked her more questions to determine why the knee was so swollen. During team camp, each team is guaranteed three games a day, but I discovered this child was playing in six games every day. I asked the coach, "How is it that she is playing that many games in a day?" Looking down at the ground, the coach replied sheepishly, "I coach the middle school and high school teams and brought both to camp this week. She is our tallest player, so I had her playing with both teams." I called the camper's mother to tell her about the knee and that I was not allowing her daughter to play anymore this week because her knee needed rest. Then I called Coach Pat Summitt, who in turn had a firm discussion with this coach.

Unfortunately, most sport programs do not require a medical presence until the collegiate level. Youth sport programs work on a skeletal medical plan. First aid and CPR-trained personnel may be the extent of the available medical care. When it comes to decision making about musculoskeletal injuries, chronic conditions, and concussions, the training is just not enough. One of our divers told me about the time she was competing as a gymnast in high school and had a history of Achilles tendonitis. Her tendonitis flared up, causing her problems during a gymnastics meet. Her coach saw the pained look on her face and asked her if she was okay. She replied that her heel was bothering her more than usual but she wanted to compete anyway. Without evaluating her, the coach allowed her to vault. On her approach run she felt a ripping sensation in the middle of her calf and fell on the runway. It's my opinion that if her Achilles had been appropriately evaluated that day, she would not have been allowed to vault. The competitive nature of both the coach and the athlete clouded their judgment and made the injury worse.

Meg McDaniel reflects on her son Christopher's pitching experience with both pride and caution. "I realized he was such a good baseball player when he was in the third grade. By the time he was in seventh grade, other kids and coaches were coming to watch him play. I remember standing by the dugout and noticing two younger boys talking excitedly about him, and when Christopher pitched the ball, it was so fast that their only response was 'Holy s—t!'" Meg's brother, who was a star pitcher, told her how to take care of Chris—to keep his arm warm and not let him throw "junk" (curve balls, sliders, split finger fast balls, or knuckle balls). Because the coach and the kids wanted to win games, there was always pressure on Chris to throw junk even when his mother asked that he be stopped from doing so. Meg said that "the coaches meant well, but they were not trained or certified to work with children, and I think that was a big flaw in the system." Unfortunately for Chris, the combination of the coach's lack of good judgment, the pressure to win, and his own carelessness resulted in a career-ending elbow injury at the age of sixteen.

Sad stories like this mobilized the medical profession to help guide the Little League in the development of rules and regulations in 2007. There is now a limit to the number of pitches a pitcher can throw in a game and how much rest he must have in between pitching appearances. Current research on pitching injuries fueled additional changes in 2010 to both pitch counts and number of rest days. The new changes are targeted to protect the youngest participants.

My assistant Catherine enrolled her daughter Mara in softball and was pleased at the first practice when the coach set the tone for the parents. He said, "I don't care if it is you, or aunts, uncles, or grandparents, if they do anything to embarrass the kids, I will personally escort them out of the park." To Catherine the message resonated loud and clear: parents were not allowed to yell at the kids, umpires, or the coach from the stands. The coach was very positive and encouraging. He was not concerned about winning and losing at their age, but rather that they learned the skills of softball and had fun. Both Mara and Catherine had a great time with youth softball.

Parents have many sports programs from which to choose. It is smart to visit team practices to observe the coach and find the one who has the personality, philosophy, training, experience, and knowledge that you determine is right for your child, because your young athlete deserves the best. And the best are those coaches who see the big picture and recognize the role they have in educating and inspiring youth. Once you have carefully checked out and approved your child's coach, relax and enjoy the ride.

Day 6: Winslow, AZ, to Gallup, NM, 127 miles

Hello Everyone,

The group galloped into Gallup, New Mexico. Unfortunately, I did not. I spent a sleepless night with a GI virus and took the trip to Gallup in the van, chewing on ice chips. And I was not alone. Four others in the group were suffering, as well. Once I got to Gallup, I visited their lovely hospital where a 102.2 temperature, high blood pressure, and dehydration called for two liters of IV fluid. Will see what happens tomorrow—now not so fun.

Day 7: Gallup, NM, to Albuquerque, NM, 145 miles

It was cold in the am (37 degrees). I was still trying to get my strength back, so I decided not to ride until the first rest stop. The weather started to warm, and the winds became favorable, so I got on my bike. More interstate riding with some very good shoulders and some not so good shoulders—but I avoided the Flat Demon. We rode through Grants, New Mexico, past the uranium plant (hope I am not glowing), and into Milan. The small towns of San Fidel, Acoma, the Laguna Indian Reservation, and Paraje really portray the Wild West. So did the big rattlesnake in the middle of the road. Mike took a picture.

It was a mental and physical day for me, trying to work through recovering from being sick. I carried a sleeve of saltine crackers in my jersey pocket and forced myself to eat two each mile to get some salt and a few calories in me. We had to cross Ten Mile Hill. It is called that because it can be seen from ten miles away; thank goodness it was only four miles long and a mild steady grade. Winslow taught me to "take it easy," so I did and went slowly. It was all downhill into Albuquerque, crossing over the Rio Grande. Unfortunately, the winds had shifted so it was "squirrelly" coming down the hill, and I could not open it up, but I still had a fun descent. It turned out to be a really nice day, sunny, warm, and breezy.

Jenny

Chapter 6

School's Out! That Summer Magic

School's out! Yay! Summer's here. When I was a kid in Skokie, a suburb of Chicago, summer meant long, endless days of playing with my friends. After breakfast we would run outside and enter a different world. It was our world, and the days belonged to us. We explored imaginary kingdoms, conquered dragons, and invented games that never ended. Balls, bats, hoops, mitts, roller skates, bikes, wagons—these were the tools of our trades, and we filled our pockets each day with treasures that we found—rocks, nuts, lost coins, shiny shards, beads and buttons, bottle caps, crumpled baseball trading cards, bright plastic bits. When we couldn't identify what we found, we knew without a doubt that it held the most power and handled it with reverence. Twice a month the knife man made his rounds on a bicycle cart with a whet stone attached. Our parents gave us scissors and knives that needed sharpening, and we watched him with fascination. Polishing each piece with a thick leather strap, the knife man sliced paper and fruit with a flourish to show off his talents.

Summer nights announced extra treats when the jingly music of the ice cream truck teased the air. We scrambled for our allowance money and ran to the truck to claim yummy delights. We savored every moment as we sat on the curb eating drumsticks, push-ups, and ice cream sandwiches—the perfect end to a full summer day.

Our park district offered day camps staffed by high school and college students. I remember days filled with kickball, games on the playground equipment, crafts, skits, swimming, and more. I'd go home tired but excited about what might happen the next day.

Summer also meant family camping when we would swim in the lake, row boats, catch sunfish and minnows, sail, and water ski. At night we'd build a campfire and make sweet s'mores, the sticky marshmallow, chocolate, and graham cracker treats, as shadows and the sounds of the tree frogs transformed our camp. I took pride in cooking the perfect, golden brown marshmallow, while my twin sister loved to burn her specimen to a crisp and then hold her stick up, a tiny glowing torch lighting up the dark sky. Dad would suddenly emit a terrifying howl, and we'd beg him, "Daddy, don't scare us," while we shivered in delicious anticipation, waiting in the spookiness for another shattering cry.

The door to the athletic training room opens to shake me from my reverie as hundreds of kids are descending on campus for summer sports camp. Our staff is ready to greet, check medical information, hydrate, assess, treat, and refer injuries, and communicate daily with parents and coaches. During the next few weeks, we will be focusing on making sure that the campers have a safe, memorable, and fun time.

All over the country, summer is filled with camps for every sport for children as young as four on up through high school. They provide opportunities for kids to learn and improve their skills. Camps may be designed for individuals or teams, residential or day camps, marketed to specific skill levels for the novice or the experienced player. All promise improved performance, skill development, and competition. Colleges and universities, civic organizations, after-school community programs, or other youth-directed sports associations may host camps. Costs vary widely from minimal charges for basic supplies to hundreds, even thousands of dollars for advanced coaching and training. We can expect to see some children decked out head-to-toe in the latest sports fashion and others wearing just the basics. While the equipment doesn't have to be expensive, it does need to be appropriate to decrease the likelihood of injuries.

Schedules and intensity levels of play vary from camp to camp. During Coach Pat Summitt's four-day overnight basketball camp, the campers have three sessions each day that include a lecture, skills work, and games. Contests, tours of facilities, and meeting the Lady Vol basketball players are high points of the camp. The experience concludes with an all-star game and an awards presentation.

Many of our campers travel great distances. The day camps used to draw children only from the local region, but now out-of-state players come for half-day sessions that focus on basic skills. I question the wisdom of sending a child, whose tee-shirt nearly drags on the floor, so far away just to learn how to dribble a ball. Given the ability, focus, and actual interest of a child of that young age, a community camp would be just fine.

However, the expenses for lodging and food and the time and money for travel seem insignificant to the parents who see their children as prodigies who might be noticed by a college coach. Our program is only one of many camp experiences scheduled for a child in the summer. When they are not at sports camp, so many spend the rest of the summer competing with the rec team or Amateur Athletic Union (AAU) or a club team, incurring all the added costs for instruction, uniforms, equipment, travel, and other required expenses.

Looking at these young people, I often think about what are they missing—family vacations, unstructured time, leisure, free play, and all the experiences of summer that bond families and friends forever. I am concerned that the single-focused summer sports camp marathon takes both a physical and emotional toll. These grand quests can actually harm the body through overuse injuries and hinder the development of a healthy, well-rounded, and balanced human being. Many issues are brought to me at camp—from upset stomachs most likely caused by homesickness, to rashes, bee stings, headaches, and injuries. This past summer a camper twisted her knee and my evaluation determined she had injured her medial collateral ligament (MCL). Luckily for her, this is a non-surgical injury; however, it requires four to six weeks of rest and rehabilitation. When I explained this to her, she said, "But I can't be out that long. I have eight more camps to go to." I suspected that she was not really hearing me or understanding the importance of being careful with this knee, so when I spoke with her mother on the phone, I emphasized over and over that her daughter needed to be seen by an orthopedist, do the rehab, be monitored closely, and that the rest of the summer camps should be cancelled.

I will always treasure my summer camp experiences. I have fond memories of attending horse camp two summers where I learned everything from riding to shoeing a horse. In middle school I wanted to improve my basketball playing so I went to a camp run by a local coach, and in high school I attended a university-sponsored one, and played in a summer league. I learned about winning and losing. Winning feels good and sets the bar for the next goal. However, sometimes it isn't about the final score at all. When we lost, the world did not end. It taught me good sportsmanship and gave me opportunities to reflect. I could take the time to think about what actions led to the loss, how I felt about it, and then—most of all—what this meant to me and about me. Experiencing this process in a safe place where the impact was minimal taught me that even losing is an important piece in building self-esteem. I still had time to learn other new things—crafts, music, and ballet. There were no trophies or report cards, but the pride I feel when I achieve something new gives me confidence, strength, and good feelings even today. I uncovered things about myself that I never knew before. When summer was over, I brought that new-found knowledge and balance to school—happy, excited, and ready for the new year.

We develop our core identity through childhood experiences. Not only is it essential for us to cross train in sports; we need to cross train in all activities—go to museums, paint a picture, read a book, visit a national park, sing, see a play, walk on the beach. Opportunities for different experiences are endless. When weighed against the rigid schedule of continuous sports camps from June through August, which would you choose for yourself and your children?

Parents defend summers devoted to sports camp with the assertion that, by developing their child's talents in one sport, they better their chances for athletic scholarships to pay for college. An estimate of total dollars spent by parents on youth sports from ages eight to eighteen ranges from $5,000 to $10,000 per year, totaling $50,000 to $100,000.[13] For the 2009–2010 academic year, tuition for a public institution averaged $12,804 and for a private institution $32,184, making four-year totals of $51,216 (public) and $128,736 (private).[14] Reliance on athletic success as the sole means to pay for a college education creates undue pressure on a child and sends the message that she won't make it through college without her sport. High school swim coach, Jeff Wobser, recalls his collegiate years as a Division I student-athlete with a scholarship: "When people commented to my parents how great it was that I could go to school for free, my father's response was always, 'College isn't free. We just paid in advance.'"

Day 8: Albuquerque, NM, day off

A day to recover, do laundry, get a massage, clean bikes, and catch up on my news to all of you. The timing is good. I still need to get more calories to increase my energy levels.

And tomorrow we get to get up and do it again—how fun!

Jenny

Day 9: Albuquerque, NM, to Las Vegas, NM, 135 miles

Hola,

Your money is safe because it's New Mexico (elevation 6,371 feet), and not Las Vegas, Nevada. The weather was grand—seventies and sunny with no wind, tail winds, and heavy cross winds by the time the day was over. I am feeling much better now.

We left Albuquerque and rode up, up, up Route 66/New Mexico 333 east into Golden (sorry, no beer) and Madrid. Madrid is a neat town with some real characters. When they founded the town, they did not do water tables, so Madrid does not have enough water for daily life. In fact, they go days without it. Needless to say, bathing is not a priority. However, I am sure we smelly cyclists had no reason to complain. Very nice people in town.

Crossing the Continental Divide provided a group picture moment. Then it was back on the Interstate 25 to Las Vegas—skipped Santa Fe in the process. This is the last day of interstate riding, and no flat tire.

"Trains" is the word for the Southwest. There are a lot of them. The railroad is alive and well in these here parts. A thunderstorm that did not amount to anything chased us all day, so we had some nice cloud cover at times. The area is beautiful, painted rock formations, desert meadows, cactus, dry river beds, etc.

And we get to get up and do it again tomorrow—how fun!

Jenny

Chapter 7

Winds of Change: The Passage of Title IX

In 1896 at the first modern Olympics, a Greek woman called Melpomene unofficially became the first female to run a marathon, completing it in 4.5 hours even though she had to hide her identity at the start and was ostracized at the end. In 1931, professional baseball pitcher Virne "Jackie" Mitchell, at the age of seventeen, made history when she struck out New York Yankees Babe Ruth and Lou Gehrig in succession during an exhibition game. She received a standing ovation. After the game Babe Ruth told the Chattanooga newspaper, "I don't know what's going to happen if they begin to let women in baseball. Of course, they will never make good. Why? Because they are too delicate. It would kill them to play ball every day." A few days later baseball's first commissioner, Kenesaw Mountain Landis, banned women from the sport, "declaring women unfit to play baseball as the game was 'too strenuous.'"[15]

In Western culture, participation in sports for men and women still follows social custom. For young men, there has traditionally been an emphasis on discipline, strong physical stamina, and competition, while young women have participated at less strenuous and less competitive levels. In the early 1900s, cycling, boating, swimming, golf, field hockey, and half-court basketball were popular for women. As years went by, they saw action in more sports—volleyball, softball, diving, gymnastics, track and field—but rules, equipment, and style of play were crafted to protect what was commonly referred to as a "gentle and fragile" body of the "physically weaker gender."

Women's sports tended to emphasize enjoyment and fitness rather than competition, with physical education classes and sport clubs serving as the chief venue for sports in elementary grades, junior high, high school, and college. Although women have always possessed a competitive spirit, desire to excel, and physical stamina, in many circles it was deemed best to keep that a secret for the good of society. Each step forward seemed to stir the powers of resistance.

Decades after baseball's first commissioner banned women from the sport, change still came slowly. In 1947 Jackie Robinson broke the racial barrier in professional baseball playing first base for the Brooklyn Dodgers, paving the way for minorities in sport. In 1954, the rights of African American students found a national stage with the *Brown v. Board of Education* Supreme Court decision that declared state laws establishing separate public schools for black and white students unconstitutional. Ten years later, the Civil Rights Act of 1964 forbade discrimination on the basis of sex as well as race in hiring, promoting, and firing. Some years after, in 1972, the Equal Rights Amendment was passed by both houses in Congress and became the subject of heated debate and political focus when it was sent to the states for ratification. The amendment proposed, "Equality of rights under the law shall not be denied or abridged by the United States or any State on account of sex."

Baseball pitcher Virne "Jackie" Mitchell, a pitcher who struck out Lou Gehrig, at left, and Babe Ruth, far right. Library of Congress. Courtesy of Andy Broome.

When I was a young girl, my mother was involved in the League of Women Voters from the early seventies to the mid-eighties and served as president of our local league in the late seventies. I remember helping her with the newsletter, flyers, and mailings, and grabbing my clipboard, going house-to-house with her to encourage people to vote. This group took on the grassroots effort to pass the ERA in Illinois and gave me my first taste of political activism. Those days were instrumental in teaching me the power and responsibility of individual citizenship.

Though the ERA did not pass with the requisite thirty-eight states (or three-fourths of the states) to become law, lawmakers succeeded in passing some legislation during these same years that addressed women's rights issues. Indiana senator Birch Bayh and Representative Edith Green of Oregon sponsored legislation to attach Title IX to the educational amendments in an effort to assure gender equity, and specifically to decrease the amount of discrimination females encountered in the educational system. Their persistence and leadership resulted in the legislation's passage on June 23, 1972.

> Title IX: No person in the United States shall, on the basis of
> sex, be excluded from participation in, be denied the benefits
> of, or be subjected to discrimination under any education
> program or activity receiving federal financial assistance.

In short, Title IX mandates gender equity in education, including athletics. I was among the early generation of young people whose lives were impacted by the legislation. But even though Title IX had passed, organized team sports for girls were scarce. Little League baseball was well established, and organized softball was not offered. I wanted to play baseball in the summer of 1975 and signed up for Little League that year as the only girl in the local league. I rode my bike to every practice and game at the VFW Park, and I'm pleased to report that I hit a home run in my third game. I was rewarded with a free hot dog and soda pop of my choice—just like the boys!

Unfortunately, not all girls had the same opportunity. My friend, women's basketball coach Heidi VanDerveer, recalls her first encounter with discrimination in sports. "When I was eleven, all I wanted to do was play Little League baseball. I showed up at tryouts with my mitt and bat, and the coach said, 'Girls don't play baseball. Only boys play baseball.'" Crying, Heidi went home and told her dad what happened. A reasonable and fair man, her dad wanted his kids to be problem-solvers. He told her to write a letter to the president of the Chautauqua Institution, a center for the arts, education, religion, and recreation. Then he went to warn the director that they would take legal action against the state of New York if they didn't rectify the injustice.

> Dear Mr. Remick
>
> Last summer I was all set to play little league. But one problem. I was born a female! I have plenty of [knowledge] on how the game is played. I also know I would be one of the best on the field. We sugested [sic] a girls team but it did not work. So then I went to Ron head of the baseball team and he made up silly excuses like too many boys on the team. And my sister went to talk to him. But he wouldn't listen. I don't want to hand out bats, or keep score. I want to play a game called baseball this summer of '75. Sure hope your [sic] with us. Yours Truly, Heidi VanDerveer Please write back soon

She did play baseball that summer.

Former collegiate athlete at the University of Wisconsin–La Crosse, Chris Hofmann remembers her experiences in the early years of Title IX. "When I started high school, the Girls' Athletics Association sponsored Play Days one or two weekends each season. It wasn't until my junior year that we had designated competitive seasons for volleyball, basketball, track and field, tennis, badminton, and softball. We were told that girls could not earn a letter in sports because our seasons were too short. I knew this wasn't fair. My senior year I was president of the Girls' Athletics Association and worked hard to change that policy. I talked with our association advisor, my coaches, and the boys' athletics director. My efforts paid off, and the policy was changed the year after I graduated. My high school coach surprised me and sent me a varsity letter."

The energy of Title IX forced open the doors for women in every sector related to education. As the dominos fell forward, women had entry into professions traditionally open only to men, found greater upward mobility in the workplace, and enjoyed new competitive challenges. The number of women in higher education increased at the bachelor level, and more pursued degrees in mathematics, sciences, and technical areas. But nowhere did Title IX find a more public stage than in athletics.

Significant change was immediate. Between the 1972–73 and the 1973–74 school years, public high schools saw more than a 59 percent increase in the number of females participating in athletic programs. During that same time period, the number of males also increased but at a lesser rate of 8 percent. The number of females participating had already more than doubled by the 1975–76 academic year, while the number of males increased by 9 percent. Between 1972–73 and 2006–07, the number of females in high school athletic programs increased by over 269 percent. Again, it is important to note that male participation in high school sports also increased measurably during that time period, by almost 15 percent. (See Appendix A.)

The impact on women's athletics astounded even those who had sponsored the legislation. Some forty years later, Senator Bayh still remembers his surprise. "I don't think any of us had any idea about the impact this would have on sports," Bayh said. "We knew what we wanted to have happen as far as equality is concerned. But I guess the reason we were surprised by the impact it had on sports was that we didn't know how bad it was to start with."

He recalled a morning several years later that made him realize women's athletics had finally arrived. While he was looking at the sports page, which he regarded as the most male chauvinist part of a newspaper, he saw that the University of Virginia had played the University of Maryland. The headline read *Maryland Tops Virginia*. "I said to myself, 'Wait a minute—that can't be. They played last week.' But this was a women's game, and this was a headline in the *Washington Post*. Wow! Then I knew that we'd made real progress!"

The second major advancement for women occurred in 1978, when all federally funded educational schools and programs were to be compliant with Title IX, and the third happened four years later, in 1982, when the National Collegiate Athletic Association (NCAA) expanded its governance to women's athletics. The all-time winningest college basketball coach, Pat Summitt of the University of Tennessee, witnessed first-hand how much those events impacted women's athletics during her career, which began at UT in 1974 and includes an Olympic silver medal as a player in 1976, an Olympic gold medal as head coach in 1984, and eight NCAA titles. "When the NCAA took over, it was the defining moment for women's athletics," Summitt explained. "That gave women's athletics instant credibility and national exposure. And so the resources were put in place throughout the country."

Title IX and single governance for men's and women's athletics set the stage for competition at new levels. Its impact has been huge and is still unfolding, affecting all ages, genders, and professions. The years leading up to the development, passage, and implementation of Title IX were characterized by vigorous arguments for and against the legislation. Even today it is still debated, celebrated, challenged, and criticized—yet it remains unchanged.

Joan Cronan, former Women's Athletics Director at the University of Tennessee, with more than 30 years of experience in collegiate athletics, believes the legal challenges of Title IX can be positive. "Every time Title IX is called into question, we have an opportunity to review it and reaffirm its intent," Cronan explained. "I know that Title IX is working—I see the results every day. Whenever I am on an airplane and seated next to a man, invariably once he knows what I do, he will turn to me with a question and a statement. (1) 'Does she stare at you like that?' and (2) 'I have a daughter or granddaughter who. . . . ' I know that the first question refers to Coach Summitt, famous for her intense stares on the basketball court; and the second statement reflects pride in a daughter or granddaughter who just might be playing for the Tennessee Lady Volunteers someday. Look how far we have come."

One word could summarize the impact of Title IX: confidence. Expanding educational opportunities in all fields of study, sports, and school activities spur women on to see possibilities never before dreamed. Violet Palmer achieved new heights as one of the first female officials, along with colleague Dee Kantner, to referee in the NBA. I was especially eager to talk with this remarkable groundbreaker and to hear her personal perspective. After more than sixteen seasons, Palmer knows that self-confidence is a reason for her success. "I was fortunate to have the opportunity to learn the rules and develop the skills to be a referee," she said. "I encountered obstacles in a 'good old boy' system that promoted the belief that women can't physically keep up with men. I was just determined to be myself and to prove that I can do it. The silver lining is achieving that common ground of understanding and recognizing that 'no' is not an acceptable answer."

Advocates remain steadfast to the intent of the law but express concerns. At the end of the first decade of Title IX, former athlete and then athletic administrator at the University of Texas at Austin Dr. Donna Lopiano saw the land mines that threatened women's sports. In her prescient talk, "A Women-Centered View of Sport," at a women's leadership conference for physical educators at the University of Iowa in 1986, she said that all men and women should have an equal opportunity to participate in sports. Dr. Lopiano reminded her audience that "sport should be a means by which one gets to know oneself, not an end in and of itself." She cautioned that sport participants must not be exploited even though growth and institutionalization of athletics would make exploitation inevitable. "It is a given

Violet Palmer makes the call. Courtesy of the National Basketball Association.

that society's dominant public institutions will inevitably seek to exploit any human activity which is valued—to make money, to retain power, to exercise power over others. . . . There will be a constant pull or struggle for the primacy of values between those preferred by the individual and those preferred by the larger society in which the individual exists." Sadly, Dr. Lopiano's premonition has come true. Like men's sports, women's sports are now driven by ticket sales, endorsements, media coverage, and championships. It's not about playing the game for the simple joy of playing. It's about the end result: winning. Every day I see pressures for perfection, skewed self-identities, and sacrifices in personal health. But somewhere in all that, we still have individuals who have a desire to play the sport they love.

The Passage of Title IX

Title IX has generated more opportunities for women to step up to new professional goals in the workplace and to have equal access to compete in sports. As an athlete and now as a professional in sports medicine, I celebrate this tremendous progress, but 40 years later we still see inequities. People have more choices than ever before, but structured sports activities are still not equal between genders. Problems arise from faulty interpretation and implementation of Title IX.

Dr. Edward H. Hammond, president of Fort Hays State University and 45-year veteran of higher education administration, told me that compliance with Title IX is a management issue. "Title IX provides institutions with three choices to measure how to offer individuals of each gender nondiscriminatory opportunities to participate in intercollegiate athletics."

This three-prong test is used to determine compliance, which requires at least one of the three. The first prong requires that opportunities for male and female athletes must reflect and be substantially proportionate to their general enrollment in the educational institution. The second requires that the school show it has a history and continuing practice of program extension to meet the interests and needs of women. The third prong requires demonstration that the institution is fully and effectively accommodating the interests and abilities of women.

According to Dr. Hammond, "Most institutions looked to the proportionality measure rather than the prong that measures interest or the one that measures the value students have for the sports. Of the three tests only the third involves the students in the process." Dr. Hammond has the right idea in listening first to the students' voice. Would that there were more like him championing student equality.

We must promote ongoing education and vigilance to assure application of the true intent and implications of Title IX. Judy Sweet, one of the first women in the nation to serve as athletics director for a combined men's and women's program at the University of California, San Diego, is a consultant for Title IX and gender equity strategies. "There have been several assaults on Title IX—efforts to weaken the law, efforts to get around the law," Sweet said. "We need to pay attention to what the intent of the law is—the moral responsibilities that go along with it—and not become complacent because things are better than they were prior to its passage. We need to make sure that there is full compliance."

When I talk with female student-athletes today, I am surprised that they are unaware of their own history—even the years just before they were born. Most have no knowledge of, much less appreciation for, the strides women have made in athletics, and so they do not realize how far we've come or how far we still have to go. The future for women's athletics definitely includes challenges. Dr. Anne Mayhew, the first woman to serve as faculty representative to the NCAA from the University of Tennessee, warns that steady vigilance is needed to assure quality athletic programs. "I worry about losing institutional memory. We need to trot out our 'baggage' for a reminder to generations just now coming of age," the academic veteran said. "For great athletic programs and high ethical practices, someone needs to keep watch."

The longstanding tradition of men's sports links the identification of a winning sports team to an outstanding educational institution, sometimes to the detriment of education itself. Not that academics, performing arts, and other areas are less important, but the national college championships in football, basketball, and other sports garner mass media recognition and generate public pride in an instant. Winning translates to multi-million dollar contracts with media organizations for regular- and post-season coverage. Winning attracts top-tier student-athletes, generates more donor dollars for building facilities, and is positive fodder for public relations. Carried too far, though, winning at any cost compromises player safety, adherence to rules, institutional integrity, fair play, allocation of financial funds, and academic success. A prudent stewardship is needed to scrutinize the commercialism of collegiate athletics and to identify and set the priorities for a balanced life for the institution and the individual.

However, the positive impact of Title IX is evident in athletics, education, and careers. Professionally, I would not be where I am without it. The winds of Title IX produced major changes and, with all the challenges and fears that emerged, the heart of the matter must not get lost. Women's desires, dreams, and capabilities have always been here. Title IX added opportunity and the possibility for women to seek and reach their goals. Congressional debate, federal regulations, and judges' rulings have withstood the onslaught of scores of challenges. The message is clear and simple: if men get to play sports, then women do, too.

Our bikes lined up outside Charlie's Spic and Span Bakery, Las Vegas. Start your engines: the most important meal of the day.

The Wall, a gigantic hill challenging us in New Mexico.

Day 10: Las Vegas, NM, to Tucumcari, NM, 110 miles

At elevation 4,085 feet, I am back in the saddle 100 percent! We got up, loaded the van, and we all road to our breakfast place—felt like a motor-cycle gang.

Holy cow! Can you say head winds? Twenty miles per hour the entire way. Everyone is exhausted! Otherwise the weather was great, seventies and sunny. We passed the 1,000-mile mark today. We went through the towns—if you could call them that; blink and you missed them—of Trujillo, Variadero, and Conchas. Conchas had a golf course with dirt fairways, brown greens, and a reservoir, a real "resort" town. The diverse terrain—desert meadows, snowcapped mountains, rock formations, look-outs, and vistas where you could see forever—was spectacular. The cows and horses had it made, no overcrowding.

We did over 4,000 feet of climbing, including a ¾-mile hill affectionately known as "The Wall." All of the climbing would have been fine, if not for that head wind . . . we were going downhill at *only* 14 mph. Up may have been a negative number.

And we get to get up and do it again tomorrow—how fun!

Jenny

Chapter 8

The Plexiglas Ceiling

As Title IX compliance rolled on, careers in athletics for women were more visible and viable. I remember the moment in high school when I recognized my desire to work in athletic training. I had always liked science, working with people, and helping others. Add to that my love of sports. I found my calling when my best friend Cindy sustained a blood blister on her heel playing basketball. Because it was not adequately treated, she developed blood poisoning and was in the hospital for two weeks. Eventually she was fine, but Cindy's experience taught me how critically important medical care is for athletes.

At that time, a career in athletic training was not widely understood. When I told people about my goal, they would respond with comments such as, "So you want to coach?" or "Hmm, a personal trainer for athletes." When I told my mother that I wanted to become an athletic trainer, she said with considerable dismay, "Oh, Jenny, no, no, you'll be picking up towels in the football players' locker room." I explained to her that athletic trainers are healthcare professionals who collaborate with physicians to prevent, treat, and rehabilitate injury. I must say that Mom does frequently lament her initial reaction. Admittedly, at that time it was a leap of faith to envision all the changes that Title IX legislation would eventually bring about.

Every summer during college I was a youth sports camp counselor, adult class instructor, and eventually an administrator at Parkside Sport and Fitness Center, a converted high school in a Chicago suburb. In this remarkable program, we worked with athletes of all ages, from preschool through high school and adults, offering a wide spectrum of classes at varying skill levels, including strength training, walking, water aerobics, karate, and wellness. Team sports included basketball and volleyball adult leagues, and the youth camps offered basketball, tumbling, softball, baseball, soccer, and swimming. Each summer we served hundreds of people in the community. There I learned to appreciate how the body moves at different ages, how to motivate people, and how to develop creative programming.

The first summer at the center, my supervisor was Beth Heiden, the world-class speed skater. An extraordinary athlete, she played tennis, soccer, and set a national record in running the mile for her age as a freshman in high school. Among her many world championship accomplishments, in 1979 Beth won the World All Round Speed Skating Championship and a bronze medal in the 3000 m at the 1980 Winter Olympics at Lake Placid. She won top honors in cycling and cross-country skiing and has been inducted into the National Speed Skating Hall of Fame. I had the good fortune to be mentored by her, and she was a true role model. Beth taught me to embrace my competitive drive and use it to send a positive message about determination, work ethic, and goal achievement. Even though she was world known, she always stayed grounded and connected to the community we were serving. It was through her guidance that I became a supervisor, gaining first-hand leadership experience in the sports world at a young age. I had to manage finances, develop and maintain budgets, schedule facilities, supervise staff, and, on a daily basis, handle unexpected customer service issues. My involvement during those three summers was as valuable to me as college. My early "real-world" experience at Parkside Sports and Fitness Center and my athletic training assistantship in graduate school readied me for early success. I was lucky to be in the right place at the right time.

I came to the University of Tennessee as the Women's Head Athletic Trainer in 1989. At 24, I was the youngest in the country in that position at a Division I program in a profession dominated by men. The National Athletic Trainers' Association (NATA) documents athletic training career demographics. Their records show that Sherry Babagian was the first female to pass the certification exam in the late 1960s. According to the earliest available data on the NATA website, in 2001 the percentage of male certified athletic trainers in all career settings—high school, collegiate, and professional sports; clinical; hospital; and industrial—outnumbered females 54 percent to 46 percent. Not an overwhelming majority by any stretch. In 2009 the scales tipped in the other direction, with females totaling 50.1 percent. (See Appendix B.)

However, a 2012 update of "Women in Intercollegiate Sport, a Longitudinal National Study" by top researchers Dr. Vivian R. Acosta and Dr. Linda Jean Carpenter determined that 99.2 percent of schools have an athletic trainer, across Divisions I, II, and III, with 30.7 percent being female and 69.3 percent male. One hundred percent of Division I schools employ athletic trainers; however, at 17.5 percent they have the lowest percentage of head athletic trainers who are female. Division III has the highest percentage at 40.5 percent. They concluded that "the duties and skills of an athletic trainer seem to be independent of the gender of the athletic trainer or the division within which the athletic trainer works. Thus, the stark variation in representation across divisions and the overall low representation of females leaves open the question of the presence of non-skill based selection processes."[16]

By 2011 only three female athletic trainers had broken into the ranks of men's professional teams, one with the Pittsburgh Steelers in the NFL and two with the Los Angeles Dodgers in major league baseball. (See Appendix C.) The findings suggest that even though comparable percentages of women and men are certified as athletic training professionals, men dominate the top career opportunities in collegiate and professional team settings.

The growth of women's athletics also has stimulated discussion regarding the significance of gender and coaching. Is it better for women to coach women? For men to coach men? I posed those questions to Dr. Donna Lopiano. "Research shows that women who have been coached by women tend to prefer women more than women who have never been coached by women, but we have no reason to believe that either gender knows more," she said. "Effective coaching depends on a value system, on training."

But employment patterns of intercollegiate head coaches show continuing disparity between men and women. In 1972, when Title IX was enacted, females coached more than 90 percent of women's teams. These positions were typically part-time, filled by graduate students in physical education programs, or were uncompensated. As colleges initiated or elevated women's varsity programs, they almost invariably hired female coaches, but salaries and positions were entry-level at best. After the NCAA became the governing body for women's sports, more men began to find their way into the coaching ranks of women's teams. The evolution of women's athletics to a highly competitive and public stage has brought money to the table and men to the jobs. As demonstrated in the Acosta and Carpenter study, the picture changed drastically. In 2012, 57 percent of women's teams have male head coaches. Virtually all of men's teams continue to be coached by males.[17]

From her vantage point, University of Tennessee women's basketball coach Pat Summitt has seen amazing growth in opportunities for females in sports, but not when it comes to coaching men. "At the Division I collegiate level, there are a lot of men coaching women's basketball teams, and nearly all have at least one female on their staff," she observed. "No female has been the head coach of a men's basketball team, and only once has a female been on the men's coaching staff. That was at Kentucky, when Bernadette Mattox served as an assistant to head coach Rick Pitino from 1990 to 1994."

Former University of California, San Diego, athletic director Judy Sweet identifies life-work balance issues as ongoing barriers to women in athletics. "We hear this particularly from female coaches," she said. "There are too many women who are not giving serious consideration to staying in the field or being a coach or an athletics administrator." Traditionally, women are the ones who have to manage daily family needs. A female collegiate coach who has been in the profession for a long time expressed her frustration. "I have three children. I have pressure to make sure my family is okay," she said. "When it comes to recruiting, speaking engagements, and community events, I have to keep balance with my family because that is the most important thing to me."

The NCAA surveyed student-athletes, administrators, coaches, and officials in the 2008–2009 school year to identify what they perceive as barriers to women pursuing athletic careers. Across the board, findings indicate that life balance issues, time commitment, family commitments, and burnout are the top reasons that women do not pursue or continue careers in athletics.

A related report by Dr. Marlene Dixon and her colleagues in the 2008 *Journal for the Study of Sports and Athletes in Education* makes the case that "[i]ntercollegiate athletic departments are culturally distinguished by high incidences of work overload for coaches, administrators, and support staff." This study by six women in academia, entitled "The Work/Life Interface in Intercollegiate Athletics," examines "this overload phenomenon, accentuated by the industry's travel demands and supervision requirements, [which] makes it particularly difficult for athletic department employees to successfully integrate work and a life outside of work on a consistent basis . . ."[18] Caregiving and domestic duties, along with societal pressure to provide the primary care for the family, continue to be issues that prompt women to leave the profession or not even to pursue a career in athletics.

Responsibilities and personal obligations can conflict in any profession. Many of my talented, hardworking, dedicated female colleagues in collegiate athletic training have been forced to make alternate career choices due to family priorities. With the 24-hour, 7-days-a-week expectations of athletics, many coaches, support staff, and administrators have resigned to take a weekday, 9-5 job to spend more time with family, while others burn out trying to balance all that is expected at work and at home.

What will it take to attract the best, the brightest, and to retain women in sport professions? Women are different and women's sports are different. These differences do not suggest that women are less deserving, talented, driven, or accomplished. Differences do not define value. It is time for all those associated with sport to embrace new creative models that lead to success and sustainability. This new vision must address multiple issues, all fueled by the pressure to win. The time demands of longer competitive seasons, increased practices, and more games during non-traditional seasons can have a bloating effect. Teams often have to share facilities, which creates scheduling conflicts that lead to early-morning or late-night practices. Recent legislation that allows coaching through the summer months and the expectation that staff be available so that athletes can train year-round adds to the work load. New conference alignments have changed the geography, greatly increasing travel times and distances. For example, the Big East Conference has teams located as far east as New York, as far west as California, as far north as Wisconsin, and as far south as Florida. Television drives the competitive schedule, with events starting late into the night. The time requirements and intensity of off- and on-campus recruiting and the need for fundraising, special events for fans, and community service expand the work schedule. In addition, summers are filled with camps that cut into family vacation time.

In order for women to enter, succeed, and remain in athletics, the new models must utilize policies and address cultures that attend to the unique needs and constraints of female employees. For the development, advancement, and retention of these valued workers, strategic elements must be incorporated that include an emphasis on leadership development and tracks for top administrative positions; female mentors who will be role models for future aspiring women coaches and administrators; the elimination of salary discrepancies to provide equal compensation; and daycare and family-need initiatives. Taking a good, hard look at the structure, culture, and climate of intercollegiate athletics to see what can be changed to improve institutional support for the work-life balance of those in the profession is a win/win for everyone.

When the 2008–2009 NCAA survey asked about gender-driven hiring practices, the respondents answered that it is most common for men to hire men. The next highest percentage of respondents said that women more often hire women; fewer than half said that there are women who only hire men; and the smallest percentage said that there are men who only hire women.

The Plexiglas Ceiling

Title IX consultant Judy Sweet expressed concern that men dominate the career of coaching. "I think we will see an increase in the number of women coaching men's team sports, but the numbers are going to be so small that I doubt that it's going to make any difference in opening opportunities for other women," Sweet said. Career paths for women coaching men have not been plentiful. At present, no woman is the head coach of a NCAA Division I men's team. The problem is that women have far fewer chances to prove their skill, knowledge, and abilities. If women coached men and failed to win games, it is highly unlikely they would be given another opportunity. On the other hand, men whose teams are not winning are not denied the chance to continue coaching women. This double standard and traditional male domination in coaching and key athletic administrative positions are apparent in studies of employment trends.

Female athletic directors in Division I are still overwhelmingly the minority. Again, according to Acosta and Carpenter, women account for 20.3 percent of all athletic director jobs across divisions, with just 10.6 percent at Division I. The number shrinks to 4.9 percent at the Football Bowl Subdivision level.[19] Reporter Andrea Adelson of the *Orlando Sentinel* attributes some of the reason for this slow progress to the "lingering perception that a woman cannot run a department that largely revolves around football."[20] Richard Lapchick, director of the Institute for Diversity and Ethics in Sport at the University of Central Florida points out, "If you're an aspiring female athletic director, you have to be discouraged by that. We've had diversity breakthroughs in pretty significant ways in a lot of different areas, and this is one area where it hasn't happened yet."[21] His observations are confirmed by the Acosta and Carpenter study. In 2012, there are still 9.2 percent of athletic programs that have no female anywhere in their administrative structures.

Inequities persist. My own experiences coupled with those of others make me wonder what college presidents perceive about the progress of women's participation and leadership in athletics. From his vantage point as president of Fort Hays University, Dr. Edward Hammond knows women are still facing equity challenges. "Women's athletics are still competing for public appreciation and popularity." He suggests that creative scheduling could invite greater interest, participation, and media coverage. Television is the stage that reaches the largest audience. Dr. Lopiano understands this. "Leaps in sport participation occur after the Olympic Games," she said. "When little girls see woman athletes on TV, they dream big. If there were one piece of the puzzle that would drive participation better than lawsuits, it is media coverage of women's sports."

Money is the driving force and the measuring stick of any business, including the sport industry. The devalued perception of "women's work" directs compensation practices throughout the workforce. Coaches of women's teams make far less, on average, than coaches of men's teams, even when they have the same responsibilities. Continuous monitoring of athletic program funding shows that the financial gaps are still wide, with women's teams accounting for just 37 percent of athletic program operating expenses. On the average, men's coaches are paid more than twice the amount paid to coaches of women's teams.[22] These disparities in all areas of athletics are appalling and call for action. The legal position of equal pay for equal work is inherent in the legislation of Title IX. Enforcement of the law requires determination, persistence, and courage. The process takes time, and even when disparity is proven, restitution is not assured due to organizational politics and budget priorities.

Dr. Anne Mayhew, professor emeritus and administrator at the University of Tennessee during my time here, points out that equity in her job arena also has yet to be achieved. "While women have gained the confidence to

Table 2. Top Ten Industries Paying Females the Least Percentage of the Dollar in Comparison with Males, 2011[1]

Industry	% of Dollar Earned by Women vs. Men
Retail	79.5%
Wholesale trade	79.3%
Public administration	78.5%
Information	75.8%
Utilities	75.8%
Durable goods	74.9%
Nondurable goods	73.8%
Healthcare/social assistance	71.8%
Professional/technical services	65.9%
Finance/insurance	62.2%

[1]Petrecca, Laura. "Number of Female 'Fortune's 500 CEO's at Record High," 27 October 2011. *USA Today* Web Site.

know that they are as able or better than their male counterparts, there is still much disparity in promotion to tenured positions. Career expectations are lowered as women feel trapped between the biological and tenure clocks," she said.

The disparity between genders is not limited to the sports and academic worlds. One doesn't need to look far to see evidence of male dominance in the business world as well. Statistics tell the story, with significant gaps between genders in position and salaries. Comparisons of salaries and numbers of women in the work force demonstrate gender differences. Female earning power still falls short of that of their male counterparts. In the 1970s, a woman earned 72 cents for every dollar earned by a man. More than forty years later it has hardly improved, with women earning only 77 cents for every dollar earned by men.

After working more than twenty-five years in collegiate athletics, I see first-hand the salary disparities and limited opportunities for advancement. Some areas of athletics show increasing numbers of women employed, but head coaching, head athletic training, and higher level administrative positions continue to be dominated by men. Paradoxically, when university administrators begin to discover that women's sports can bring big dollars and publicity, it is not uncommon to see the hiring of a man over a woman even when the woman is more qualified. This practice maintains the gridlock that stymies career growth, experience, and equal compensation.

Sociologist Dr. Jay Coakley cites traditional negative views of strong women as a barrier to the growth of women's athletics. "Strong women challenge the gender logic that underlies the norms, legal definitions, and opportunity structures that define and describe the conditions under which men and women form identities, live their lives, and relate to each other," he explained. "People who gain by the prevailing gender logic in society see strong women as a threat and do all they can to return to the 'good old days,' when men played sports and women watched and cheered."[23]

Judy Sweet considers resistance to change as a major threat to achieving equity. "People have difficulty whenever there is change. Unfortunately, those who have enjoyed a certain style of living are concerned when there are changes that provide equity and possibly have to share some of the benefits that were enjoyed by a few," she observes. "They are going to blame Title IX for changes in what they perceive as their quality of life." This argument is unfounded. While the power of Title IX significantly increased the number of women in sports, it did not hinder the continuing growth of men's participation.

Men still occupy the top administrative levels of the sport industry. As long as girls do not have women as career role models in decision-making positions, progress for women in sports will be slow. The glass ceiling has, if anything, lowered and is now made out of nearly unbreakable Plexiglas.

Resources and benefits have improved since Title IX's passage, but they fall short of what equity requires. Attorney Stacey Sisco looks forward to the time when legislation will not be needed to assure parity. She maintains that the legal activities that challenge inequities are not nearly enough. "We hear people talking about the inequities but rarely see anybody taking action," she says. "Fortunately now more individuals within an institution are no longer assuming inequality is acceptable, and they are taking action. More progress is being made in this form than in court decisions. In my mind that is encouraging." Sisco also urges women to be persistent. "So many people just will not stay with it. Equity shouldn't have to be discussed. It should just simply be. I hope that in the future equality is not a part of the discussion; it's just a part of life."

Day II: Tucumcari, NM, to Dalhart, TX, 96 miles

Howdy y'all!

Sorry this is late—the hotel in Dalhart TX was having trouble with their Internet connections. You talk about twenty-five very unhappy people. We are all prisoners to our computers.

It was supposed to be an easy day since it was under 100 miles, but head winds of 12–15 mph changed that. It was also cold—high temp 57 degrees, and at midday it was only 50 degrees, not including wind chill. Cloudy. At least the forecasted rain held off—that would have been too much and would have taken away the fun! Talk about a lonely stretch of highway. We traveled on 54 East, a nice smooth road, and as far as the eye can see were pastures with trains, trains, trains going by. The mountains are gone.

We passed through the towns of Logan and Nara Visa, New Mexico. Nara Visa was literally a ghost town with everything boarded up, run down, and vacant. I was really hoping for a hot tea at this point to warm my chilled bones, but no such luck. At fifty-four miles, we crossed the state line into Texas. The road got rough at this point, and there was very little change in scenery. Ten miles outside of Dalhart, Texas, the feedlots started. We were

The ghost town of Nara Visa, New Mexico.

thankful because it was cool with a strong breeze. The feedlots are incredible. I could never have imagined seeing so many cattle in one place and packed in so tight, row after row in huge facilities on both sides of the road.

The town of Dalhart has a distinct odor and a train that goes by our hotel every couple of hours, all night long. A real cowboy town.

And we get to get up and do it again tomorrow—how fun!

Jenny

Chapter 9

Homophobia in Sport

German psychologist Karolyn Maria Benkert first coined the term "homosexuality" in the late nineteenth century. While the word is relatively modern, lesbians, gays, bisexuals, and transgendered (LGBT) people have always existed. Historically, the ancient Greeks accepted and celebrated same-sex relationships through the teachings of Plato and the writings of Aristophanes. Voices of the fifth century BCE speak of gender attraction as a personal matter rather than a moral issue. In the present day, sexual orientation and gender expression are serious points of contention, sparking emotional, political, religious, and civil debate. In the sports world, homophobia, which is a generalized fear or intolerance of lesbians, gay men, bisexuals, and transgendered people, is rampant.

Because people fear difference, the fear of LGBT people is not so surprising. Homophobia rages in almost every segment of American society: young, middle-aged, and elderly; poor, middle-class, and rich; male and female. It can be found in every religion and in every city and town. It impacts workers in arts and culture, professional, and laboring positions. And of course, in sport.

What does this fear have to do with sport? Everything and nothing. Everything, because sport is not immune to social ills. Historically, people in all areas of sport were actively discriminated against based on race, gender, ethnicity, and religion. Racism played a key role in denying access to professional sports. Women once were perceived to be too weak for marathon running, weight lifting, and cycling. Following Hitler's rise to power in 1933, Nazi officials expelled top German athletes who were Jewish. Today, sexual orientation is the target of overt and silent discrimination at every level of sports—professional, Olympic, college, high school, and youth. And fear should have nothing to do with sports, because—just as with an athlete's race, gender, ethnicity, or religion—sexual orientation or identity has no bearing on athletic ability, leadership skills, or capacity for sportsmanship and heart.

Dr. Pat Griffin, Professor Emerita at the University of Massachusetts, Amherst, and author of *Strong Women, Deep Closets: Lesbians and Homophobia in Sport*, is working with the Gay, Lesbian and Straight Education Network (GLSEN) to address bias and behavior in sports at the K-12 levels. With a history of more than thirty years in higher education, Dr. Griffin has witnessed a changing climate regarding attitudes and acceptance. "When I started doing this work, I was a lone voice in the wilderness. It is good to see change and so many more people doing the work."

While LGBT people have gained some visibility and acceptance in the general culture through the media, athletic culture lags behind. Dr. Griffin feels that we need to consider the role sport has played historically in the larger culture. "Sport has defined masculinity. Sport is where boys learn to be men," Dr. Griffin explains. "I think that whether it is women in general or gay men and lesbians in particular who want to participate, they are a threat to that historical function."

Homophobia is so menacing and powerful that it stops people from coming out, from being who they are, from reaching their full potential, and it discourages them from playing sports or participating fully in society. In athletics, males and females can experience this differently. Athletics has historically been defined by masculinity and perpetuates a culture that is binary—male or female—with only two ways to fit. In general women can stretch the binary rules of male and female and be accepted as tomboys. Males are not allowed to stretch these rules with the effeminate stereotypes of gay men. The macho locker room is an inner sanctum populated by all the strong masculine stereotypes and follows the scripted military policy (at least until recently) of "Don't ask; don't tell."

Consider a quarterback of a top-ten college team or an All-America point guard. Their images have been cast in a mold that does not allow for differences. Universities have rich though sometimes narrow traditions. The phenomenon of student-athletes representing these traditions to alumni, fans, and the general public leaves little room for diversity.

Coming out is often a difficult decision. A few athletes choose to do so while at the peak of their career, some after their career has ended, and some are out long before they become involved in sports. It is rarely easy; it is sometimes disastrous; sometimes it is nearly a non-event. The positive side to coming out allows you to be true to self; puts an end to lies; often encourages others to come out; helps biased people realize they already knew and loved a gay person; and helps to normalize LGBT people to others. The negative aspects of coming out may include rejection and ridicule by family, friends, teammates, coaches, fans; ridicule by opponents; hate actions and threats; loss of endorsements; and loss of popularity. In spite of the possible negative ramifications, the widespread consensus is that life is better after coming out.

The number of professional athletes who have come out is miniscule. Most have done so after their playing careers have ended. Some of these sport greats include tennis icon Billie Jean King; football stars Esera Tauolo and David Kopay; baseball's Billy Bean and Glen Burke; and basketball center John Amaechi. A fine example of an athlete who came out during her playing career is tennis superstar Martina Navratilova. One bold sport administrator has come out while on the job. Rick Welts, then president and chief executive officer of the NBA Phoenix Suns, came out as gay on May 15, 2011, in an interview with the *New York Times*. The following fall he took a similar job with the Golden State Warriors in northern California to be closer to his partner. By comparison, the number of college athletes who have come out is astronomical, though in the grand scheme of things it is still quite small.

Andrew Langenfeld grew up playing sports. He also grew up knowing that he was different. As early as age six he vividly remembers asking his parents questions about sex and roles in male/female relationships, and by age seven he realized he was gay. He confided in his mother, but she convinced him that he would outgrow this phase. Growing up in a small midwestern town, Andrew says that he worried most about how close friends and family members would respond when he came out. He feared abandonment. When he was eighteen years old, he again told his mom that he was gay, and then in college, where he experienced his first relationship, he came out publicly. A standout swimmer, he earned a scholarship at the University of West Virginia and then transferred to Purdue University. He not only came out to his teammates, but he also took on the responsibility to educate them and carry the message to others.

Knowing the challenges that gay athletes can face, I asked Andrew how he found the strength to step forward. "Being a student-athlete is one of the most incredible experiences of your life, and you really want to have no regrets," he said. "I know a lot of people give up sport because they know they are gay, when really all they want is to be able to integrate all the parts that make up who they are."

Andrew has encountered positive and negative reactions. "At West Virginia, a friend and fellow athlete had preconceived ideas, but when he learned that I am gay, he realized that people are people. We started to hang out together. Then when some of his friends began asking him if we were dating, that really scared him. Eventually he told me that he could not continue to be friends with me because other people would think he was gay, too. That hurt."

At Purdue University, Andrew continued to be an advocate for gay athletes. When he became aware of derogatory language in the locker room, he suggested that he and his teammates write an email calling for change. "We were not just competitors in the pool. We were a family. There are athletes everywhere who don't have a gay teammate or who don't know another gay athlete. We realized there needed to be leadership and role models. This really sparked us to create an organization to help other student-athletes and form a national support network."

Andrew advises gay athletes to take it one step at a time. "Coming out is a process. I made sure that before I came out, I met a few other gay people so I had someone to talk to. I told a straight friend, and then I told my mom, taking my time, on my own terms. This pace made it so much easier for me. Word spreads quickly through a team. Make sure that you have a support group that's going to be there for you."

Dr. Sue Rankin, research associate in the Center for the Study of Higher Education at Pennsylvania State University, finds that individuals come out selectively to people they trust. "Out is on a continuum: out to your friends is one part; out to your nuclear family is another; out to your extended family; out to professional colleagues, if you are a coach, for example. There are very secretive pockets in athletics. Coming out is a daily process and is incredibly stressful."

Mother of a gay son, Meg McDaniel urges youth to love themselves first and find the courage to be who they are. Then, she says, they will find those who will love and embrace them. Meg says, "I have grown and learned so much from both of my sons. My message to parents of children who are LGBT is to let them know that your love is unconditional. My favorite quote is from author Anne Wilson Schaef, 'Children are the best teachers for helping us unlearn what we have learned.'" Meg says that she now knows that her son kept a lot of his thoughts and feelings from her because he was so conflicted about being gay. "I wish with all my heart I would have known what he was going through, because I would have been his chief ally."

Gay people are coming out much younger because of social networking, media exposure to role models, and greater public acceptance. Athletics, however, continues to perpetuate the binary culture that makes it impossible to be different in this system, according to Dr. Rankin. "If you don't fit what it means to be masculine or feminine, then you don't fit on that athletic team, and so you are weeded out; and in youth sports I think athletes experience that early."

Lee Turner played basketball as a child, and his experiences bear witness to Dr. Rankin's observations. Lee knew that he was different from other boys, and when he was in second grade, he began to understand that he is gay. He protected his secret until graduating from college. Lee remembers the alienation and isolation he experienced in the midst of homophobic comments and attitudes, particularly in sports. The male macho culture was frightening to him. "I never felt comfortable in the locker room and really would have preferred tennis to the team sports that were most popular for boys to play. Even though my brother was very good at baseball, I never played. The macho environment of that sport scared me."

One of the areas where homophobia is prevalent is in athletic recruiting. In "The Positive Approach: Recognizing, Challenging And Eliminating Negative Recruiting Based On Sexual Orientation," a paper Dr. Pat Griffin co-authored, she defined negative recruiting as when "coaches or other school representatives make negative comments or inferences about other schools and athletic programs rather than focusing on the positive qualities of their own school."[24] Negative recruiting is alive and well in women's athletics. One of our student-athletes told me that she experienced it. "On recruiting visits to another school the coaches reassured me and my family that we didn't have to worry about lesbianism—'We don't do that,' they boasted, and they were saying this to the parents of a girl who is gay." The actual or perceived sexual orientation of any coach, player, or staff member has no place in the recruiting process.

The documentary *Training Rules* tells the story of the destructive tragedy of homophobic practices by Rene Portland, the former women's head basketball coach at Penn State, and investigates why the university, which established policies to protect gay students, had done nothing to end this common form of victimization of their student-athletes. Coach Portland enforced three rules during her 26-year career: "(1) No drinking, (2) No drugs, and (3) No lesbians." The film's synopsis offers a chilling description of this real-life story: "Training Rules examines how a wealthy athletic department, enabled by the silence of a complacent university [blinded by winning records], allowed talented athletes, thought to be gay, to be dismissed from their college team. In 2006, student-athlete Jennifer Harris, in conjunction with the National Center for Lesbian Rights, filed charges against Penn State and Coach Portland for discrimination based on sexual orientation. This lawsuit inspired others whose lives were shattered during [her] reign to come forward."[25]

I saw Coach Portland's homophobic creed in action when I was an athletic trainer at Penn State from 1988–1989. One day I was covering a women's basketball practice as the softball team walked through the gym. Coach Portland said to me, "They are all a bunch of lesbians, and my goal is to get that team off this campus." As a lesbian, I knew I could not work with an actively homophobic coach in that targeted, unhealthy environment. That summer I accepted a position at the University of Tennessee.

Dr. Rankin finds that while progress in the battle against homophobia has been made on an institutional level, its impact has not been significantly felt for athletics. One student-athlete confided to her, "My coach and I kind of had a bumpy road in my career. He didn't communicate with me; he kind of cut me off. He was trying to get me to leave, and I never really understood why—all the older players warned me about him. Sometimes the coaches would say 'you need to be careful about who you hang out with' or they'd warn younger players not to hang out with certain teams, 'they will get you.'" Lauren P. shared her experience about being a lesbian collegiate volleyball player. "Being in the closet absolutely had an effect on me as a player. I find that a lot of energy goes into hiding a part of yourself from everybody around you. This is all driven by anxiety worrying about what everybody is going to think if they find out. It's sad when you can't be honest with the people you are closest to. This process is exhausting and depressing. It absolutely affected how I played. By the time you reach Division I college athletics, I truly believe it's about 20 percent physical and 80 percent mental. Generally, everybody at this level is physically similar, so the more successful athletes are the mentally tough ones. To carry on a charade like this affected my focus. I didn't feel that I could let down my guard and just relax because I was afraid. I always had to be 'on.' I don't feel that my teammates got to know the real me. It's not that being gay is such a huge part of who I am, but when you work so hard to hide it from other people, you end up hiding other parts of yourself."

Lauren P. went on to say, "My junior year I started to come out to a select few. When my roommate found out, she did not speak to me for three months and ended up transferring. That was a very difficult time. I heard gay slurs in the athletic department and all over campus. I eventually found a support network that made all the difference. I began to feel comfortable with myself and came out to family and friends. I remember when I came out to my sister, and she encouraged me to come out to my parents as well. I was terrified. She told me 'you need to give Mom and Dad more credit.' And she was right. My dad, who used the term 'faggot' more than I care to admit, now writes letters to the editor of our Ohio small town newspaper about his daughter having the right to marry just like anyone else. It was a pretty amazing transformation."

Endorsements, playing time, scholarships, coaching positions, and teaching and working with youth may be compromised when a female athlete discloses her sexual orientation. Sociologist Dr. Jay Coakley warns that "homophobia affects all women, lesbian and straight alike; it creates fears, it pressures women to conform to traditional gender roles, and it silences and makes invisible the lesbians who manage, coach, and play sports."[26]

One woman who preferred to remain completely anonymous told me, "When I was in high school and getting ready for college, I was deep in the closet and really feminine. Nobody ever suspected I was gay. I had a personal trainer who was an All-American, and one of the first things she talked to me about was that her first roommate was gay and to be careful. Little did she know, she was warning the wrong person." All through college she remained closeted to everyone except the select few she could trust.

With a desire to go into coaching, she feared her silence needed to continue, and this fear was confirmed. As a young club team coach, she was approached by some of the team's parents with an offer to help her select an interview outfit for a college coaching job. "They said, 'We will help you out—we can get something that looks professional, and still look feminine enough because you don't want to be labeled one of those dykey coaches.'" She said, "I know that there's a lot of homophobia in my sport, and it's a big concern for me. I know that I can't be out and be coaching."

Gay and lesbian coaches experience discrimination, as well. Lisa Howe, former soccer coach at Belmont University in Nashville, Tennessee, told me her story. She had been a head soccer coach for seventeen years in collegiate athletics. During her six years at Belmont, she won the 2008 Atlantic Sun Conference tournament and participated in the NCAA tournament for the first time in school history. Coach Howe found herself thrown into the national spotlight in December 2010 when, at the height of her career, this celebrated coach was forced to sign a "mutual agreement" with the university ending her coaching position. This agreement was made after she came out to her team as a lesbian and informed them that she was having a baby with her partner, Wendy. The team was very supportive; the administration was not. Her players and others close to the program told reporters she was fired for revealing the fact she was having a baby with her partner. Lisa grieved, saying, "I felt sad, angry, and, as my family's financial provider, fearful." The support poured in from faculty, students, and boosters, and from the local community and people across the country. The media took notice, creating a frenzy of debate with the majority speaking out against the injustice of the university's actions. Although Lisa is no longer coaching, her courage resulted in progress at Belmont. In January 2011, the board of trustees added sexual orientation to the school's non-discrimination policy. Lisa and Wendy named their little daughter Hope.

Lisa is currently executive director of the Nashville GLBT Chamber of Commerce. She knows that sport success is tied to diversity, and her goal is to show businesses that diversity and equality increase capacity and are positively tied to performance. Her advice to other lesbian and gay coaches is, "You are not alone. There is nothing more important to me than to live my life honestly and authentically. I know that people have to feel safe. Everyone has their own timing, and it's a very personal journey. You are not alone; there are lots of us out there."

The most recent LGBT issue in athletics today is the transgendered athlete. This issue is the only sexual orientation/gender identity topic addressed by NCAA legislation. The NCAA Inclusion of Transgender Student-Athletes policy "ensures transgendered student-athletes fair, respectful and legal access to college sports teams based on current medical and legal knowledge." The policy guides institutions to safeguard the privacy, safety, and dignity of transgendered student-athletes. Kye Allums is the first Division I transgendered student-athlete—female to male—basketball player on the George Washington University women's basketball team. He was allowed to continue playing on the team as long as he did not take the male hormone testosterone. In all other aspects he was treated as a male.

He had access to male locker rooms and restroom facilities in accordance with the Washington, D.C., law that ensures individuals the right to use gender-specific facilities that are consistent with their gender identity or expression. Male pronouns were used in the media guide, marketing, and coaching. Kye felt a great relief and satisfaction with his decision to be who he really is. He told the NCAA, "With the love and respect of the people around me, I no longer feel like I have to choose between being true to myself and staying in school playing the sport I love."[27]

Dr. Rankin makes a strong case for the prevention of prejudicial behavior through education. "Educate—get rid of the ignorance. Parents and institutional policy makers need to be educated. The discussion needs to be about power—who has it; what is it; how is it used; what privilege comes along with that power?"

Society dictates power and privilege according to how people are identified. White privilege is defined as a "right, advantage, or immunity granted to or enjoyed by white persons beyond the common advantage of all others."[28] White privilege is prevalent in our society, and most whites have no idea that they are privileged, which in and of itself proves that they are. Not long ago, a Caucasian friend of mine was at a convention with several colleagues. Due to a check-out time misunderstanding, the key to her hotel room did not work. She went to the front desk and asked for a new key. The clerk readily gave her one. Shortly thereafter, an African American colleague also asked for a new key. The clerk asked to see her ID.

Privilege extends to gender as well. Recently, my sister went to buy a car. The salesperson directed all eye contact and conversation to her husband, even saying, "Will the little lady be driving it as well?" They immediately walked out of the dealership. Ironically, at this time in their professional careers, she was the breadwinner of the household.

Occurrences of privilege exist even when the power characteristic is not overtly visible but assumed. Two qualified female candidates were the finalists for an assistant strength and conditioning position. One had more experience and stronger references; however, a key member of the search committee dismissed her, saying she was "not a good fit." While the actual words were not spoken, the rest of the committee assumed it was because she appeared to be a lesbian. The other candidate was hired.

In virtually every group, even those whose members have been discriminated against historically in this country, privilege and power exist. My brother overheard his African American neighbors talking about a Hispanic landscaping crew working next door. One said, "Bet those guys are illegals—ten bucks says they don't have papers."

Dr. Rankin is so right when she goes on to say, "We need people to be free to talk about what they think and how they feel about these issues," because a way to eliminate fear is to engage in open, inter-group dialogue. Putting names, faces, personal experiences, and emotions front and center will help us realize that we can accept people for who they are and celebrate our differences. I participated on campus with other administrators in a workshop designed to educate, stimulate conversation, resolve issues of conflict, and evaluate our current status as a just and diverse university. After getting to know me through group dialogue activities, one white, heterosexual, middle-aged male administrator came away with understanding, a greater awareness, compassion, and respect for gay people and is now actively working to improve our campus climate.

Struggles for acceptance in the sports world are not limited to athletes. Lindsy McLean, the highly respected head athletic trainer for the San Francisco 49ers, spent twenty-four years living in two worlds before his retirement. As McLean talked with me about his experiences, I felt anger for what he went through and admiration for the courage he brought to his athletic training room every day. McLean says he was aware of his sexual orientation as early as grammar school, when he had a crush on a classmate. Societal messages clearly denounced same sex dating, and McLean held onto the possibility that he might outgrow it. After dating a few women, he accepted that he is gay.

From 1968 to 1979, McLean was head athletic trainer at the University of Michigan, and during this time he came out to friend and colleague Dr. Robert Anderson, Michigan's team physician, whom he trusted. Although McLean found support within athletics, he did not experience that security across the board. One assistant football coach told McLean that he thought he had been "come on to" in the locker room at another school, saying, "I beat the pulp out of that guy." Despite the intolerance and even hostility he encountered, McLean said, "I still got up and did my job every day."

In 1979, he became the head athletic trainer for the San Francisco 49ers. McLean had a partner and didn't hide his sexual orientation, but he didn't go out of his way to mention it either. "I was working in a profession that wasn't accepting of gays, especially the players. I heard talk in the locker room that made me aware that they knew, and they didn't know quite how to deal with it, and that made me uncomfortable about coming out." At times he did feel supported by assistant athletic trainers, head coaches, and general managers.

During his career, he did suffer some physical and emotional attacks by players. Through it all, he remained professional and valued by the organization. Reflecting on those times, he theorizes why people are so homophobic. "It is something people don't understand, and they are fearful of the unknown." When McLean announced his retirement from the 49ers, a reporter from the *Santa Rosa Press Democrat* wrote a story about him that included his sexual orientation. "Before I agreed to do the article, I thought about it, talked to my partner, and I read a book, *Setting Them Straight: You CAN Do Something about Bigotry and Homophobia in Your Life*, by Betty Berzon. She motivated me when she wrote, 'The single most effective thing you can do to eliminate homophobia and bigotry is to come out.' So that convinced me to do the article."

He said that he feels almost universal support from peers across the profession. When I asked him how he would advise others who are gay, McLean said, "I don't suggest that they stay in the closet. Live your life without compromises but don't flaunt the fact that you are gay. If you let little comments get to you, you just can't survive. Earn respect by doing your job." A member of the National Athletic Trainers' Association Hall of Fame, Lindsy McLean's exemplary career illustrates that one's sexual orientation should not be an issue.

However, today, a person can be fired for their sexuality in twenty-nine states. Homophobia is pervasive. I feel gut-wrenching outrage at the unwillingness of educational institutions, governing sports organizations, and administrators to step up and say, "No more." During my twenty-five years, I have seen athletes leave their treasured sports because of their coach's prejudicial behavior toward them. To blend in, athletes change how they dress, how they act, how they talk—all attempts to hide who they really are. I have seen them create a phantom date or guy back home to disguise their lesbianism. I have seen academic troubles, falling grades, affected performance, and depression. I have seen an athlete be open to one person or group and closeted to another. I have seen conflict with parents and family as they apply pressure to conform to beliefs taught in their religious faith. I have heard the general athletic training room talk, the thoughtless use of slang such as the phrase, "that's so gay," and seen its powerful impact on the faces of athletes in the room. I have seen an athlete kicked off a team for vague reasons listed under the heading of attitude, when the true reason is that she is a lesbian or thought to be. I have seen athletes turn to alcohol for comfort in order to cope with their fear, because they feel they have no place to turn and no real protection. I have seen their spirits slip away bit by bit.

We must work to educate people who express homophobic and other discriminatory behaviors that threaten individuals. I am a leader on my campus, working with colleagues, faculty, and students to ensure that equality, acceptance, and respect are championed at the very top level and throughout the organization. I continue to educate my staff and athletes and create a culture where every individual can be their best regardless of sexual orientation or gender identity. One of the focal points in the athletic training room is my office's Diversity Window with its collage of stickers with slogans, symbols, and pictures of various cultures, religions, ethnicities, sexual orientations, and disabilities. It gets a lot of attention and encourages dialogue.

Diversity window.

I have seen young women simply eager to grow, make lasting friends, develop their talents, become contributing citizens and find personal meaning just like everybody else. Athletes ask me advice about coming out. I tell them, "Be great at what you do. Be respectful, positive, and pleasant to everyone. If you are someone who people want to be around, how can they hate you? When you do come out, be comfortable with people who accept you and patient with those who don't."

The slow change in culture, politics, and sport is frustrating. Equality will be attained through policy and governance to bring about social justice nationally and culturally by changing one person at a time. It requires commitment, courage to confront obstacles, patience, daily vigilance, and an open door. These are some of the very qualities that define a high-performing athlete. Despite how behind the culture of sport is regarding homophobia, I choose to believe that one day it will be a non-issue.

Day 12: Dalhart, TX, to Pampa, TX, 112 miles

Howdy y'all,

Holy cow (and not cause we are in Texas)! Started the day in a hard rain; middle of the day was steady rain; end of the day was torrential rain and lightning. We pushed it the last two miles to get to the hotel—at least I got there before the hail started.

Hail the size of golf balls, near Pampa, Texas.

The locals told us at breakfast that it had not rained in thirty-five days. At least someone was happy about it—lucky us, again. The temperature was a high of 53 degrees and there were head winds of 10–20 mph all day. There were no sights to see because the entire area was cloudy, misty, and rainy, with poor visibility.

This was a day of small favors: hoping a large semi-truck would buzz by to create a little back-draft push for you (and you did not care about the wet spray); winds dying down to 10 mph; patches of road work for a smoother surface; a small town with a mini-mart to get something hot to drink. This was a test of wills or sanity; I still have not figured out which. (I know many of you are answering this question for me . . . thanks).

We traveled through the towns of Hartley, Dumas (thank goodness for the mini-mart), Borger (thank goodness for yet another mini-mart), and into Pampa. Nothing much in between except pastures, and even the cows were hiding from the rain.

A hot shower was a blessing. We will not talk about the forecast for tomorrow. I want sweet dreams tonight.

And we get to get up and do it again tomorrow—but still having fun.

Jenny

Through rain, sleet, and hail.

Chapter 10

Breaking News

In 1976, Mel Greenberg of the *Philadelphia Inquirer* was the first sports writer for a major daily newspaper to cover women's basketball. He sounded the call to rank women's collegiate teams and was instrumental in developing the sport's first top-twenty poll. Greenberg's persistence brought national prominence to women's sports.

Today technology brings every imaginable sports event to homes throughout the world in real time. What's your passion? Cycling? Gymnastics? Figure skating? Boxing? Sailing? Triathlons? All that and much more are yours for the watching. Entire networks are dedicated solely to around-the-clock sports coverage. Channels feature single sports such as football, basketball, car racing, tennis, and golf. There are even channels solely dedicated to collegiate sports. Because of Title IX, the opportunities for girls and women to participate in sport have grown accordingly, with the media showcasing the product.

During her 35+ years in women's athletics, Debby Jennings, retired associate athletics director for media relations at the University of Tennessee, has witnessed the astounding transformation of media and women's sports. "In the early days of Title IX we couldn't generate a lot of ink. The newspaper was the main source for coverage, and I used to measure the column inches dedicated to men's and women's sports," she told me. "Women definitely had to earn credibility with the media. We always have had female athletes willing to step up and bare their souls. I think women are different from men in their communication styles, and I believe their genuine enthusiasm and honesty endeared us to the media."

Jennings remembers moments that stand out as turning points. "As television began covering the Olympic Games, female athletes and coaches were recognized and held up as role models. Television first covered the Olympic Games nationally in 1976, and as our country watched, it provided us with a model for the developing role of media."

I recall my first glimpses at women competing in those Winter Games. Riveted in front of the television, I watched champion figure skater Dorothy Hamill win the gold medal and the collective American heart. That same year I was transfixed watching the battle for Eastern Bloc supremacy in gymnastics between Russia's Olga Korbut and Romania's Nadia Comaneci during the Summer Olympics. I would pretend that I was one of these champions, fully believing that one day it could be me.

The relationship of the media with athletics is a two-sided coin, with both positive and negative implications. On one side, coverage of athletic programs helps attract a fan base, instills pride in the team and school, enhances recruiting, generates revenue, and informs the public. On the flip side, media exposure feeds a culture that is driven by commercialism, image, and winning with little concern for the human beings involved. Privacy boundaries are frequently pushed or blatantly ignored to the detriment of nearly every aspect of sport and the people associated with it.

The first time I found myself on the public radar was in 1997. The HBO special *A Cinderella Season* told the story of the 1996 Tennessee Lady Volunteer basketball season, when the team lost ten games before improbably winning the national championship. Senior point guard Kellie Jolly had suffered an anterior cruciate ligament (ACL) injury early in the season, but, also improbably, returned three months and three weeks later to lead the team to the title. This quick recovery was most unusual, and the media took notice. The conditions that contributed to her recovery were key. Since she had injured the same ACL previously, she understood the process. Highly motivated, she did exactly what she was instructed to do throughout her rehabilitation. Her injury did not involve other structures such as other ligaments or the meniscus, and she responded favorably to treatment. Because all of these elements came together and she experienced only minimal swelling, she was able to complete the season. Yes, she had top-quality medical care every step of the way, but her case was unique and therefore not a good indicator for measuring ACL recovery, which usually takes much longer. I am always working to educate injured athletes, their parents, coaches, and even the media to understand that rehabilitation prescriptions and timelines, even those for identical injuries, do not follow a template.

Media attention to athletes' injuries has helped to explain what athletic trainers do. Before games, my friends teasingly tell me that they hope they won't see me on television. When an athlete suffers an injury, the camera zooms in on her and the athletic training staff. Because commentators and observers can be all too quick to draw conclusions based on what they think has happened, we shield our conversations and injury assessment from the microphones and cameras to protect the athlete's privacy. Before any information on her injury is made public, the athlete approves what is reported in our press release. When an injury takes a player out of the game, diagnosis will likely require examinations over a period of time. Recovery depends on many factors. I have learned to deliver vague but true responses, such as "Right-knee injury. Further evaluation will be conducted," or "We will make decisions on a day-by-day basis."

In many cases, disseminating information about injuries is a positive move, because it raises public awareness and generates support for research, treatment, and prevention. Media exposure has shown the relationship between overtraining and injuries, made ACL a commonly understood acronym, underscored the risks of performance-enhancing drugs, and most recently heightened serious concerns about concussion recognition and management. The media has helped the medical profession to spread the word about such serious conditions as dehydration, heat illness, sudden death due to cardiac conditions, sickle cell trait, depression, eating disorders, and addiction. The news helps to educate athletes to listen to their bodies, and parents and coaches to recognize problems and to seek early medical assistance. Stories help us identify with athletes. We feel a personal connection. We cheer them, sweat with them, cry with them, and celebrate with them.

A vigilant media is a powerful tool for investigating systematic wrongdoing in collegiate sports. Exposing and reporting on a series of major violations can effectively take down the perpetrators—athletes, coaches, athletic administrations, and even the president of an institution. To their considerable credit, media watchdogs have reestablished the level playing field in a number of conferences. Yet, I do question whether it is fair to scandalize an athlete's encounter with the law, skipping classes, drinking, or using performance-enhancing drugs when there is not a whisper of publicity about the misdeeds of their non-athlete peers. When athletes violate the law or break the rules, there must be serious consequences. What is not fair is when the reports of the transgression linger on in the public's mind, unduly damaging the athlete's reputation.

In this age of instant information, it is not good enough to report the story—you must be the first to do so. My concern is that in their haste to form opinions and find answers, the media often fail to produce in-depth, factual coverage. Case in point: Coach Pat Summitt scheduled a team meeting on a Tuesday afternoon at 2:30 to tell her players about her medical condition of early dementia, the Alzheimer's type. Earlier that afternoon I received a text message from an assistant coach summoning me to the office. When I arrived, I learned the story had already been leaked. While they were in class, athletes had received phone calls, text messages, and tweets from parents and friends telling them about their coach. Coach Summitt was extremely disappointed that she was unable to be the first to share her personal news with her team.

On the other hand, the media exposure of Coach Summitt's condition brought needed attention to the cause of Alzheimer's research and treatment funding. Her willingness to be open and forthright with her story about this terrible disease produced greater public awareness and understanding and may be instrumental in improving the quality of life for many and in helping to hasten a cure.

Widespread communication brings new challenges. Armed with cell phones, computer gadgets, and the Internet, anyone can communicate anything—thoughts, opinions, facts, concerns, and pictures—with no assurance of accuracy. Everyone has access and there are no boundaries. Personal privacy doesn't exist on the Internet. It only takes one compromising picture on a blog to destroy an athlete's career.

I am constantly warning athletes, their teammates, and their families to be careful about what they post on their websites. The medical world has adopted stricter privacy standards, yet our lives have become open books. A naive comment can violate an individual's privacy. This hit home for me when, on a drive back to campus from the doctor's office, my athlete posted her medical diagnosis on her social network page. I was barely out of the car when my phone rang, and a person outside the athletic department asked me about her injury. I immediately turned to her and asked, "Don't you think we should have told your parents and coaches first?"

The media's push to deliver breaking news raises the question: does the public demand for instant knowledge let the media off the hook? "A source within the athletic department who is not authorized to speak on the subject" may have intentionally leaked information to control the message by the department. At other times, information is never intended for the public. In either case the news becomes "fact," and the public eats it up. Who is responsible ethically? Yes, the media can overstep their bounds. At the same time, it acts as a watchdog. As long as fans are excited and obsessed with their sports teams, the media feeds the frenzy. The fault line in the sand is not always clear.

Satellite television puts a human face to every sport, especially during the Olympic Games. Unfamiliar sports that were rarely discussed at the water cooler are becoming more popular. In the southern United States, where many have never seen snow or ice ponds, curling is now offered in local ice skating rinks, thanks to the exposure this sport received in one recent Winter Olympic broadcast. We can watch several sporting events at once in real time with three-dimensional, split-screen technology. High-definition TV dramatically reveals the strategy, skill and techniques, stunning beauty, explosive power, sheer strength, grace, will, and artistry of the athlete. Who can ever forget when television captured the grace and strength of Michael Jordan's extraordinary flight to the basket? Technologies will continue to find ways to take the public behind the scenes and into the game, the event, the locker room, the coaches' minds, and even into athletes' off-court lives. You only need to watch the news, read the paper, scan the web, or check your cell phone to know this is good news and bad news.

Day 13: Pampa, TX, to Elk City, OK, 97 miles

More rain in the morning and cold (51 degrees), so on went the Gortex. We delayed the start about thirty minutes to have the bad stuff pass. Another day of head and cross winds 10–15 mph. Whatever happened to the wind blowing from west to east?

We left Pampa, Texas, in Gray County, which has some bumpy shoulders! I was standing on my pedals as much as I could to save my bottom. But then we entered Wheeler County on the way to Wheeler, and thank goodness for the oil wells, because their roads and shoulder were *smooooth*. Again, when you have rain, head winds, and cool temperatures, it is the small things that make it fun.

The rain did stop about midday and only spit on us occasionally after that. Besides oil, cattle is the main industry. We passed many a feedlot along the way. That it was not warm was a plus; my nose is thankful. Otherwise, not much for entertainment.

We crossed the Oklahoma state line and into a town called Spot of Sweetwater. It did not taste sweet to me, though it was refreshing.

Even the turtles are bigger here. Saw a dead armadillo—don't worry, no picture of that—looking forward to a live one. For those in the South, an armadillo is a possum on the half-shell. Then into Elk City. Rain is supposed to be moving out, so it's time to clean my steed, the bike.

And we get to get up and do it all again tomorrow—how fun!

Jenny

Chapter 11

Beyond Grades and Wins

Wins? Grades? The University of Tennessee takes both very seriously, and our student-athletes are expected to do the same. I'm proud to say they do. On Day One, when women athletes walk into a classroom, they are expected to follow an established protocol that sets them on the right road academically. They are required to sit in the first three rows of their classes; they must introduce themselves to their professors and make an effort to develop a relationship with them; and if they have an unexcused absence and miss a class, they miss a competition. Tough stuff.

Setting high standards on the field, court, or pool produces champions. Setting high standards in the classroom produces graduates, and I have the statistics to prove it. Women's basketball, cross country/track and field, tennis, and volleyball at the University of Tennessee have a 100 percent graduation rate according to an October 2011 report.[29] The entire Athletic Department graduation rate for men and women is 76 percent, compared to an overall four-year student body rate of 36 percent and a five-year rate of 59 percent.[30]

That there is life beyond wins and grades is something I remind athletes of during the course of their collegiate careers. The college experience is about expanding horizons, learning about one's self and the world, and maturing into an adult. But it also is in the athletes' best interest to understand that when they become "civilians" again, like the rest of us, they will need to focus on fitness to maintain a healthy lifestyle.

I do see some student-athletes enter college with a single-minded, one-dimensional focus that is counterproductive to experiencing the full gamut of college life. That can and will change if they jump right into the college culture that encourages creativity, independence, free expression, self-exploration, and respectful debate, as well as learning. For some, that's a difficult transition, but one well worth making. Curiosity, eagerness to try new things, and willingness to explore different ideas garner success in college. Traditional students have the flexibility to vary the number of classes they take, change majors, take part in extracurricular programs, and join campus organizations. However, student-athletes do not enjoy this same level of flexibility because of the demands of their sport, their team requirements, and NCAA rules.

Kerry Howland, former assistant director at the University of Tennessee Thornton Athletics Student Life Center, worked directly with student-athletes to assure that they achieve their academic goals. "All students follow academic plans set by their majors," she noted. "The student-athlete, however, deals with the added demands of practice, play, and travel. Experiencing campus life beyond the classroom in clubs and in social and special events is even more difficult. Student-athletes have very little margin of error."

Voicing her seasoned perspective as an academician and faculty representative to the NCAA, Dr. Anne Mayhew admits that participation in college athletics can impede a student's academic development and intellectual curiosity. "The time demands on student-athletes are sometimes a roadblock to their academic development," she explained. "College is more than achieving passing grades; college is about developing the intellect. The accepted standard is to make the grade, but the academic experience is about exploring and discovery."

When I consider our athletes' schedules, I am amazed that they can keep their heads above water. A student-athlete's week day or weekend day is dictated by one of four scenarios: (1) practice, (2) home competition, (3) travel, or (4) away competition. The schedules vary from sport to sport, but the elements are the same. A typical practice day includes classes, study hall/tutors, treatments and rehabilitation, and three to four hours of practice, team meetings, film sessions, and weight training. Additional responsibilities may include community service and mentor programs.

If it is on a week day, home competition includes classes, a shorter practice, film session, pre-game meal, pre-game treatment and rehab, and the competition. Afterwards there are media interviews, an autograph session, and post-game treatment and rehab.

A travel day involves going to classes, traveling to a destination via bus or airplane, treatment and rehab, practice, film session, group study hall, restaurant meals, sleeping in a hotel, and curfew.

An away competition day means a shorter practice, film session, treatment and rehab, individual study time, pre-game meal, the competition, and travel home, usually arriving in the wee hours with the expectation of being in class the next morning. It is no wonder that athletes have little extra time and can easily be isolated from other college experiences.

In spite of their demanding schedules, student-athletes can take advantage of their unique situation. Traveling to new places can expand their interests, pique their curiosity, and open their world to different cultures. Community service is emphasized, with activities that provide athletes an understanding of their many blessings and instill a "give-back" philosophy. Their tight schedules teach discipline and time management. Athletes tell me that their grades are often better during the competitive season because they have to be focused and efficient with the time they have to study. They learn to set goals and work very hard to achieve them. They also learn how to win and lose with sportsmanship and grace. The relationships they develop with their teammates are priceless. Strongly bonded, athletes are very often friends for life.

Although the student-athlete experience differs from that of other college students, I see that our athletes who do embrace their many opportunities are transformed from inexperienced freshmen to graduates ready to take on the world. How rewarding it is to be a part of their growth.

A very small percentage of college athletes will make a living playing their sport as a professional athlete. The majority joins the ranks of the recreational athlete with the rest of us—at least optimally they do. I encourage student-athletes to make physical activity a big part of their life long after their time at Tennessee. I also encourage them to decrease the calories they consume, since their activity level will diminish. Obviously, this advice works for non-athletes as well, because as we age, we all benefit significantly from being physically active and curbing our calorie intake.

Medical and research experts are the first to say that adults live longer when they stay fit, physically and mentally. Exercise strengthens the body/mind/spirit connection. An active lifestyle decreases the chances of heart disease and stroke, high blood pressure, noninsulin-dependent diabetes, obesity, back pain, and osteoporosis. It can boost your energy level, improve sleep and your moods, and help you manage stress. Experts recommend that you do twenty to thirty minutes of aerobic exercises three or more times a week that involve large muscle groups in sustained, rhythmic movements, for example, running, cycling, walking, hiking, swimming, or using an elliptical machine. At least twice a week you should do some type of strength training in the form of weight training, body weight resistance, bands, or other resistance devices to help you move with greater ease.

Stretching is important too. Although the research is not conclusive, stretching can help to increase flexibility, which may improve your performance in physical activities or decrease your risk of injuries by helping your joints move through their full range of motion. Stretching also increases blood flow to muscles.

It doesn't matter whether you were once a highly competitive athlete or just want to start moving again. If you have been inactive for some time, I encourage you to begin with swimming or walking at a comfortable pace without straining your body. Once you are in better shape, you can gradually do more strenuous exercise.

Physical fitness can be integrated with mental and spiritual development. Many people feel a spiritual connection with nature when they hike, canoe, and scuba dive. During the last decade, yoga has gained popularity in the United States. Originated in ancient India, yoga is a physical, mental, and spiritual discipline, with the goal of achieving balance and tranquility. Tai chi, another non-traditional form of exercise developed in China, is a graceful form of exercise that is used for stress reduction and a variety of other health conditions. Described as "meditation in motion" it promotes serenity through gentle movements, connecting the mind and body.

As we get older, our body may tell us when it is time to move from our activity of choice to an activity our body can handle more easily. I advise: (1) take some time off—as we get older it takes longer for our bodies to recover and heal; (2) cross train with alternate activities to stimulate different muscle groups; (3) if one activity is detrimental, find an alternative—aging may not allow you to run without breaking down and getting injured, but you may be able to cycle, swim, or walk without consequences; and (4) add mind- and spirit-stimulating activities—reading, music, art, theatre, meditation, and nature.

Just as your children have many chances to engage in youth sport activities, there are numerous recreational leagues, teams, and organizations offering sport and fitness opportunities for adults. From the highly competitive weekend warrior to the neighborhood walking group, from the pottery to the photography class, from yoga to tai chi, health benefits and good times await you.

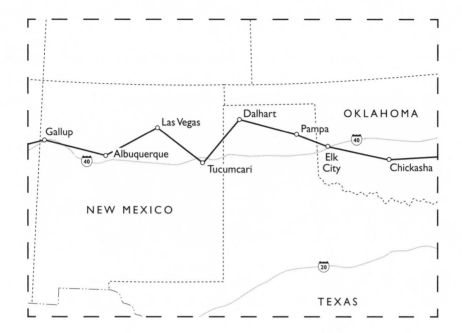

Day 14: Elk City, OK, to Chickasha, OK, 125 miles

Howdy y'all!

What a superb day of cycling. Very little wind, which is surprising considering that Oklahoma is the best flag-flying state in the Union. Mild temperatures—mid-fifties to start, then up to the high sixties—and cloud cover.

The roads were wonderful—smooth, very little to no traffic (being Sunday helped), peaceful, scenic, and pristine. Absolutely ideal. Most of the roads were unmarked, so we had to watch our mileage carefully, and it helped when you came to an intersection and only one of the roads was paved. Wheat fields everywhere. As a vegetarian, I may not contribute to the local beef economy, but I do consume more than my fair share of wheat products.

We went through the towns of Sentinel, Rocky (Yo, Adrian!), and Cloud Chief. Since it was Sunday, no stores or gas stations were open; thank goodness the world is a bathroom, at least according to cyclists and cows. The only thing open was a little store in NOWHERE, OKLAHOMA.

Sunday oasis in Nowhere, Oklahoma.

We rode around Fort Cobb Lake and across the dam, which was at least a mile long; pretty cool. The lake was large with lots of fishing, and some recreation boats were out. Traveled through the towns of Anadarko and Verden on the way to Chickasha. What few people we did see took a keen interest in our expedition, asking questions, cheering, waving at these funnily dressed, two-wheeled strangers in town. What I have come to realize, though, is that, when you talk to someone local and they ask you where you are coming from and where you are going, you cannot say, "Costa Mesa, California, to Savannah, Georgia." This means nothing to them. However, when you say, "from Elk City to Chickasha," they are amazed and grasp the trek. Then they make a suggestion about a better way to go.

And who said Oklahoma is flat? We did over 5,000 feet of climbing today, lots of high rollers—no wonder I'm tired. Today we crossed the halfway point of the trip.

And we get to get up and do it again tomorrow—how fun!

Jenny

Chapter 12

Burnout and the Press of Stress

I had to be strong and healthy for my ride across America, but I was not always that way. I have toyed with some unhealthy behaviors—as a college student I sometimes drank too much and played food games. A pivotal time in my life came at the beginning of my career. I fell into an exercise-at-all-cost mentality and was trapped by issues of perfectionism. I was young and invincible, driven to put my career and myself on the map, working eighteen-hour days, eating on the run if at all, until I crashed. I was on a fast track to burnout. Here I was, a newly minted athletic trainer, teaching others how to take care of themselves, and I certainly wasn't taking care of me. Thankfully, our team physician recognized my dangerous course. A very smart woman, she came up with a wonderful cure. She gave me a golden retriever puppy and said, "If you're not going to take care of yourself, go home and take care of her." I named my new savior Rehab. That sweet dog brought a healthful degree of balance to my life and helped me to learn well how to live what I teach every day.

My personal code has developed over time. It encompasses leading by example and listening to my body, eating properly, getting healthy exercise, satisfying my spirit, expressing and nurturing my emotions, valuing relationships, and embracing every moment of the journey.

Altogether this prescription makes for good balance in life. For an athlete there are some compelling complications, however. Most dedicated athletes routinely face physical, mental, and emotional demands that make sport/life balance difficult. At an early age they embrace the message that the goals in sports are to earn the highest honors, win the most games or events, progress to higher levels every year, earn a collegiate athletic scholarship, and become a professional athlete.

The formula for accomplishing these goals seems clear, but its dictates can be worrisome and detrimental if they follow the accepted progression.

Select your sport at a young age and commit to it. Attend all team practices and competitions. Practice on your own. Work with a coach/personal trainer. Make your sport your number-one priority. Specialize in your position. Play your sport year-round. Engage in the highest competition possible (club teams, travel teams, AAU teams, training academies, sports camps, etc.) even if it requires living away from home.

At this point, the formula can actually lead to an early exit from sport participation, because when sports are organized in a way that is regimented play, the activity becomes much like work. I know this from my own experiences but was curious to learn if this rings true for others. I talked with Steve Moore, a recreational athlete. Even though he is well into his adult years, Steve remembers the exact moment when he no longer wanted to participate in youth sports. He was tall, strong, and excelled in basketball. He played throughout his childhood on community and school teams. Early in high school, though, the game became something different. "The coach was more intense and focused on winning," Steve recalled. "In a team meeting he told us that we needed to make a choice between everything else in our lives and playing basketball." Steve wanted to do so much more in his life. He wanted to be with his friends outside of sports and participate in a variety of activities. He walked away from basketball because the fun was no longer there. It had become work. "My parents were disappointed but supported my decision. My coach and some of my teammates ignored me from that point on," he said. Steve's story underscores the kind of pressure that kids feel at a time when sports should be a part, but not the whole, of their lives. His decision took courage.

As the popularity of sports and athletics increases, so does the campaign for more games to add revenue. The National Football League (NFL) is considering adding two regular season games to its schedule; some NCAA men's basketball coaches are advocating growing its playoff tournament field from 65 to 96 teams; and the geographic expansion of collegiate athletic conferences requires more travel. The time allowed for competition preparation has also increased—now collegiate women's basketball begins official practices two weeks earlier than in the past.

When is enough enough? Burnout caused by the grueling demands of sport is the price so many athletes pay. For some athletes, the fear of letting others down or being viewed as a "quitter," not meeting expectations, and the possibility of losing their scholarship can be intimidating barriers to recognizing and articulating their needs. I have seen athletes display signs and symptoms of burnout—loss of appetite, trouble sleeping, apathy, depression, fatigue, withdrawal, and falling grades. Burnout can also manifest as a physical injury. An athlete will complain of pain, but evaluation and testing reveal no physical cause. Though the pain is real, it cannot be fixed with ice, rehabilitation, or surgery. In these cases, I suspect that burnout is finding its way to expression. Consciously or unconsciously, the athlete is searching for change. My evidence of this, though anecdotal, is based on over a quarter century of working with highly competitive athletes.

Burnout is debilitating and can be life changing. Amidst the gloom, here is a dramatic example with a happy ending. Elena Delle Donne is a sports heroine of the finest kind. At the age of seven, this young woman was spotted as a basketball superstar in the making. With a private trainer, she worked obsessively, driven to be the best. A guard at six-foot-four, Delle Donne worked magic with the ball and could shoot like no other. When she was thirteen, she had a strong gut feeling that basketball wasn't fun anymore. However, sometime later when she was asked if she was feeling drained by a sport she played twelve months of the year, abiding by expectations Delle Donne said that "burnout" was not in her vocabulary. Unfortunately, no longer was the word "fun."

The 2008 Naismith National High School Basketball Player of the Year, she accepted a scholarship to the University of Connecticut, with the likelihood of four national titles and a glittering career in the WNBA. Just two days after arriving on campus, Delle Donne walked away, not only from UConn, but from basketball itself. Her fans were stunned. How could anyone so talented turn her back on such a promising future? Connecticut women's basketball coach Geno Auriemma had no explanation for this reversal. "I don't know how you can play that much basketball and be that good at it and say, 'I hate[d] it since the time I was thirteen.' To me, those two things don't go together . . . that you would be that good at something and not enjoy any of it. I'm still not able to see how that makes any sense. I didn't understand it and haven't understood it right from the beginning."[31]

Those who saw that Delle Donne was walking toward family, joy, and balance understand completely. In her own words, "You can't understand burnout unless you've been burned out. It's just doing something you have absolutely no passion for."[32] As a student at the University of Delaware, Delle Donne opted to walk onto the volleyball team, forego any athletic scholarship opportunity, and play in front of much smaller crowds. She was named to the Colonial Athletic Association All-Rookie Team for volleyball. Commenting on her new sport, Delle Donne says, "Now that I play volleyball, I know how it feels to have a passion for your sport. Before, I just thought, 'Maybe everyone's faking it, because this is horrible.' . . . I'd rather be a face for happiness and doing things that you have a passion for, rather than faking it and pretending like I'm this face of women's basketball when I can't stand the sport at all."[33] Elena Delle Donne sends a message that resonates with truth and caution when we consider the relentless push to be the best at all costs in sports today.

After a year-long break from basketball Delle Donne has since returned to the sport. She joined the team at the University of Delaware, this time with a new set of expectations and boundaries. She plays with a healthy attitude and a renewed love for the game. She showed maturity and fortitude when she acted on what she was truly feeling.

Going through the motions, dreading doing "same ole same ole," losing interest in what has become to you a mindless activity, and questioning why you are even involved are sure signs of burnout. But once you recognize burnout, you can make changes and take a new path. However, be realistic. There are no guarantees of smooth sailing if you do change course and tack in a new direction because you will likely encounter stress, a partner of burnout.

Stress is an inevitable part of life, but it is not always a bad thing. In small amounts it can be a motivator to help us perform under pressure. When we recognize stress and know the ways to reduce its impact, we can bring about balance and accomplish our goals. Stress is a normal response to events that threaten us in some way. Our heart pounds faster, muscles tighten, blood pressure rises, breath quickens, and senses become sharper. It can be caused by external factors such as major life changes, work, public speaking, relationship difficulties, financial problems, health concerns, demanding schedules, children, and family, and by internal factors generated by pessimism, negative self-talk, and an inability to accept uncertainty. Stress affects the mind, the body, and the spirit. It may create unrealistic expectations, perfectionism, and lack of assertiveness. It can lead to serious health problems: high blood pressure, a suppressed immune system, and an increased risk of heart attack and stroke. It can contribute to infertility, speed up the aging process, lead to anxiety and depression, and cause pain, digestive problems, sleep problems, and obesity. Everyone reacts differently.

In sports, stress is good and bad. The good type of stress, called "eustress," comes from the challenge of a pleasant activity. When I was preparing for my bike ride from coast to coast, I was excited and thrilled at the prospect. I was also stressed. I worried that I wouldn't be able to keep pace with the other cyclists and that my competitive drive would be detrimental to the overall goal. What if I pushed myself too early and then wasn't able to sustain the energy and physical demands that I would need? Questions like these continued to bug me. On Day One, I was determined not to be last, so on the first leg of the ride I did not stop at a restroom, though I should have. By the time I reached the first official SAG, or rest stop, almost two hours later at 32.5 miles, I was really aching because I had to go. That's stress! However, the adrenalin this stress produced was beneficial, because I was able keep pace with the main group. At the end of the day, 122 miles later, I felt fine and knew I belonged on the ride.

Distress, the bad type of stress, arises when we are experiencing too many negative demands. Athletes at all age levels can fall prey to it. At the beginning of each year, our soccer athletes are required to complete a fitness test to be officially on the team. Even though they practice and pass the fitness test over and over in the summer, when the head coach comes out with the stopwatch, the distress kicks in. Some stress and panic to the point that they don't finish the test in time.

Another source of distress can come from the persistent emphasis on winning. The expectations of parents, coaches, and fans can create competition anxiety for the athlete, resulting in overwork, overtraining, and subsequently, burnout. University of California, San Diego, head basketball coach Heidi VanDerveer observes, "Some of our student-athletes are trying to live up to the expectations of their parents. Sometimes they are mainly participating to please them," says VanDerveer. "Looking through 'mother-colored' glasses, parents don't always see what their children are feeling, saying, and doing." It is time for a wake-up call when the costs of competition outweigh the personal rewards.

One of the top stressors for student-athletes is time management. Balancing school and sports is not easy. University of West Virginia head soccer coach Nikki Izzo-Brown acknowledges the pressures student-athletes face. "Time management is a big challenge for them. We are asking a lot academically and athletically. Balancing both aspects is very difficult. Playing their best and making a difference on the field is huge. They have pressure from their family, pressure to succeed from their coaches, so it can be a struggle."

The University of Findlay diving coach Jane Wobser also recognizes the tough rigors athletes have to deal with. "If you take the amount of their scholarship and divide it by the hours they put in during the academic year and in the summer and subtract what they give up during school, it's a pretty brutal, low-paying, part-time job," said Wobser. "If fun and true love for the sport are not top priorities, it's difficult to stay the course. If there are injuries, they hurt even more." When their activities are balanced, there is less wear and tear on their bodies, and they are more likely to be prepared for the pressures.

It is important to keep all things in perspective. Of the many benefits of sport, the one factor above all others is to have fun. Student-athletes carry a heavy load of high expectations, their own and those of others. The toughest of critics, Coach Summitt understands that expectations create stress. As a person who demands and strives for perfection, she knows that perfection is unattainable. Her advice? "Do the next thing right, and you will be as close to perfect as any person can be."

Here are some strategies that I recommend to our student-athletes to help them deal with stress. They'll help you, too.

- Use statements of affirmation to turn stress in a positive direction. For example, I encourage our students who say, "I'm not ready for this test," even though they are well prepared, to turn that around and say, "I am prepared. I know the material. I am ready."
- Use breathing techniques to decrease anxiety. Long, slow breaths in through the nose and out through the mouth. In a pressure free-throw situation, we have taught many of our athletes to take a deep breath before they step to the line and begin their free-throw.
- When knots build up or their muscles spasm, I encourage athletes to deliberately tense up that muscle group, release the tension, and shake it out.
- Treat yourself to a massage to release stress-induced muscle tension.
- Visualize your happy place. For some it may be a beach, the mountains, or a bike ride.
- Eliminate negative self-talk. Don't ever forget that you are your own best friend.
- Treat yourself to some "chill" time—even 30 minutes of watching TV, going for a leisurely walk, listening to music, or taking a hot bath—to renew your energy to tackle the next big hurdle.
- Discuss your problems with a counselor. Friends are great, and we all need them to support us, but an objective pro-

fessional will give you the skills to cope and to process situations.

- Give your body a fighting chance to combat stress. Get plenty of rest and eat well.
- Exercise regularly to stimulate the body and the mind. Exercise moves fluids, strengthens muscles, improves cardiac function, gives a sense of accomplishment, and releases the body's endorphins.
- Laugh a lot. Laughter stimulates organs, soothes tension, improves your immune system, relieves pain, and increases personal satisfaction.

Stress will always be a part of our lives. How you handle it is up to you. Overall, and you have read it here before, my magic elixir to transform your life is balance of mind, body, and spirit. Go for it.

Day 15: Chickasha, OK, to McAlester, OK, 145 miles

Howdy Everyone,
   Whew! Long day.
Last night in Chickasha I had a big Mexican meal with my friends, Nancy and Kelly, from Oklahoma City. And it was a good thing, too, because I needed all the energy I could get. At 2 a.m. we were all awakened by severe thunderstorms and warning sirens. So, not a great night's rest.

The good news is the storms moved out before we started our ride in the morning at 7 a.m. Four miles into the ride, a dog decided to escort a pack of riders just in front of me. This dog was the Energizer Bunny—we clocked him and he hung with the pack for four straight miles at speeds of 13–14 mph. At one point I thought it might be his last run, because he nearly got hit by a truck weaving in and out through the riders and traffic. I am sure he is going to sleep well for the next few days after that workout.

We rolled through the town of Dibble where many of us needed to navigate around school traffic, but the kids gave us great waves of encouragement. Then into the towns of Purcell, Lexington, Asher, and Konawa. At this point the lead pack (or "The Hammers," as we call them) took a wrong turn and ended up in the town of Ada. Needless to say, they covered over 150 miles and missed a rest stop to refuel and hydrate. They were not happy campers.

An isolated thunderstorm crept up on us, and several of us sought shelter for about fifteen minutes in an abandoned building that was once Ray's Trading Post. If it had been open, I would have been willing to trade for a fresh pair of legs. Besides the little pop-up storm, the weather was very good, seventies and partly cloudy. The Oklahoma winds were flying the flags today, a cross wind from the south at 10–15 mph—annoying! Again, where are the west to east winds that are supposed to carry me?

We pedaled, pedaled, and pedaled through the towns of Allen, Atwood, Calvin, Arpelar, and finally into McAlester. A rooster farm entertained us just before Allen. On such a long day, we decided to help pass the miles by keeping count of the number of road kill armadillos we saw. The total count was twenty-one, and this was after the first fifty miles before the game began. Yes, we are getting a little warped at this stage of the tour. There were also a ton of turtles trying to cross the road. Why? Of course, to get to the other side, silly. Thankfully, most of them were alive when we passed them.

Another day of hills, long steep rollers. We climbed 5,100 feet, adding to the insult of the mileage total. I know, making us tougher! The roads were good—more traffic, since it was Monday. And we figured out Mike's theme: why ride state roads when you can find county roads with hills? Great.

The group has taken it upon itself to expose our British rider, "the Brit," to all the finer American snack foods that will survive nuclear fallout. Yesterday was the Twinkie, and today was the Snoball. I think she is riding faster. We get to sleep in tomorrow and start riding at 8 a.m. I guess Mike figures we need the additional rest. I am grateful after the sleepless night before.

And we get to get up and do it again tomorrow—how fun!

Jenny

Chapter 13

Flat Tires

Pffff!

Aarrgh, that depressing sound of a bicycle tire losing air. It's tough, make that almost impossible, to ride down the road with a flat tire. It absolutely has to be fixed. You stop and change it. Similarly, it is difficult, often impossible, for an athlete to carry on with an injury. Although injuries are an innate part of sport, today's persistent push for high performance too often ignores their impact to deleterious effect.

Athletes are bigger, faster, and stronger than they were thirty years ago. They are more explosive, harder hitting, and quicker. The games have changed. Seasons are longer, and more games are played, so there is less time to rest and recover. Injuries cause lost playing and practice time. Ankle sprains, hamstring muscle tears, thigh bruises, knee ligament tears, dislocated shoulders, broken bones, and head injuries are fairly common and take an athlete immediately out of the game. Some may require surgery. All require rest and rehabilitation and, in my world, lots of ice.

The rising numbers of young athletes who suffer injuries are startling. According to the American Academy of Orthopaedic Surgeons, more than 3.5 million children age fourteen and younger are treated for sports injuries every year. The CDC estimates that high school athletes sustain 2 million injuries, visit doctors 500,000 times because of them, and undergo 30,000 hospitalizations annually. A former student-athlete and diver, Dr. Lauren Loberg shared with me her personal case in point. "I began gymnastics when I was three years old. At the age of nine I was on a first-name basis with my orthopedist."

A national movement named the STOP Sports Injuries campaign is committed to calling attention to the issue. Created by a coalition of medical and fitness organizations and healthcare corporations to prevent athletic overuse and trauma injuries in kids, STOP Sports Injuries has established a Council of Champions that includes business, sports, and medical leaders to bring this message to youth sports parents, coaches, athletes, and healthcare providers. According to its website, the campaign battles the "growing epidemic of preventable youth sports injuries that are dismantling kids' athletic hopes and dreams at an early age."[34] Dr. James Andrews, president of the American Orthopaedic Society for Sports Medicine and co-chair of the campaign, is dedicated to the cause. He strongly feels that "the escalation of injuries in kids is alarming. . . . Armed with the correct information and tools, today's young athletes can remain healthy, play safe, and stay in the game for life."[35]

Today, middle school and secondary public school athletic programs fall far short in caring for the well-being of their young athletes because many do not have the services of athletic trainers. The early recognition, proper assessment, and immediate treatment of athletic injuries by a certified athletic trainer can make all the difference in a young athlete's life. Scripps-Howard writer Lee Bowman reports that, "[w]hile most of the nearly 2 million injuries among U.S. high school athletes each year are not life threatening, half are serious enough to require medical attention and at least one day off the field."[36] While 18,400 public and private high schools offer interscholastic sports, athletic trainers working in secondary schools across the United States number about 6,400 according to the National Athletic Trainers' Association (NATA).

The National Center for Catastrophic Sports Injury Research at the University of North Carolina at Chapel Hill, under the direction of Dr. Fred Mueller, has been instrumental in several rule changes improving the safety of sports. The center, which is funded by grants from the NCAA, the American Football Coaches Association, and the National Federation of State High School Associations, collects and disseminates death and permanent disability sports injury data that involve brain and/or spinal cord injuries. Dr. Mueller has been tracking down information related to catastrophic injuries of high school and collegiate athletes for more than forty years. "The number of injuries keeps piling up, and in the early years when we had thirty-six football deaths in a year and young kids with permanent disabilities, something had to be done," said Dr. Mueller. "One catastrophic injury is too many."

His research has led to new rules that increase safety and decrease injuries. One of the most momentous changes came in 1976 in high school and college football whereby initiating contact with any part of the helmet was made a rule infraction. This "spearing" rule change caused a dramatic reduction in the number of quadriplegic injuries. In 1976, twenty-five cases of paralysis were reported, but in 1984 a total of four incidents demonstrated an 82 percent decrease. Other sports have benefited from his research as well. Pole vault pits have been expanded and surrounded with softer padding, minimum depths have been established in swimming pools, and cheerleading pyramids have been limited to two people high.

Dr. Mueller has definite ideas about the future assurance of sport safety. "It is not fair to put sole responsibility for medical care and liability on a coach," he reasoned. "The coach's focus is on strategy and winning the game. Healthcare professionals are responsible for preventing and treating injuries; yet less than half of high schools have certified athletic trainers, and many of them are caring for multiple sports at one time."

I know first-hand that high schools have limited resources. For twelve years I was an athletic trainer on Friday nights for an area high school. The upside was that I provided on-the-spot injury assessment and emergency care during a game. The downside was that I was not available every day at practices or to do follow-up and rehabilitation, let alone to incorporate injury prevention programs. I remember one hot August Friday night when one of the players dislocated his shoulder. He told me this was not the first time. When it had happened in the previous spring, he went to the emergency room but did not follow up with a physician as the ER doctor advised him to do. Throughout the summer he continued to have problems, each time going to the emergency room, but still he never saw an orthopedist. By the time I saw him, the damage had been done. Repair required extensive surgery, and his shoulder would never be the same. His coaches believed he had the ability to play on the collegiate level, but his shoulder told him otherwise. I'm sure that if the team had had an athletic trainer working with them on a daily basis, the outcome would have been different.

When medical professionals are not available at the youth league, middle school, and high school levels, Dr. Mueller advises parents to take an active role. "Parents should check on the background and training of the coach," Dr. Mueller explains. "Is there an emergency plan? What kind of equipment are they using? What are the coach's plans for hot weather? Can an athlete approach the coach and say, 'I hurt, or I don't feel well,'" and be assured the coach will listen?

I educate our coaches to understand that although they are recruiting "high-performance sports cars," these cars already have a lot of mileage on them. It's not a matter of just getting from point A to point B and scoring. What is important is that athletes go from point A to point B in the correct way to prevent injuries, so they can be in the game and not on the sidelines.

Young people need to be establishing the right patterns of movement in addition to developing their athletic skills. Performance coach Loren Seagrave puts this model into practice. "I developed the concept of teaching movement because movement is the language of sport. We teach body control as the athlete matures, provide challenging, novel tasks at the level that the athlete is able to absorb and learn, thus taking a competency approach to performance training," Seagrave says. All athletes can adopt this concept when they eventually specialize in one sport. The athletes whose play is based on a foundation of balance, great body control, and proper movement techniques do not get injured as often as the athletes lacking these attributes. By the time they reach the collegiate level, it is almost too late to change them. Their habits are so ingrained that when the lights go on and the ball comes into play, they revert back to what they have relied on for years. It should be the responsibility of parents and youth coaches, but we work hard to change bad habits when necessary to prevent injury. That said, I have a greater success rate in helping athletes change when they sustain a time-loss injury. When they lose the function of an injured body part, I use the equipment of their particular sport during daily rehabilitation to break down poor patterns and replace them with corrected ones for their return to play.

I am saddened that a number of student-athletes arrive with tired spirits and high mileage bodies that show the wear and tear more commonly seen in adults middle-aged or older. My colleague, physician Rebecca Morgan, observes that with their injuries and illnesses they bring a troubling sense of urgency. "Athletes say, 'I need you to fix me now because I don't have time for this.'" One soccer player started her freshman year at the University of Tennessee suffering from severe ankle pain and tendonitis. When I told her to take a week off and not engage in any form of training, her eyes got wide and she panicked, saying she had never taken more than three days off since she began playing soccer as a little kid. To her, rest was a scary and foreign concept.

Dr. Morgan points to one area as especially significant for athletes today. "In my thirteen years as a team physician, I have seen a dramatic increase in the number and types of overuse injuries in college freshmen. Long-term implications regarding these injuries will not be known for many years to come." Chronic tendonitis, stress fractures, low back degenerative discs, early arthritis in joints, hip ailments, and sports hernias rarely or never seen before in youngsters are now becoming prevalent. "Today the injuries I see

Chapter 14

Connection

When I began working in my first full-time job as an athletic trainer in 1988, I could not have predicted the incredible advances in health care, research, and medical technology that would come about. We continue to learn so much about how the body works and heals and the intricacies of this amazing machine. In the past, surgeries required a time of immobilization. Today protocols have the patient moving as soon as possible. Rehabilitation techniques are more functional and aggressive. Injuries that once were career ending can now be healed. Athletes return to their sport more quickly. Years back in some instances I felt that my treatment and care were similar to applying a Band-Aid. Now my approach to healing is holistic, one that takes advantage of the many new medical developments. I look at how the body, mind, and spirit all play a role, especially when there is an injury.

Considering the entire body as a whole, I have been successful in getting to the root of the problem. Pain is a signal that something is wrong. Yet, the source of the injury may not be at the point of pain. For example, an athlete may be experiencing tendonitis in the knee, yet there could be several other causes, including core instability, hip rotation, or foot mechanics. If the tendon is the only thing treated, the athlete will feel better temporarily, but the injury is not healed.

When Olympic-caliber diver Tracy Bonner pulled her hip muscle, I initially focused on the injured muscle and used stretching, massage, ultrasound, electrical stimulation, and anti-inflammatories. We were getting nowhere. Puzzled by her lack of progress, I looked away from the injury itself to find out what other parts of the body might be involved. It dawned on me that all those times a diver enters the water without perfect form the head bears the brunt of the impact. This force can lock the sutures—or joints—that join the bones in the skull. I gently rubbed her head with my thumbs to release the sutures and the hip flexor muscle responded. Releasing the connective tissue around the skull subsequently allowed her body's connective tissue around the muscle and the hip to relax. The hip flexor loosened and began to heal. Tracy returned to the boards to capture an NCAA title and a career as a professional diver in the Las Vegas "O" Show by Cirque du Soleil. Treating her led me to consider new ways to do rehabilitation and expanded my skills.

The mind is a powerful tool for healing. I had a basketball player who tore a ligament in her knee. After the surgery, her mind disowned her leg. She would not bathe it, move it, touch it, nor bear weight on it. Though I implored, tried to motivate her, and forced her to meet the minimal requirements, I could not get her to do the exercises, because in her mind the leg didn't exist. After two years of nearly fruitless effort, she returned to the court. However, I suspected her leg was not ready to handle the rigors of basketball. And sure enough, she favored the injured leg and developed a stress fracture in the other leg, which sidelined her for the rest of the season. If her mind had been engaged in the healing process, I am sure the results would have been different.

The human spirit touches us on a deep level, connects us to one another, and inspires us. It puts passion to our beliefs, employs emotion, and ignites the heart. When I think of spirit, Cait McMahan comes to mind. From early on, she and her mother bonded through their love of basketball. When Cait entered the University of Tennessee as a Lady Volunteer, the family learned that her mother's cancer was spreading, and there was not much more doctors could do. When basketball practice started in October, Cait's knee began to bother her. It was swollen, painful, and gave out on her. An MRI revealed bone surface damage, a byproduct of the anterior cruciate ligament (ACL) she tore in high school. Our orthopedic surgeon outlined her options. The best option was surgical repair and sitting out a year. However, that would mean Cait's mom would probably not see her play in a Tennessee uniform. Cait opted for a temporary surgical fix and the shorter rehab time. She knew that this choice could likely mean that her condition would worsen over time. To Cait, this sacrifice was small compared to what her mother was enduring and the joy she could give to her biggest fan. That year Cait's mom exceeded doctor's expectations; she lived long enough to cheer on her daughter as the Lady Vols won the 2007 NCAA National Championship. Cait's spirit carried her mother and the team to victory.

Teresa McMahan passed away in May. A week later Cait underwent extensive surgery to permanently address her knee injury and the lengthy rehabilitation required her to sit out the 2007–2008 season. Seemingly recovered and ready to go she was cleared to begin practice in October 2008. Cait brought a "blue-collar" work ethic to the game and only knew one speed—fast and furious. Five games into the season her knee started giving her trouble. It "gave-out" several times during a practice and while I was attending to her, she looked at me, crying, and said, "I'm done, aren't I?" I too began to cry and nodded my head. I saw in that moment all the pain, the physical, emotional, and spiritual struggles that she endured. Cait could have easily lost her self. Instead she rechanneled her energy, focus, and passion into a career in music—closing one chapter of her life to open another.

When I treat an injury, I don't just see body parts anymore; I see the whole person. I consider where the athlete comes from, where she is currently, and where she wants to go. Now I care for athletes in terms of connection—balancing their body, mind, and spirit. One of these three may take over temporarily when an injury occurs, but if healing is to take place, the imbalance cannot be sustained for long. This new approach has a positive influence on the kind of care I give my athletes and the way I live my life.

Day 17: Fort Smith, AR, day off

Hi Y'all,

A very productive day—extra sleep, clean clothes, full belly (several times), clean bike, and new supplies, rehabs on some hurting cyclists and staff (just cannot take the athletic trainer out of me), a wonderful massage for me (have to take care of me, as well), and caught up on work emails and phone calls. The storms blew through, bringing a forecast of good weather.

Day 18: Fort Smith, AR to Conway, AR, 123 miles

Hi Y'all,

ALRIGHT!!!!!!!!!!!! Tail winds! Everyone was jumping for joy this morning. Finally tail winds, and they were blowing anywhere from 15–25 mph. Just what we needed to help us climb 3,100 feet today. Temperature in the morning was 60 degrees and got up to 70 degrees, with good sun. Kept the sunscreen flowing.

Seven new people joined the group for this last portion of the ride, just as I was getting a handle on the names of the original clan.

We streamed through a lot of cute small towns with populations of less than five hundred people: Charleston, Paris, and New Blaine. Following the

Knoxville Avenue in Dardanelle, Arkansas.

valley of the Arkansas River, very pretty. We had our lunch stop in Dardanelle and crossed the Arkansas River. At this point we headed north into the cross wind—how dare they—good thing it was only five miles. I almost turned down Knoxville Avenue, but alas, that would have been a wrong turn.

Then off to the east again, to Russellville, where we blew by a huge Tyson chicken packing facility with truck after truck leaving to bring chicken to your table, "Because Your Family Deserves It." I have been fairly quiet about my vegetarianism in all these meat laden states.

The Brit's junk food experience today was a Suzie Q.

Sailing through the towns of Atkins and Morrilton, I finished my first sub–five hour century in 4:58.24, a personal best and a very happy moment. Did I mention we had killer tail winds? Heck yeah, it counts! My top speed was 32.9 mph. I passed a group of riders and when we got to the rest stop, one of them imitated an Arkansas state trooper and tried to give me a speeding ticket. As far as I was concerned, the next twenty-three miles was a cool down. And we were still flying.

The town of Menifee's main industry is a paper mill, and it looked like Tinker Toys to me. Between Menifee and Conway, we flew past rice fields (pretty cool) and yes, I'll take a ten-pound bag to go, please. Conway's population is over 43,000, and there's lots of traffic. Of course we are staying close to the Wal-Mart.

And we get to get up and do it again tomorrow—how fun!

Jenny

Chapter 15

ACL: "The Pop"

Picture this: a basketball player jumps up for a rebound, lands on one leg, and twists her knee. She feels the pop, screams, buckles to the floor, grabs her knee with both hands, and curls up into the fetal position. The cameras catch the awkward and painful moment. The audience gasps at the replay on the big screen. I run out on the court to help her. She is terrified that she has torn her anterior cruciate ligament (ACL). Regrettably, I am all too familiar with this season-ending injury.

The ACL is one of four ligaments that stabilize the knee. Ligaments attach bone to bone. "Anterior" means front, and "cruciate" means cross. Thus the ACL is the ligament that crosses from the back of the knee on the thigh bone (femur) and attaches to the front of the knee on the shin bone (tibia).

Most often, ACL tears happen as non-contact injuries. The knee is vulnerable to changes of direction, sudden stops, and improper jumps and landings. The athlete feels the infamous "pop." Two common mechanisms cause ACL tears. One is hyperextension of the knee when it moves beyond its fully straight position. That often occurs when a basketball player lands from a rebound and her knee buckles backwards. The other common cause is pivoting, which can lead to excessive inward rotation of the lower leg. A sudden change of direction is usually the culprit here.

The ACL can tear in contact injuries as well, such as when a lineman is blocking, and a player falls or rolls on the back of his leg.

To complicate things even more, an ACL rupture can be coupled with a torn meniscus, the shock absorbing cartilage in the knee. The tear happens in about two-thirds of ACL injuries and requires more extensive surgery and a more conservative approach to rehabilitation. Other injuries may also be associated with ACLs, including knee ligament sprains, bone bruises, disruption of the joint surfaces, and the beginning of arthritis.

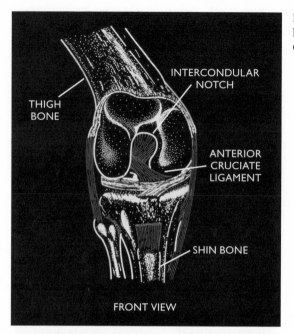

Diagram of knee, highlighting the Anterior Cruciate Ligament (ACL).

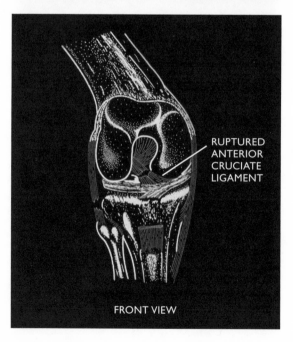

Diagram featuring a ruptured ACL.

Plant, twist, pop. Common ACL injury.

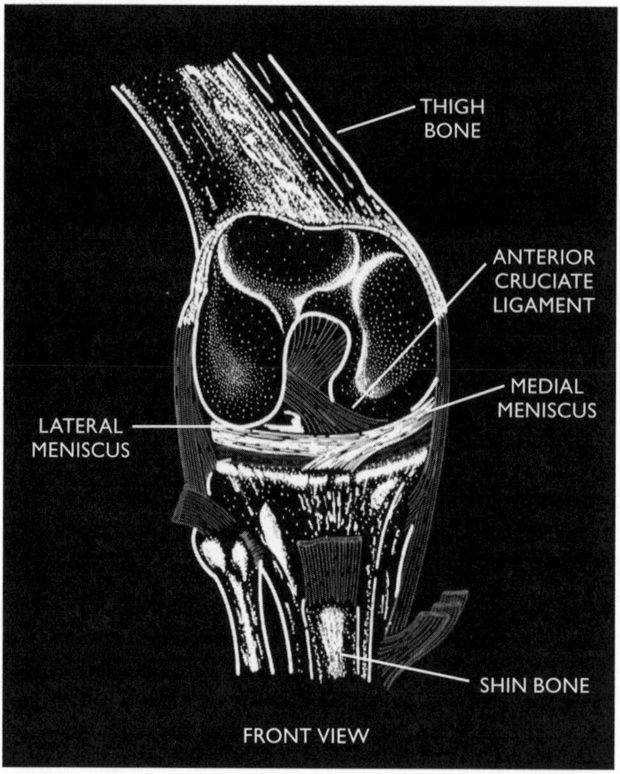

Diagram featuring medial and lateral meniscus.

THIGH BONE

ANTERIOR CRUCIATE LIGAMENT

MEDIAL MENISCUS

LATERAL MENISCUS

SHIN BONE

FRONT VIEW

Thirty years ago, tearing the ACL would likely have ended an athlete's career, but due to advances in medical, surgical, and rehabilitation techniques, an injured ACL usually results only in the loss of a season. Older athletes can show you their railroad track scars running up and down their leg from the open surgical techniques. Today that's all changed because of arthroscopy. Commonly used, it is a minimally invasive surgical procedure with small incisions that employs a camera, a viewing monitor, and smaller instruments. Arthroscopy reduces surgical trauma to the joints and tissue, reduces recovery time, lessens scarring, and leads to more aggressive and functional rehabilitation. Arthroscopic ACL surgery costs about $25,000 and requires anywhere from six to twelve months of healing time.

Injury to the ACL is more prevalent with female athletes. Research shows that they have a four to eight times higher incidence of ACL tears than their male counterparts.[38] This injury is not new in its frequency; however, extensive media coverage has raised public awareness and made ACL

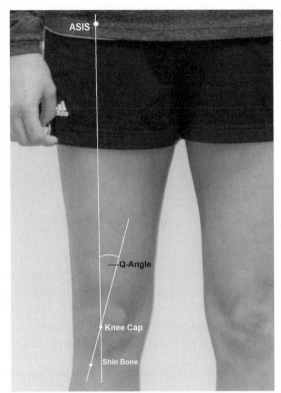

Q-angle—the angle formed by the thigh bone and the shin bone—influences how the knee moves in relationship to the hip.

an everyday term. As more females play sports, the injury has reached near epidemic proportions. Dr. William Youmans, an orthopedic surgeon for over forty-five years, recalls the time when he began to see ACL injuries increase. "It happened when women's basketball went from the half-court to the full-court game. There was much less acceleration during the half-court days. Now the game requires a combination of greater speed down the floor and the jump stop."

Many factors, often interrelated, contribute to widespread ACL tears among female athletes.[39] To explain why, I have to get technical here. Sit back, relax, have a healthy snack or a nice cup of tea, and read on. These factors can be divided into two categories: (1) those inside the body that we have little control over; and (2) those outside the body that we can affect.

The inside factors are anatomical and hormonal. The anatomical differences include bone structure and ligament size. Remember this familiar ditty? "The foot bone's connected to ankle bone; the ankle bone's connected to the shin bone; the shin bone's connected to the knee bone; the knee bone's connected to the hip bone." It's true—it is all connected, so to get to the bottom of this, we need to turn our attention away from the knee.

Starting at the hip, the quadriceps angle (Q-angle) influences how the knee moves in relationship to the hip. The degree of the angle is measured by (a) drawing a line from the anterior superior iliac spine (ASIS), which is a part of the hip, to the middle of the knee cap and (b) drawing a line from where the patellar (kneecap) tendon attaches on the shin bone through the middle of the knee cap. The two intersecting lines form the Q-angle.

The Q-angle primarily measures between 14 and 22 degrees. The wider the angle, the more stress on the knee. Men, with their narrower hips, occupy the lower ranges while women, whose bodies are designed to bear children and thus have wider hips, are in the higher ranges.

The intercondylar notch is the anatomical archway on the thigh bone that allows the ACL to pass from the back of the knee to the front of the knee. Orthopedic surgeons are finding that a male's intercondylar notch is shaped like an inverted U, allowing more room for the ACL to pass through the archway as the knee bends and straightens. A female's intercondylar notch is shaped like an inverted A, decreasing the overall arch dimension and so providing less room for the ACL. If we were talking about grades, this is the one time when the U (unsatisfactory) beats the A.

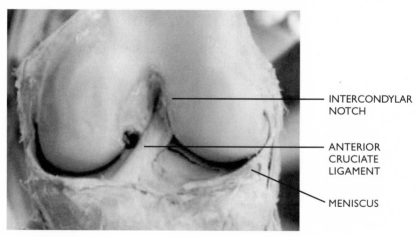

INTERCONDYLAR NOTCH

ANTERIOR CRUCIATE LIGAMENT

MENISCUS

Intercondylar notch. Courtesy of Marisa Colston, University of Tennessee, Chattanooga.

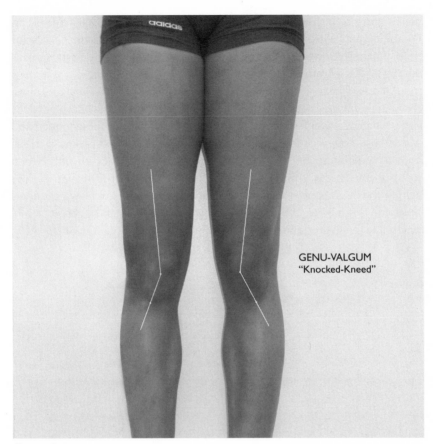

GENU-VALGUM
"Knocked-Kneed"

Genu valgum.

Genu valgum, the Latin term for knock-kneed, is a developmental condition in which the knees are touching or are very close together and the ankles are apart when the person is standing. This results in a person's weight shifting to the inside of the knee, adding uneven stress to it and the ACL. Because of an increased Q-angle, women are more susceptible to genu valgum.

Another anatomical factor is foot pronation. It occurs as the foot rolls inward, and the arch of the foot flattens. This is a normal part of the walking and running cycle and helps absorb shock. However, excessive pronation, or flat feet, can cause the knees to turn inward and produce knock-knees. Flat feet causing knock-knees can occur in both genders, but the condition places more stress on a female's knee when you factor in her wider hips. We use orthotics, which are custom-made shoe inserts, to correct excessive pronation and to keep the foot in a more neutral position, which straightens out the knee and reduces strain on the ACL.

All joints have a certain amount of play, or laxity, so they can move through their range of motion; however, some people are like "Gumby" dolls and have increased joint laxity. This is commonly called double-jointed and is seen more often in females. An individual who is double-jointed in the knee can go into hyperextension, a condition known as back-kneed, or genu recruvatum. The ACL prevents the shin bone, which naturally sits slightly behind the thigh bone when seen from above, from moving forward underneath the thigh bone. If the knee is already sitting back in hyperextension, it will take a smaller amount of movement and less force to tear the ACL.

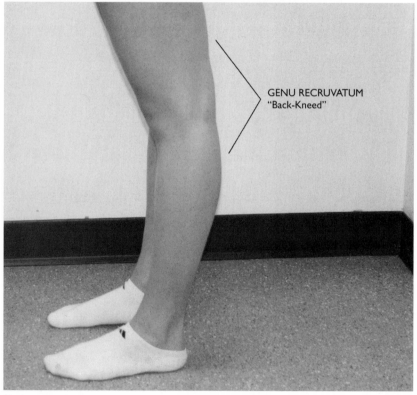

GENU RECRUVATUM
"Back-Kneed"

Genu recruvatum.

We teach our hyperextended, or back-kneed, athletes to play in a more bent-knee position, sitting back on their hips.

The actual size or volume of the ACL also may play a role in its vulnerability. When the ACL tears, the fibers tend to fray like a rope. The thicker the "rope"—or the more fibers an ACL has—the stronger it is. The female's ACL has less volume than a male's. Researchers are hoping to study whether the ACL itself can be made stronger, larger, or both when a child is still growing and developing. This could eventually lead to another option in ACL injury prevention.

Hormones, the second "inside" factor, can contribute to a higher incidence of ACL injuries among females as compared to males. Female hormone levels of estrogen and progesterone may affect ACL stability. Recent studies have shown a correlation between the fluctuation of hormone levels during the menstrual cycle and increased ligament laxity.[40] It's been found that females are three times more likely to tear their ACL when in their menstrual cycle. Researchers are looking into the relationship between the use of oral contraceptives and a reduction in ACL injuries. Findings are not definitive, and the use of oral contraceptives for ACL injury prevention is controversial.[41]

We can't do much, if anything, about the various internal factors. As Dr. Youmans predicted, "If you get a knock-kneed, ACL-dependent knee that is loosely constructed, that person will more than likely tear her ACL. I don't think it's caused by just one thing." However, there are a number of factors outside the body that we can influence to decrease the occurrence of tears. These include movement patterns, balance, muscular function, and flexibility.[42] Males tend to play flexed or bent and move from their hips, with the hamstrings and buttock muscles dominating. Their movement looks like they are squatting to sit on a chair. Females have a tendency to play in an erect and upright position, moving from their knees, using the quadriceps (front of the thigh) as the primary muscles. This movement resembles sitting down on a stool and causes the knees to move beyond the toes. This puts the knee in a vulnerable position and lends to pivot injuries. So far medical research has not found a reason for the differences in muscle group dominance between males and females. I believe it is due to females having wider hips, which places more stress on the knee (Q-angle) and forces the quadriceps muscles to overdevelop in compensation. Therefore, females should focus on the hip, hamstring, and buttock muscle strengthening. The hips are made up of more and stronger muscles than the knees and are built to generate and absorb forces.

Poor movement patterns affect an athlete's ability to jump and land safely. We spend a lot of time teaching our women athletes to jump, land, and change direction from their hips. Unfortunately, many enter our program jumping with their knees over their toes and landing with their knees turned inward. We work to change these poor habits to prevent injury. Our strength and conditioning coach sends the same messages but with the intention of improving performance. Using your hips allows you to jump higher. Who wouldn't be excited to increase their vertical? We break down the skills into two parts: the jump and the landing.

Jump

Sit back and load your hips.

Keep your head up and chest out.

Maintain neutral knees, with the middle of the knee cap in line with the second toe.

Swing your arms at the same time that you are jumping.

Explode upward.

Reach for the sky.

Landing

Sit back and load your hips.

Maintain soft, neutral knees, with the middle of the knee cap in line with the second toe.

Land softly on the balls of both feet and then release the heel, making almost no sound.

Stay light as a feather.

Keep your head and chest up.

Be on balance.

Changing directions is a skill required in almost all sports. A softball player rounds third base and sees the ball thrown to the catcher. She realizes she will not make it home to score and turns around to head back to third. Her foot plants, her body goes one way, and her knee goes the other. The likely result is an ACL injury. Some injuries, including ACL tears, are associated with a rotational force and being off balance.[43] All of our movements in daily life and sport have rotational components. When imbalance comes into play, there's trouble. To prevent that scenario, we focus on the athlete's core strength, core stability, and hip strength and mobility. We use specific exercises to improve their ability to maintain their center of gravity, change directions safely, and enhance efficiency of movement. And what is the added bonus? Better performance.

Our coaches consistently remind our athletes to "play on balance." I like hearing this from coaches because, in addition to improving performance, playing on balance prevents injury. A lack of balance increases the potential for ACL injuries. This is why balance exercises are such an important part of ACL rehabilitation.

Although the ACL is one of the four stabilizing ligaments of the knee, it doesn't do a very good job. Look at the injury stats. As a restraint ligament, the ACL has the poorest design of the four. However, in terms of balance, it does have the advantage of being a proprioceptive ligament, with little sensors that signal where the knee is in space and time. To improve an athlete's balance, we create an unstable environment. For example, we use mini-trampolines, balancing disks, rocker boards, and vibration platforms. Balancing with their eyes closed and balancing with ball tosses (not every one catchable) are just some of the challenges we put them through.

I tell our athletes that "the world is rehab," and I show them why and how whenever we go on the road. A hotel can instantly become a rehab laboratory. We get questions and amused looks as we ride the elevator up and down doing balance exercises. Stairwells are sites for a variety of exercises, and the beds become treatment tables. And of course, we hit the pool for aqua therapy. My ACL athletes sometimes tell me their leg that had the surgery works better than their other leg. While it sounds nice on the surface, that comment alerts me to the fact that we need to do the rehab exercises with both legs.

Muscular function, including strength, endurance, and power, plays a role in ACL injuries as well. Female athletes tend to be more quadriceps-dominant and weaker in the hamstrings. The hamstring muscle group actually assists the ACL in preventing the shin bone from moving forward underneath the thigh bone, providing 35 percent of the ACL's stabilizing ability. If these muscles are weak, slow to contract, or tire easily, the ACL is more susceptible to injury. Our strength and conditioning program emphasizes the hamstrings two to one over quadriceps exercises.

In the case of ACL injury, the tendency for women to have overly flexible hamstrings can be problematic. Because a lengthened muscle is slow to contract, the hamstring may fail to assist the ACL in stabilizing the knee. Looking back, many of my ACL injured basketball players had very flexible hamstrings. However, tight hamstrings can place undue stress on the knees. Having appropriately flexible hamstrings that allow for full knee and hip range of motion will decrease general knee and low back pain.

Notable forms of prevention involve specialized training programs that focus on neuromuscular control of the knee. Exercises and drills can be designed specifically to decrease the injury-producing forces on the ACL. Helpful strategies involve the ability to recruit muscles at the appropriate time and correct sport movements, including instruction on proper jumping and landing techniques, and balance training. Increased muscle strength, power, endurance, and core stability reduce ACL injury rates.

Training programs are most effective during the middle and high school years when movement and motor patterns can be reset and properly taught. It is critical that coaches, athletes, and educators be well versed about prevention strategies and integrate proven ACL injury prevention programs into their training plans. With the new medical knowledge and data available today, the number of ACL injuries can definitely be decreased. It's time to stop the epidemic. Let's pop some corn and skip the knee pops!

Day 19: Conway, AR, to Brinkley, AR, 100 miles

Hi Y'all,

Brinkley, Arkansas, is the home of the ivory-billed woodpecker, once thought to be extinct.

Another gorgeous day on the bike. Temperature in the morning 60 degrees, getting up to 74, and sunny. Tail winds again, 5 mph in the morning, and getting up to 10–15 mph in the afternoon, straight from the west.

Arkansas is really a beautiful state. Oklahoma was a very pleasant surprise, as well. I am seeing parts of this country that are hidden secrets. The locals are very proud of their towns and states, as they should be. One woman told me, "Arkansas could have cut itself off from all other states and not need anything from them, because they had oil and gas, agriculture, water, wood, and livestock." And you know, she is right. I would have also added retail, with Wal-Mart. And I have seen them all. I was amazed by the acres and acres of rice fields. The wheat fields were beautiful blowing in the wind. Feel free to break out into song.

We rode through the towns of Ward, Des Arc, Hazen, De Valls Bluff, Biscoe, and into Brinkley. We crossed the White River and rode by and through the Cache River National Wildlife Refuge, which has waterfowl viewing, houseboats, and hiking.

The group decided to make this a recovery day—easy pacing and enjoying the fabulous weather—so large groups (fifteen or more riders) rode together. It was neat descending on these small towns in all our colors. People were cheering and waving us on. Even the Big Dog riders took it easy today. We still have over a week of riding left, and our other assumed recovery days earlier in the trip were met with head winds and rain. So an easy day was smart on everyone's part.

It was a fairly flat route, only about 1,900 feet of climbing. Just some small hills to tackle. We did have to work a little today though; for a ten-mile stretch, the route turned us due south, so we had a strong cross wind to fight. We actually had to ride leaning sideways for most of it.

We all got in before 2 p.m., nice early day. Our hotel is across the street from Wal-Mart.

While sitting here in the lobby documenting the day and taking advantage of the free Wi-Fi, I watched two sweaty and tired workmen drag in, make their way to the front desk, and ask for two rooms. "We are sold out for the night," the clerk told them. "We have no rooms available." One guy said, "But there are no cars in the parking lot." "Right, they all got here on bicycles" she told them. They looked at me, I shrugged my shoulders, and they left in search of another refuge.

And we get to get up and do it again tomorrow—how fun!

Jenny

Chapter 16

Concussions—Heads Up!

You got your bell rung!
Shake off the cobwebs!
Get the smelling salts!

Sadly, these used to be the common reactions to a concussion. Thankfully, not so much anymore because there is a growing understanding that all concussions are serious and need to be managed accordingly. Given the horrific revelations about the effect of concussions on NFL players, a spotlight is on the telling need for education about the ramifications of the injury and its proper management.

The word "concussion" comes from the Latin *concutere*, which means to shake violently. A concussion, also called mild traumatic brain injury, is a transient alteration of brain function. Our brains are suspended in cerebrospinal fluid (CSF), similar to an egg yolk inside its shell. If the head sustains a violent blow and the brain is shaken during a sudden acceleration or deceleration or is spun around during a whiplash, it "sloshes" inside the skull.

The traditional diagnostic tests, including CT and MRI scans, assess physical damage to the brain, including skull fractures and dangerous bleeds in and around the brain, but do not provide adequate information to measure the concussion injury. In fact, people misunderstand the situation when the doctors tell them the CT scan was normal. Patients automatically assume they are fine and can resume their regular routines. But the fact is, if a patient has a concussion, that patient is not fine and needs to see a medical professional trained in concussion management, which includes an initial, thorough evaluation and frequent monitoring of the athlete's symptoms and the brain's ability to function. The athlete should not be allowed to return to play until the brain is fully healed and is medically cleared. Recovery from a concussion is a process and may take days, weeks, or months. Unfortunately, in rare cases, an individual may never fully recover and will have to retire. When concussions are managed properly, most athletes are able to successfully and safely return to their sport.

Today, the good news is that concussion diagnosis and management are better understood, since the medical world reached consensus on the injury. In 2008, medical and research professionals convened in Zurich, Switzerland, to discuss mild traumatic brain injuries. A revolutionary approach was developed that now manages concussions with new and unified guidelines for diagnosis and treatment.

We use baseline testing as part of an athlete's initial physical exam to gather pre-concussion information, which includes collecting extensive data regarding symptom reporting, cognitive function, and balance. For example, we ask athletes to describe how they are feeling—do you have a headache, are you feeling in a fog or dizzy? We have them do a memory word recall and number/symbol recognition. We test their balance by having them stand on one leg with their eyes closed. A detailed computerized test assesses reaction time, recognition, and memory. After an athlete sustains a head injury, we use these same tests to guide our diagnosis and management.

Certain language previously used to categorize concussions is no longer meaningful. There is no need to label the concussion grade I, II, III, or mild, moderate, severe. If there are any symptoms, the determination is that the athlete has a concussion, and it must be managed.

In sports, the danger lies in "second impact syndrome," when a concussed athlete returns to play before he is fully recovered and sustains another injury to the brain. This new injury has the likely potential to cause severe damage, permanent disability, and even death.

I dealt with the most challenging concussion case in my experience when Kelley Cain, a post player on our basketball team, suffered a concussion during a car accident in July 2009. The CT scan at the hospital did not show a skull fracture or a bleed in the brain. She was advised not to participate in physical activity for the rest of the summer. In her pre-season physical exam in August she was cleared to play basketball. In late November, during a game against Texas, Kelley went up for a rebound and was hit in the head by an opponent's elbow. She left the game with a headache and dizziness. We followed our concussion protocol to the letter, and Kelley returned to basketball in just over a week.

However, as the year went on, Kelley's grades began to suffer. She came to me and said her classes used to be easier for her. At first she thought her courses were just getting harder because she was deep in her major in business logistics and marketing. She said that in class she would have headaches and would become dizzy and sick to her stomach when she read or took notes, and she had trouble concentrating. Her parents were worried when she told them that she did not feel like herself. Although basketball was going well, it became obvious that she was having problems off the court. We realized we needed to look more carefully at her condition, ask questions, and find some answers. So Kelley and I flew to Pittsburgh to see Dr. Michael Collins. A neuropsychologist, he is the assistant director of the Sports Concussion Program at the University of Pittsburgh Medical Center for Sports Medicine and a leading expert on concussions and mild traumatic brain injury. Dr. Collins explained to us that, "mild concussions can become severe and severe concussions can become mild."

Concussions are a neuro-metabolic dysfunction, or a chemical change in the brain. The brain is made up of billions of nerve cells called neurons. Describing the physiology of concussions, Dr. Collins told us that once the brain shifts inside the skull, potassium is released from the neurons, creating an opening for calcium, which normally circulates outside the cells, to enter. "The calcium restricts the flow of blood to the brain. At the very time that the brain needs more blood to bring nutrition and energy to the neurons, the blood supply is reduced," he said.

His evaluation of Kelley showed that her concussion continued to affect how her brain was functioning. He determined that she was suffering from post-concussion syndrome, a collection of cascading and very hard-to-describe symptoms that can be incapacitating and life altering. "Young people especially can experience chronic symptoms such as headaches, dizziness, fatigue, light and noise sensitivity, balance issues, chronic mood changes, anxiety, and depression," Dr. Collins explained. The syndrome may continue for weeks, months, or occasionally, years.

To reset her brain chemistry Dr. Collins prescribed medication and specialized physical therapy exercises involving hand-eye coordination, memory recall, concentration, eye tracking, and balance. Additionally, he advised that certain academic accommodations be made, including having someone take notes for her, receiving additional time for tests and assignments, and having the option to take oral tests. We followed his advice. Her follow-up appointment with Dr. Collins two months later showed she was improving. He strongly advocates that rest from the rigors of academics is often pivotal in proper concussion management. "The worst way to treat student-athletes who have had a concussion is to push them academically, because that is going to make this injury worse," he said.

Physicians need to work with professors and academic support systems to make sure that academic accommodations are built into a good concussion protocol. The less severely injured may not have to be taken out of class, but they still may need special accommodations such as less work, tests read to them, testing in a separate room, extensions on assignments, books on tape, and rest.

Once the spring semester was over, we told Kelley not to enroll in summer classes and restricted her physical activity to reduce her chances of another concussion. At the end of August 2010, over a year after the car accident, her assessment numbers returned to her pre-concussion baseline scores. Now well, she was solid and productive during her last basketball season and graduated in May 2011.

The effects of concussions differ between genders and among age groups. People with a history of migraines have more difficulties recovering from the injury, and female migraine incidences outnumber males four to one. "There is evolving research that shows that females may not only ex-

Basketball siblings. Courtesy of the Crispin-Pischea family.

hibit acute difficulties, but they also may have longer and more complicated recoveries," Dr. Collins said.

Young people are especially vulnerable to concussive injuries for a variety of reasons. Dr. Collins cites glutamate as a key factor in this vulnerability. Glutamate is the most common neurotransmitter in our brains and is involved in the cognitive functions of learning and memory. Basically, a neurotransmitter is a chemical that helps a message jump across a synapse, the space between a nerve and its target cell. (Your body is entirely made up of cells, from muscle cells, to organ cells, to complex brain cells.) A concussion causes the release of more of the glutamate neurotransmitter, creating a state of chaos so that the brain has trouble processing and remembering new information. "Children are three times more glutamate sensitive than adults, which is probably why they are more vulnerable to the injury and why we see young people taking longer to recover," explained Dr. Collins. "We know that the brain continues to be developing in people under the age of twenty-five."

In children, the strength of their necks also plays a role in their vulnerability to concussions. For all of our athletes, we incorporate neck resistance exercises in our strength programs to develop their neck muscles. The stronger the neck, the better the forces are transferred from the head through the neck to the body.

The severity of concussive injuries can be impacted by force differentials. Some youths are very strong, big, and fast, and some are not. In high school, there can be a huge discrepancy in size when preadolescent freshmen go head to head with physically mature seniors. In college, the changing size and weight of athletes over the years has also increased the potential for concussions. Dr. William Youmans, who was our team orthopedist for over thirty-five years, has witnessed the collective growth spurt. "When I began my practice, a collegiate offensive lineman might have weighed 250 pounds. I never would have predicted that a starting offensive lineman would average 320 pounds, as they do today," he told me. "It's a different game because of it."

"I am very aware of the changes in the size and height of female athletes, as well. Women 6 feet and taller are not unusual, and we even see players who are 6 feet 8 inches." In 1995, the number of officials for women's basketball increased from two to three to keep up with the speed and physicality of the game. Recently the rules were changed with the three-point line moving back a foot, equal to the men's distance of 20 feet 9 inches. Women are beginning to play above the rim. Although these changes make for a more exciting game, they also increase the chance and severity of concussions.

Many myths are associated with concussions. It's time to debunk the most common among them.

Myth: The head must actually be hit in order to sustain a concussion.

Fact: False! A concussion can be sustained in any situation or during any accident that shakes the brain in the skull. I personally experienced this when I was a student athletic trainer for the ice hockey team at Western Michigan University, where I did my undergraduate work. I stepped on the ice during a practice to assist one of the athletes, and suddenly my legs flew out from under me, and I crashed down on my butt. I hit the ice so hard that I felt the jarring in my head. Two athletes helped me off the ice. I had a headache, was dizzy, spaced out, and dazed. The team physician evaluated me. His diagnosis: concussion.

Myth: Concussions occur only in contact sports.

Fact: This is definitely not true. Concussions can occur in any sport and in any situation when the brain is shaken. One of our golfers slipped and fell as she walked up a set of steps on campus. Her concussion lasted over two months, keeping her off the course and in the clubhouse. Athletes don't have a corner on the market. A concussion can happen to anyone at any time: car accidents, hitting your head on the corner of a countertop, or being jostled on a roller coaster.

Myth: A concussion involves loss of consciousness.

Fact: Most of the time the injury does not involve loss of consciousness. There is no correlation between the two. Both Kelley and the golfer had concussions, but neither lost consciousness. On the other hand, I have seen athletes lose consciousness and yet return to their sport symptom free and fully recovered in less than a week.

Myth: After a head injury, it is important to wake up or stay awake for a period of time.

Fact: Actually, Dr. Collins cautions against that. "Waking someone during the night will make the concussion worse. After we have done a CT scan and ruled out any kind of bleed, the brain needs to rest." Rest is the main treatment for a concussion. The last thing you want to do is interrupt the healing process.

Myth: Helmets prevent concussion.

Fact: Not so. Dr. Collins asserts that "helmets do an incredible job of preventing skull fractures and internal bleeds. What the helmet can't do is prevent the brain from moving inside the skull." I found this out when I was hit by a car while riding my bike. My helmet cracked in three places, saving my skull, but I still sustained a concussion.

Dr. Kevin Guskiewicz, athletic trainer and researcher at the University of North Carolina at Chapel Hill and recipient of a MacArthur Foundation "genius grant," has conducted extensive research on the assessment of sport-related concussion and its long-term effects. He has determined that concussion is a predisposition for future injury. To find out what happens to football players during practice or in a game, he placed force sensors in their helmets. Dr. Guskiewicz found a significant connection between player position and impacts and has identified the correlating factors of the forces on a concussion. That is, a hard hit does not necessarily lead to a concussion; on the other hand, a light hit may result in one. On football weekends, we often see and hear two behemoths smash into each other with a resounding crash, and both get up unhurt. A few plays later, we might see a running back downed by a typical tackle from behind leave the game with a concussion.

Myth: Mouth guards decrease the severity of a concussion.

Fact: Research shows there is no evidence that mouth guards have any effect on reducing or preventing concussions. However, they are effective in preventing or reducing injury to teeth, gums, lips, the tongue, and the jaw. Without them, I see severe lip lacerations and broken and knocked-out teeth. Elbows do fly, so I strongly encourage our basketball team to wear mouth guards. Although they do not prevent concussions, they do protect your pearly whites.

A concussion can be a frustrating and maddening injury for coaches and athletes alike, because the injury is not an obvious one, with no visible evidence of treatment such as tape, bandage, or ice. The athlete looks fine. People who don't understand concussions may question an athlete's toughness, and that can be troubling and embarrassing for the player. An athlete's strong desire to participate sometimes leads to a reluctance to report symptoms honestly. Medical staffs are also frustrated by the injury. Concussions require rest and time to heal. No one can predict how long recovery will take. As an athletic trainer, I too find it frustrating that I cannot speed up the healing process as I can with other injuries. My rehabilitation skills, icing, and high-tech modalities are ineffective and sit idle. Concussions require patience, honest symptom reporting by the athlete, and understanding from coaches, teammates, parents, and fans.

I learned so much from Kelley's case and our visits with Dr. Collins. Concussion management is much more complex than has been previously recognized, and every case is different. When I was dealing with a concussed point guard who had not been practicing for over three weeks, I heard her teammates teasing her, calling her "Headache" and questioning her toughness. I exploded. I would have thought they would have known better after seeing what Kelley went through. This was a teachable moment if there ever was one. They got the message loud and clear. They apologized to their teammate and to me. I talk regularly to my athletes about concussions, constantly reminding them that all head injuries, big and small, are serious. You only have one brain. Take care of it.

Dr. Collins views concussions as manageable injuries. He says, "The best form of treatment is making certain that the athlete is 100 percent fully recovered before going back into play." A host of people with professional expertise surrounds every athlete, yet decisions do not always reflect the wisdom of these resources. Regrettably, if a parent, coach, or athlete disagrees with a medical recommendation, they will sometimes shop around for the answer they want, often to the detriment of the athlete who should not be playing.

We must do a better job in educating athletes, parents, and coaches about what they need to look for, and it is imperative that athletes honestly report their symptoms. Dr. Collins says, "It is really hard to get an athlete to be honest at the end of the day when it is fourth down and two, and the athlete wants to go back into the game. This culture has to be changed."

Day 20: Brinkley, AR, to Senatobia, MS, 113 miles

Hey Y'all,

Ah, back in the Deep South: hot and humid, kudzu, catfish fry, a slower pace, and thick accents. It is funny when I am the interpreter for many in the group.

We started this morning in a light rain. We packed up and rode to breakfast at Gene's BBQ and descended on the locals in Brinkley, Arkansas. They had to put us in the back room because the regulars had their tables, and we were not to break their routine—no bad karma! They are really proud of their ivory-billed woodpecker—great for tourism.

After about the first thirty minutes of riding, the rain stopped and the humidity started. It was 60 degrees when we left Brinkley, and the temps rose quickly to about 80 degrees. We had cloud cover for most of the morning, and then it was bright and sunny. Unfortunately, all good things have to come to an end. We had head winds 10–15 mph today. At least we kept jockeying between going east and south, so we had head winds, then cross winds. And wouldn't you know it, after we got to the hotel in Senatobia, the winds shifted to tail winds. Oh well, maybe we will have them tomorrow.

We rode through the towns of Moro, Marianna, Walnut Corner, Helena, and across the mighty Mississippi River. I was able to take a picture before crossing, but not on the bridge because getting over it was a bit technical— very narrow, road debris and lots of fast moving, truck hauling traffic crossing over the state line into Mississippi.

Into the towns of Lula and Rich and through the back roads of Mississippi. Our lunch stop was on the side of the road in a field. We took Crenshaw by storm, as many of us stopped at a local store for ice cream and cold beverages. The town folk were very curious about us, our bikes, what we were doing, and so on, and again, I was the interpreter and did most of the talking.

Today was a really flat terrain day; however, between Crenshaw and Senatobia the hills began, short, steep rollers. I felt like I was in east Tennessee.

Giant ivory-billed woodpecker sign, alongside souvenier shop, in Brinkley, Arkansas, where sightings of the bird, long thought to be extinct, have been reported.

Heads Up

Riders noticed my comfort level with them right away, and one of them said, "Ah, your training terrain." My answer, "You got that right." We rode on one really rough road, and my hands, feet, and buttocks hurt. It did not matter if you went fast or slow, the jarring hurt the fillings in your teeth. The route sheet indicated we were on the road for nine miles before turning off and, just when I was thinking about walking the last four miles of it, the road all of a sudden smoothed out, and we all looked up and said "thank you!" to the cycling gods.

Senatobia has a cute, southern city center. I did some bike tinkering with Mechanic Jim tonight (probably due to the road from he@#), ate, and did a quick load of laundry. Tomorrow is a longer mileage day, and laundry is further away, so I thought I would get ahead of the game. Under 1,000 miles to go. Dreaming of tail winds.

And we get to get up and do it again tomorrow. Fun!

Jenny

Chapter 17

Back on Track

Candace Parker is, hands down, one of the best female professional basketball players today, an accolade that doesn't come by chance. I remember the first time I saw her as a freshman, when she had a badly swollen knee that required surgery in September. She set her goal to play by January, even though this surgery typically requires eight to nine months of rehabilitation. Candace's therapy went so well, and she was so ahead of schedule, that our orthopedic surgeon cleared her for practice at the end of December. To the delight of Coach Pat Summitt, during one of her first times back on the floor, Candace dunked the basketball. Although her performance on the court was astounding, the knee did not respond as we would have liked. She experienced pain and swelling. Even though she could have contributed to the team on a limited basis, she did not want to begin her collegiate career short of her best effort. She opted to sit out that freshman year and continue to strengthen her knee. Her decision in the midst of the expectations of others was remarkable and showed maturity well beyond her years.

It is not surprising that student-athletes who are completely immersed in their sport inevitably experience great difficulty when faced with a season or career-ending injury. It can be devastating if one's sense of worth and identity is solely built around sport. My life as an athletic trainer puts me up-close and personal with injuries and how athletes respond to them. If I were to write a formula for overcoming injury, it would be the following:

> hard work + motivation + working through the pain + active rest + positive attitude = athlete on the mend

Meeting adversity with determination and vigor will have a favorable outcome. It may take a village to raise a child, and it also takes a village to heal an injured athlete. They rely on medical staff, teammates, family, coaches, and friends to support them through this traumatic time.

Candace Parker. Courtesy of Intercollegiate Athletics, The University of Tennessee.

Looking back on her collegiate career, Candace takes a positive approach to her injuries. "I took injuries very hard. Once I fell in love with basketball, it was my outlet through very tough times in my life. If I was upset about something, I would shoot hoops. When I was injured, I couldn't go shoot; it was really tough for me," she reminisces. "But I had the best athletic trainer and support staff to help me to get through and over it. I believe that everything happens for a reason. I am the person and the basketball player that I am today because of the adversity that I had to overcome."

Candace is exemplary in every facet of life. She approached rehabilitation as she faced every other challenge in her life—with a fierce determination. She was a student not only of basketball, but also of the rehab process. Working with her, I felt as if I were educating a student of athletic training. She wanted to understand how her body worked and how it healed—what more she could do to return to the court sooner. When I commented on her resolve, Candace responded without hesitation. "There comes a time when you have to look at yourself in the mirror, and say, 'OK, this happened, so now what are you going to do about it?'"

What did Candace do about it? She kept a journal and wrote down all her goals—how far she was going to bend her knee by a certain day, how she would work to improve her balance, how much weight she was going to lift, and how long she would ride the stationary bike. She set her goals and met them. It is my job to create the environment to heal, and the athlete has to do the work to heal. Setting goals and meeting them is the way to heal.

As a professional in the WNBA, Parker sustained a season-ending injury in 2010. Co-owner of the Los Angeles Sparks Kathy Goodman told the *Los Angeles Times*, "We can't replace Candace. Nobody can. . . . Bad things happen . . . Then you have to persevere. She'll be a role model on how to deal with personal adversity."[44]

No athlete wants to hear that they cannot practice or play. However, there are times when the body just can't go on. My job is to keep those times to a minimum. This is why I incorporate the principle of "active rest" during the time of a player's rehab. A seemingly contradictory term, the concept is essential to healing. It means sparing one part of the body from overuse or harm while keeping other parts in motion. A good example is an injured athlete who cannot and should not run on the road but may be able to run in the pool. The water provides buoyancy and reduces pounding. The athlete will still feel like an athlete because she is moving, exerting energy, and sweating. Active rest also applies to the mental aspect of the game. The athlete sidelined from practice can find ways to sharpen strategic and problem-solving skills in the fun of video and board games. For example, we used puzzles, marbles, and other similar toys to break up the monotony of hand rehab for one of our golfers.

Active rest does not only apply in times of injury. The healthiest way to develop as an athlete is to follow the "work smarter, not harder" philosophy. This translates into cross-training, modifying the intensity level, changing activities, taking time off, and listening to your body. Some days, for various reasons, an athlete may be feeling less than great. It happens to all of us. I often tell them to maximize their effort on a given day—no matter how they feel. If they give their best, they know that tomorrow will be even better. Of course, if low output days become a pattern, there may be a need to evaluate other physical factors such as sleep patterns, iron levels, allergies, asthma, continued soreness, lack of recovery, undisclosed minor injuries, and nutrition—which may include not eating enough calories to meet their energy needs. Mental and emotional factors should not be overlooked either. These include stress, anxiety, depression, eating disorders, and unrecognized learning disabilities.

In today's culture, rest is not popular in certain circles. Achievers are expected to be always on and always pushing. Too often the pressure to be constantly productive defines success. Rest may be viewed as a negative—a sign that an athlete is lazy, selfish, and idle. The reality is that rest increases productivity when used appropriately. When you break your arm, everyone understands it needs to be put in a cast to heal. When your body or spirit is broken, you must recognize the restorative powers you need to heal. Take the time to rest so you can recover physically, mentally, or emotionally.

My prescription for recovery from strenuous training and competition entails the following:

>   Cross-training—doing a different activity that will give you similar benefits. For example, a runner can cross train with cycling.

>   Resting—taking a day off from the physical and mental requirements of your sport. No one should feel guilty about this; it takes ten to fourteen days for a well-trained body to begin deconditioning.

>   Refueling—ingesting carbohydrates and proteins within an hour after physical activity to replenish your energy stores and repair muscle breakdown.

Playing—breaking up your workouts with activities that are fun whenever possible. If you can't connect your effort to the essential joy that attracted you to your sport in the first place, it will be hard for you to continue.

Pursuing diverse activities—challenging your mind and spirit to nurture interests other than sports to create a well-balanced life.

Listening to your body—paying attention to the small aches and pains before they become actual injuries. Use the ice!

Day 21: Senatobia, MS, to Aberdeen, MS, 138 miles

Hey Y'all,

Happy Mother's Day! Yes, I called mine.

Phew! I'm tired—in fact the entire group looks a little fried. I think it is the cumulative effect. Of course 138 miles today was no picnic; that is a lo-o-o-ng way. The temperature was in the low sixties when we started, with some clouds, but no rain. It got hotter as the day went on, but not as hot as it could have been. It only reached 74, with a lot of sunshine. The tan lines are very distinct. There was not much of a wind for most of the day, only 5–10

Cyclist cooling off.

mph, but that is a good thing, because the route sheet today had us turning forty-two times. We obviously ended up further east, but we went round about ways to get there. Rode mostly in the middle of nowhere.

We left the motel at 7:30 a.m. and headed out of town on Yellow Dog Road. After eight turns, we hit Harmontown, the first town. Now, since it was Sunday in the South, all of those towns we went through were like ghost towns, with nothing open and no one around. Of course, the church parking lots were full. Abbeville, Toccopola, Pontotoc, Troy, Algoma, Egypt, and Toxish were very small. Even Aberdeen was closed down tonight. It is a good thing the restaurant in the hotel was open. Our gang made the restaurant's monthly quota.

Again to my surprise, Mississippi is very hilly—or maybe Mike can just find 'em. The first forty miles was steep interval rollers, like home, and then the next seventy miles was a series of long steady hills. It did not flatten out until the last twenty-five miles or so of the ride. At least we were headed due east at that point and had a tail wind that picked up to about 15 mph. That really helped mentally.

Everyone was so tired by lunch, the 87-mile point, that a couple of riders tried to gas up their bikes for the rest of the way to the hotel.

Our leaders told us that the lunch stop would be in the parking lot of a local ice cream shop. That was all motivation one rider needed for the day. When we arrived, to his dismay, the shop was not open on Sundays. Barb mentioned to him that there was probably packaged ice cream at the convenience store he passed half a mile back. He replied, "Doug doesn't go backwards."

In the later afternoon, we began to see more people and there were a lot of friendly waves. And the drivers here are very courteous; they wait for us to top a hill, pass all the way over on the left and no one buzzed us. I really did not see much industry or agriculture—some corn, soybeans, area woodlands, and cattle but there was a lot of land not used for anything.

Nothing against Mississippi; however, they have the roughest roads of any state we have been through. My vote: Arkansas for best roads. Mississippi wins the dog state award. Lots of dogs who like to chase bikes. The most common breed was Border collie; our dog Sami would be proud. The good news was many of the dogs were tired from chasing the riders ahead of me, so it was only a token effort when I went by.

Full tummy, time for an early evening to get energy and rest. It is supposed to be a hill day all the way into Alabama.

And we get to get up and do it again tomorrow—how fun!

Jenny

Fill 'er up.

Chapter 18

Nutrition: Fuel for Fun

Maintaining good health. Winning performances. Both are admirable goals. How to reach them? Let's talk nutrition.

Good nutrition is essential for everyone. The adage, "You are what you eat," may be a common one but, in spite of its wisdom, so many of us continue to fill our bellies with junk. More and more, the medical profession, the government, educators, media outlets, and the public are focusing on the subject. Proper nutrition is in the limelight, front and center on the main stage, playing a critical role in all aspects of life; it affects longevity, energy levels, the ability to ward off illness, and the healing of injuries; it impacts attitudes and moods, mobility, and overall health.

One of the reasons nutrition is getting so much attention these days is because our nation's people are growing, and not in a good way. No matter the age group, obesity is a national health crisis, and everyone pays the cost. Risks include cardiovascular disease, such as high cholesterol levels, high blood pressure, and coronary heart disease; type 2 diabetes; breast, endometrial, and colon cancers; stroke, liver, and gall bladder diseases; sleep apnea and respiratory problems; osteoarthritis; abnormal menses; and infertility. Over twenty-five years ago I decided not to repeat my family's diabetic history. I gave up sugar for Lent. After forty days, I realized I could live without it. To this day I do not eat desserts. I truly believe that I have increased my odds against succumbing to this awful disease. Food is fuel. The right foods on a reasonable schedule replenish the energy that sports and physical activity expend. With energy being their stock in trade, it would seem logical that college athletes would sign on to the concept that they have specific nutritional needs. But for too many, nutrition is not a priority—it's practically an exotic notion that rarely appears on their radar screens. They skip meals, especially breakfast, eat late at night because of busy schedules, eat way too much fast food, and drink high-sugar, caffeinated beverages.

Some time ago, our basketball coaches asked me to work with a player from the Deep South who would tire too quickly in practice. When I talked with her about what she was eating and drinking, she said that she downed seven to ten glasses of Hawaiian Punch every day. I was appalled. "But Jenny, it says 'juice' on the can," she said, convinced she was making a healthy choice. Score one for marketing! I explained that actually it only contains 5 percent fruit juice in a whole lot of sugar, but I could see that she really didn't get it. So I made a deal with her. I gave her a squeeze water bottle and asked her to halve the number of Hawaiian Punches she drank in a day for one month, replacing them with water and keeping track of what she was drinking each day. In exchange, I would give her one day off from rehab each week. After three weeks, she had lost eleven pounds, had more energy, and saved some money. Basketball practices not only became easier for her, she also appreciated that what she put into her body made a big difference. Important lesson learned.

When I speak to groups about nutrition, I often compare the human body to a sports car. For top performance, a car needs high-grade fuel, oil, water, lubricants, exhaust removal, and regular service maintenance. With the proper fuel, a car can accelerate from zero to sixty miles per hour in seconds. Just like the car, your body ought to function smoothly whenever you ask it to. Take meticulous care of the most important and expensive vehicle you will ever own—your body. It needs the carbohydrates in whole grains, fruits, and vegetables to fuel the energy that our bodies want. It requires proteins, the building blocks of muscle, to aid in recovery and help repair damage. It uses the fat stores it has in reserve to go the distance, provide insulation, and protect vital organs. It also requires vitamins and minerals to make the machinery of our cells work. All vehicles—muscle cars, Rolls-Royces, SUVs, sedate sedans, pickup trucks, custom vans, semis, motorcycles, and clunkers—need fluids—oil, brake fluid, coolant, water—to cool systems, clean parts, and remove byproducts. Our bodies, too, no matter the type, need fluids to cool us, remove waste products, keep us hydrated, fight illness, and keep our organs working.

Too many athletes, coaches, and parents don't understand nutrition and its effect on performance. We need to emphasize nutrition as much as we emphasize practice. To improve your game, you need to practice once a day, but to win, you must eat at least three meals a day plus energizing snacks. Basic nutritional needs are not being met in this fast food society, with its over-scheduling and the disappearing family meal. Parents are succumbing to marketing campaign claims for meal replacements such as energy bars, shakes, powders, and smoothies. With a little creative thought, you can rustle up healthy meals on the go. Most supermarkets have salad bars. Call ahead to a restaurant with healthy menu options for an easy take-out meal. Learning to eat nutritionally just takes planning.

I use every means I can to promote good nutrition. In our athletic training room we have posters showing the nutritional value of foods in popular fast food restaurants so that those late-night munchies or meals on the go can be chosen with nutrition in mind. We have developed a comprehensive, hands-on program for our athletes. Our sports nutritionist holds "food court," teaching all aspects of healthy eating—creative cooking in a microwave, making healthier fast food choices, getting a bang for your buck at the grocery store, making trail mix for late-night snacks, grabbing a good on-the-run breakfast, antioxidant-rich smoothies, and thirty-minute dinners.

But we can't watch athletes 24/7, so demanding that they eat a certain way or lose weight will never work. We learned that, to be successful, we need to meet the athletes where they are with their eating habits. Otherwise, they will never take responsibility and buy into the goal. Back in the day, when we had athlete weigh-ins, one track coach had what she called "breakfast club." She required her athletes who were overweight to do extra bike and elliptical workouts every morning at 6 a.m. After six weeks of this, not one person lost weight, and some even gained. She finally figured out that they were revolting and eating even more junk food.

Now we tackle poor eating habits gradually with negotiable exchanges. When the team is traveling to a game, a restaurant meal on the road presents the perfect opportunity to take a step forward to a healthy choice. If an athlete decides she wants a New York strip rather than a grilled chicken breast, we discuss selecting a salad instead of an appetizer and a baked potato instead of fries. Great! And she can live with that. Another good nutrition lesson learned.

At the age of twenty-five, elite athlete Kara Lawson had to get serious about nutrition, because she got sick to the point that it was affecting her WNBA play. She had no energy, felt she didn't recover after the games, and had joint pain. Her doctor told her she needed more rest, better nutrition, and more water. She started focusing on what she was eating and the timing of her meals. At this time, she was dating her future husband, Damien, who was following a sound nutrition plan that was helpful to her new regimen. Eight weeks later, she had lost twelve pounds and her body fat decreased 6 percent. She had more energy, recovered faster game to game, and her joint pain went away. "I realized that there was a correlation between what I was eating and how I felt. When I ate the right food, I felt good; when I ate the wrong food, I felt bad," she said. Now six years into her eating routine, she is in the best health ever. When she isn't playing professional ball, she is an analyst with ESPN. Her flourishing career in broadcasting requires extensive travel to big and small towns all over the country, so meal planning can be a challenge. She often takes healthy food along with her because of maddening delays in airports or on planes.

Taking a cue from Kara, it's always smart to evaluate your eating habits. Good or bad they make a difference in the performances of your life. Athletes, be it at the high school, college, professional, or recreational level, often must make significant adjustments to their diet as they age and their level of activity decreases. Athletes in sports that require large body mass, such as football or heavyweight wrestling, may struggle even more when their career is over. Within a six-year span, eight former University of Tennessee football players died under the age of fifty. Associate athletics director for administration, Carmen Tegano, decided to do something about it, so he started the 76 Club in honor of Harry Galbreath, who wore the number 76 as a UT offensive lineman and professional player, and who died at the age of forty-five. Designed to provide former athletes with an exercise and nutrition education program, the club meets every weekday at 6 a.m. on the UT campus. The members, who currently number seventeen, walk, do body weight exercises and light strength training, and learn about good nutrition. If retired athletes' eating habits don't change, their future after sport may look completely different. The rates of obesity for athletes and former athletes are part of a broader story on the increasing rates of obesity among adults nationwide. Table 3 contains the most recent data on obesity percentages for each state. What is most disturbing is watching childhood obesity rise and knowing children aren't the ones responsible for the epidemic. Children are not being taught how to eat or the importance of physical activity. But there is hope that by recognizing and confronting the nutritional challenges—and by highly visible athletes and public figures who can be especially effective in bringing the sound nutrition message to young people—significant inroads can be made in solving the problems.

One of our former track athletes is doing just that. Four-time Olympian Joetta Clark Diggs, considered by track enthusiasts as the most prolific 800-meter runner of all time, has created a foundation to educate children about nutrition and exercise. She appreciates the visibility of her success as an opportunity to have an impact. "An elite athlete has a public platform,"

Table 3. The Percentage of Obese Adults by State.[1]

State	%	State	%
1. Mississippi	34.9	27. Wisconsin	27.7
2. Louisiana	33.4	28. Alaska	27.4
3. West Virginia	32.4	29. Illinois	27.1
4. Alabama	32.0	30. Idaho	27.0
5. Michigan	31.3	31. Oregon	26.7
6. Oklahoma	31.1	32. Florida	26.6
7. Arkansas	30.9	33. Washington	26.5
8. (tie) Indiana and South Carolina	30.8	34. New Mexico	26.3
		35. New Hampshire	26.2
10. (tie) Kentucky and Texas	30.4	36. Minnesota	25.7
12. Missouri	30.3	37. (tie) Rhode Island and Vermont	25.4
13. (tie) Kansas and Ohio	29.6	39. Wyoming	25.0
		40. Arizona	24.7
15. (tie) Tennessee and Virginia	29.2	41. Montana	24.6
17. North Carolina	29.1	42. (tie) Connecticut, Nevada and New York	24.5
18. Iowa	29.0		
19. Delaware	28.8	45. Utah	24.4
20. Pennsylvania	28.6	46. California	23.8
21. Nebraska	28.4	47. (tie) District of Columbia and New Jersey	23.7
22. Maryland	28.3		
23. South Dakota	28.1	49. Massachusetts	22.7
24. Georgia	28.0	50. Hawaii	21.8
25. (tie) Maine and North Dakota	27.8	51. Colorado	20.7

[1]Compiled from Centers for Disease Control and Prevention and *Trust for America's Health*, 2012. Individuals with a body mass index (a calculation based on weight and height ratios) of 30 or higher are considered obese.

explains Clark Diggs. "Through our programs we reach approximately 5,000 children each year and hope to make a difference so that they can live full and healthy lives."

First Lady Michelle Obama has taken on the challenge by launching a program called Solving the Problem of Childhood Obesity within a Generation. "For the first time, the nation will have goals, benchmarks, and measurable outcomes that will help us tackle the childhood obesity epidemic one child, one family, and one community at a time," Mrs. Obama said. "We want to marshal every resource—public and private sector, mayors and governors, parents and educators, business owners and healthcare providers, coaches and athletes—to ensure that we are providing each and every child the happy, healthy future they deserve."[45]

When I speak to groups about healthy eating, I rarely refer to it as a diet. I prefer meal plan. To me, diet is a four letter word for RESTRICTION. Following a nutritional plan is a common sense strategy for maintaining a healthy body. The following guidelines have been around for generations. There are no short cuts. Be fad-free. Here's what to do:

Eat a variety of foods.

Pay attention to portion sizes.

Eat more whole grains—such as whole-wheat, bran, oat breads and cereals, whole wheat pasta, and brown rice—to increase fiber in your diet.

Include a variety of vegetables and fruits, especially dark red, orange, and green varieties, to get more antioxidant nutrients like beta carotene and lycopene, which reduce the harmful molecular chain reactions that cause damage or death to a cell.

Have fruits and vegetables more often than their juice to reduce acid and get more fiber.

Keep your meals moderate in total fat, low in saturated fats, and eliminate trans fats for a healthy heart. Eat low-fat dairy products, lean meats, and foods prepared without added fat.

Balance the amount of food you eat with the amount of physical activity you do.

Limit your consumption of salty and processed foods to keep your blood pressure in a healthy range.

Drink eight 8-ounce glasses of water a day to keep your body hydrated and cool, and to assist your cells' essential metabolic functions.

Cut back on high-caffeine beverages, which are dehydrating and may interfere with bone health.

Consume only moderate amounts of alcoholic beverages (beer, wine, and liquor).

Do not skip meals. Breakfast is the most important meal of the day. Have a protein source with breakfast (milk, peanut butter, cheese, or eggs).

Bodies spend energy through exercise and physical activity. Within an hour of exercise, you should consume 100 grams of carbohydrates to replenish your energy stores—for example, an orange and a bagel. Carbohydrates are also brain fuel. One of our volleyball players finished workouts and went straight to class, neglecting to grab a snack after practice. She promptly fell asleep because her brain didn't have the energy to pay attention and stay awake. The professor noticed, turned out the lights, and took the class out into the hallway, leaving the athlete to her dreams. What a nightmare! Not only was she embarrassed, but she also had to face her coach's discipline and sit out the next game. Want to bet she ate after the next practice?

To your revitalizing snack, add a protein source—cheese, peanut butter, slice of turkey, chocolate milk—after a really hard workout such as weight training or a long practice, during which muscle breaks down. Protein plays a pivotal role in recovery. I knew this going into my bicycle ride across the country. I am a lacto-ovo (dairy and eggs) vegetarian. Riding over one hundred miles every day, I knew that I would need extra protein to get back on my bike each day. I made a conscious effort to have several sources at every meal. For me, no meat is necessary. Nuts, tofu, beans, eggs, milk, cheese, yogurt, and peanut butter are my staples at meals and in my snack pack.

If you are working out in extreme heat, traveling by plane, susceptible to muscle cramps, or experiencing vomiting or diarrhea, you need to replenish your electrolytes such as sodium, calcium, and potassium with a non-carbonated sports drink. When one of our sprinters pulled a hamstring muscle, she thought she was doing everything she could to recover—icing, stretching, elastic bandage, fancy modalities, massage, heat, stretching, and more stretching. Her hamstring wasn't responding as well as we hoped. When I asked her about her eating and drinking habits, she told me she drank a lot of caffeinated sodas and very little water. I asked her how often she peed and if her urine was the color of apple juice or lemonade. When she told me she didn't go often and when she did, her urine was a dark apple juice color and had a strong odor, I knew then that she was dehydrated, and her hamstring muscle was not getting the fluid it needed to heal. After she switched to water and electrolyte sport drinks, she went to the restroom more often and her urine was odorless and light in color. When I massaged her hamstring, I could feel the tissue become more supple and pliable. Her stretching was less painful, and her hamstring started to heal.

As common sense as those tips sound, we are an impatient society that demands immediate results. I am particularly concerned about the widespread and excessive use of supplements. The Food and Drug Administration (FDA) does not have the resources to regulate and investigate dietary supplements for safety, accuracy of ingredients, or effectiveness. Protein drinks, for example, contain ingredients such as herbs and elements that are not listed on the label. These elements can be harmful in and of themselves and potentially can react with other medications. The term supplement means "in addition to." Supplements were never intended to replace meals or proper nutrition. There is no pill, powder, or bar that can substitute for good, balanced nutritional practices. Ideally, you should consult a physician and/or nutritionist when creating a healthy nutrition plan.

We have to be especially mindful of the dangers of these products to children. Dr. Kristine Clark, director of sports nutrition at Pennsylvania State University, shares her concern. "Believe it or not, I had the parents of a six-year-old call me and ask if they should start their son on supplements for pee-wee football," she said.

A toxicologist and founder of Sciencecorps, Kathy Burns, investigated a sampling of protein supplements at an independent lab. She found varying levels of arsenic, cadmium, or lead present in fifteen protein powders and drinks. "When these toxic heavy metals are combined in a product that is marketed for daily use, that raises serious public health concerns, especially for pregnant women, children, and young adults."[46]

Energy drinks contain high levels of caffeine, sugar, vitamins, and various herbal ingredients. They are marketed at sporting events, concerts, and festivals, and are readily available at grocery and convenient stores. They have no therapeutic benefit and in fact may be dangerous. These products complicate diabetes and can cause rapid heart rates, high blood pressure, seizures, anxiety, sleeplessness, headaches, fatigue, drug dependency, kidney stones, cardiac arrest, and even death. A cyclist friend was on a West Coast ride from northern Oregon to southern California when he left the ride in severe pain, ending up in a hospital in Santa Cruz. He was diagnosed with a large kidney stone. The urologist asked him if he drank a lot of energy drinks. Case in point. I had been hounding him for years to stop drinking that stuff. Now he tells me, "You'll never see or hear of me drinking another one. Sometimes it takes a hammer to the head." Or the worst pain you will ever endure.

Chapter 19

Body Image vs. Performance

Prevailing and persistent gender issues haunt the body images female athletes have of themselves. Shape, weight, and size are troubling subjects in sports. Athletes will come into the training room and tell me they want to lose five pounds. My response is, "Why five pounds? Why not three or eight?" And they can't answer those questions. Their coaches and parents have pressured them to believe that a particular weight is the magic number for performance, image, and acceptance. Bombarded with these external beliefs, the athletes predictably compare themselves to a variety of famous ones who exhibit the "ideal" look. And if that's not enough, they struggle with their own internal pressures to please.

Add unfortunate typecasting to the mix. The model images of athletic women prevalent today rightly celebrate strength and fitness, but they also send a mixed message. The athletes are not valued simply because they are talented and accomplished; they are also expected to be sexy, thin, and shapely.

I see the misguided stereotypes of females every day. Young women get caught in a tug of war. They are told they have to be faster, stronger, physical, and aggressive—the best athlete—and oh, by the way, they have to appear feminine and look like a Barbie doll. I see athletes putting on make-up and styling their hair as part of their pre-game ritual only to go out and sweat and compete.

There are societal pressures with regard to females and what they look like in a swimsuit or in a skin-tight volleyball or gymnastics uniform. Sport nutrition expert Dr. Kristine Clark shared her observations with me, pointing out that women's faultless, perfect, Photoshopped images are in direct conflict with reality. "I think we're all mistaken if we don't think that being on television or in front of the fans has something to do with body image and the uniforms that women wear," Dr. Clark said. "The very fact is that many of their uniforms—or in the case of gymnastics, their costumes—are extraordinarily revealing. They wear make-up, they have their hair done, they wear ribbons and glitter. They are performing, and they know they're being looked at. They know they are being evaluated aesthetically, not just for their athleticism."

Former Division I swimmer Bryttany Curran confirms that body image is a common struggle for athletes. "There are two different messages that we confront. One is body image: what society decrees we are supposed to look like. The second is having the perfect body for your sport and what that looks like. There is no perfect body; there is no perfect stroke; there is no perfect way to race. There is only what works best for you."

Society has different expectations of the male and female body. As females enter adolescence, they typically want to look attractive based on mainstream standards that focus on weight and body shape. Males also can be conscious of cultural standards of muscular size and body mass. Dr. Clark notes that women generally want to lose weight, while men are motivated to gain weight in the form of muscle mass. Both behaviors can lead to distorted body images and such unhealthy behaviors as disordered eating patterns, use of laxatives and dietary supplements, fasting, and excessive exercising.

We cannot take misperceptions of body image lightly. Even subtle comments from coaches, parents, and peers can have devastating effects. One real-life example of this I know about played out when a coach off-handedly commented to an athlete when she returned from summer vacation that she "looked healthy." The coach was making a positive statement, but the athlete mistook the comment to mean that she looked fat. Subsequently, she spiraled into an eating disorder.

"*Shape* magazine and *Self* magazine talk about fitness, and *Runner's World* talks about fitness, but there isn't a woman in any of those magazines who hasn't a model image," according to Dr. Clark, who points out the pressures women face today to meet societal expectations. "Many, many female athletes will say, 'I don't want to bulk up. I don't want to get any bigger. I don't want to gain weight.'" I have experienced that same response when it comes to medical issues. Female athletes will hesitate to take various medications with side effects that include possible weight gain. They often refuse to eat after surgery, for fear of gaining weight because their activity level is so low; ironically, this is just at the time when their bodies need food the most in order to heal.

I always try to educate coaches to talk to their athletes in terms of performance only—how fast, high, far and so on—rather than comment on weight, shape, and size. Their weight should never be discussed. It shouldn't matter how an athlete looks—only how she performs. There is no correlation between body weight/body composition and performance. In fact, at Tennessee, the athletes' weights are not listed in media guides for the women's teams. Any discussion about weight or body composition is only between the athlete and our sports dietitian.

Youth soccer coach Josh Gray notes that societal images of gender have a definite impact at the high school level. "I have a player on my team who would be an elite athlete anywhere in the country. But she isn't really interested in college. She is interested in her boyfriend who doesn't care about her sport, doesn't want her to go to practice, and just wants her to hang out. I see this a lot. Caught up in that normal high school peer pressure, the girls too often are judged by how they look—not by how many goals they score and how good a soccer player they are."

When individuals are judged by others based on physical characteristics, their confidence and self-image are no longer their own. Being defined by others can lead to a physical, mental, emotional, or spiritual demise. Since body image so often is linked to self-esteem, it can directly affect performance. We have a far way to go to change that, but if an athlete is made aware of the connection, confronting it can make a difference. Rather than focusing on shape and size, coaches need to focus on what each athlete contributes. Look at their passion and commitment. These are the very factors that carry the correct weight every time!

Day 23: Tuscaloosa, AL, to Prattville, AL, 117 miles

Hey Y'all,

Prattville, Alabama, is the hometown of ride leaders Mike and Barbara Munk, a noble couple who function like a well-oiled machine, and whose tag line is, "Do you ask the man in charge or the woman who knows." We woke up to another cool morning with temperatures in the low fifties, no rain forecasted and very little wind. Any wind we did have was in favorable directions from the west and northwest. It got up to the low seventies with sunshine. We are thankful not to have the humidity.

The hotel had Twinkies on the continental breakfast buffet. "Twinkies, not just for after school anymore."

The Big Dogs were anxious, as they are every morning, to get on the road, but Mike was not loading luggage until 7 a.m., so I got a picture of two of them itching to leave while waiting "patiently" in their rooms.

The Big Dogs ready to roll, first thing in the morning.

Today was a day of climbing . . . over 6,000 feet. If there was a hill in Alabama, we climbed it. It was the third biggest climbing day of the tour, and everyone was feeling it—it was the talk, or should I say the complaint, at each rest stop.

We explored the hilly neighborhoods of Tuscaloosa before leaving town, nice houses, streets, and people. We even went through two roundabouts. Most of the roads were good, but we had some long stretches of "chip and seal" where crews throw down chips of asphalt and let them seal themselves by vehicles driving over them—very rough. Not only is it a rough ride, but there is less roll on your tires, so the ascents are harder and the descents are slower.

Not much exists between Tuscaloosa and Prattville, just the towns of Centerville, with nothing open when we went through at 9:30 a.m., and Antioch. That was basically it. And all we saw were a church and cemetery in Antioch. Good thing the grass grows tall: just watch out for snakes, poison ivy, and fire ants. The challenges and adventures never end.

We saw some great views from high on the hilltops that we climbed and climbed. The dogs were more active today, so add a little sprint work with the climbing. We had many of the roads to ourselves with very little traffic, so you could really relax and hear your own labored breathing.

For those of you who are not from the south, kudzu is a vine that was introduced from Japan to prevent erosion, and it has taken over! It climbs trees, telephone poles, billboards, and the sides of hills, and it cannot be killed.

The city center of Prattville is really nice, with cute shops, restaurants, and an old cotton gin factory. Of course, there were more hills to climb before getting to the hotel.

And we get to get up and do it again tomorrow—how fun!

Jenny

Chapter 20

Three Spokes: The Female Athlete Triad

It's time to give three big hurrahs to celebrate the enticing and increasing prospects for girls and women in sports. The physical, social, mental, emotional, and spiritual benefits are many. Physically, the athletes are more likely to maintain a healthy weight, which can help lower blood sugar levels, cholesterol, triglycerides, and blood pressure, thereby decreasing the incidence of obesity-related diseases like diabetes, hypertension, and heart disease. Two more advantages of participating in sport are preventing osteoporosis and decreasing the risk of breast cancer. In general, female athletes are more likely not to smoke or abuse drugs and alcohol and, if single, they become pregnant at less than half the rate of non-athletes.

They benefit socially as well and are more apt to be successful academically and graduate from high school. Sports teach women how to take risks, be aggressive, set goals, and maintain the focus needed to achieve them. Involvement in sports develops leadership skills, teamwork, strategic thinking, and the pursuit of excellence in performance—all skills necessary for success in the workplace. The mental and emotional benefits are also significant. Among them are a more positive body image, higher self-esteem, and reduced stress and depression. Athletes report being happier, more energetic, and having a better overall quality of life.

However, the demands of sport can negatively impact them in some serious ways. When their participation lacks balance, they may have low energy, fatigue, and susceptibility to illness; easy bruising; stress reactions; stress fractures; and irregular or absent menstrual cycles. All are the signs and symptoms of the Female Athlete Triad, three interrelated conditions that include energy-deficiency/disordered eating; menstrual disturbances/amenorrhea; and bone loss/osteoporosis, on a continuum of severity.

In essence, the Triad creates a domino effect that typically starts with energy-deficiency. An issue of balance, it may be in the form of insufficient calorie consumption, purging, or over-exercising. When the body's energy needs are not being met over time, the menstrual cycle becomes irregular or ceases and hormonal function is altered. This in turn compromises bone strength.

Each component of the continuum may have its own level of severity. Energy-deficiency/disordered eating can range from inadequate calorie intake based on energy expenditure needs to grave eating disorders such as anorexia and bulimia. Menstrual disturbances can vary from irregular to absent, and bone loss/osteoporosis can be diagnosed as mild, moderate, or severe. The consequences of this devastating trio can be ruinous—an athlete's worst nightmare—leading to impaired performance; an increased risk of injury; impaired mental functioning; dehydration; malnourishment, which can cause electrolyte imbalances and loss of reproductive ability. The ultimate cost is starvation, organ failure, and even death.

At various times, female athletes may be anywhere along this spectrum of health and disease. The ideal athlete is to the far right on the spectrum, which defines a healthy state. However, research studies tell us that many are not. A study by Byrne and McLean published in the *Journal of Science and Medicine in Sport* found eating disorders in 31 percent of elite female athletes in sports that emphasized a thin build, such as gymnastics, cross country, diving, ice skating, cheerleading, and light-weight rowing, compared to 5.5 percent of the control population. Another study in the *Clinical Journal of Sports Medicine* by Sundgot-Borgen and Torstveit found that 25 percent of female elite athletes in endurance sports, aesthetic sports, and weight-class sports had clinical eating disorders, compared to 9 percent of the general population.[47] Menstrual disturbances vary widely by sport, age, training volume, and body weight. Small sample size studies have reported 69 percent of dancers, and 65 percent of distance runners experience amenorrhea. Researchers admit unreliability in gathering data and determining the prevalence of Female Athlete Triad components, as these issues are difficult for individuals to recognize in themselves and even more difficult, perhaps, to admit. Some conditions predispose a female athlete to the Triad. Athletes who participate in the aforementioned sports are at greatest risk for low energy when they restrict food intake, exercise more than necessary, and limit the types of food they will eat.

Dieting at a young age is found to be the greatest contributor to disordered eating and eating disorders. Other factors include playing sports that require weigh-ins, punitive consequences for weight gain, low self-esteem, social isolation, family dysfunction, and a history of abuse. An early start of sport-specific training, injury, a sudden increase in the amount of training, pressure to win at all costs, and controlling parents or coaches all add to the problem. Stress fractures result from low bone mineral density, menstrual disturbances, late onset of menses, dietary insufficiency (especially as it relates to vitamin D and calcium intake), genetic predisposition, over-training or increasing training volume and intensity too quickly, and biomechanical abnormalities.

The warning signs affiliated with the Female Athlete Triad are numerous and not difficult to recognize in others. An athlete who complains of always feeling tired or fatigued, having trouble sleeping, obsessively talks about food, counts calories, or restricts food intake, focuses on body shape and size, and constantly strives to be thin is displaying symptoms affiliated with the Triad. Physical signs, such as irregular or absent menstrual cycles, stress fractures, frequent or recurrent injuries, lingering illnesses, and cold hands and feet maybe present as well.

The Female Athlete Triad is a prime example of the intricacies of balancing the body, mind, and spirit. Ideally, treatment of these three health problems involves multiple disciplines. If a friend, parent, or coach suspects an athlete has fallen prey to the Triad, they should seek professional help. A physician must address the hormonal role of low estrogen due to the menstrual disturbances. A nutritionist is best equipped to educate the athlete on eating properly to fuel her body to match energy demands, aid recovery, and maintain normal bone density. A mental health expert is needed to help the athlete process a wide spectrum of issues—mood changes, low self-esteem, perfectionism, drive for thinness, stress, and emotional trauma—that may play a role in this distressing continuum.

At the University of Tennessee in 1992, we created the innovative model program, Team ENHANCE (Enhancing Nutrition Health Athletic Performance Networking Community and Education), for our student-athletes to address the Female Athlete Triad and other mental and emotional health issues. An interdisciplinary support service, Team ENHANCE provides a safe, caring, and confidential environment where young women can seek help in their daily lives and in their pursuit of athletic excellence.

A heart-wrenching example of a young woman who suffered from the Female Athlete Triad was a cross country runner I worked with, who was diagnosed with an eating disorder in high school and underwent inpatient treatment. When she arrived on campus, we established a comprehensive plan and support system for her through Team ENHANCE. Initially, this young student-athlete's recovery was stable and she ran well, but as time

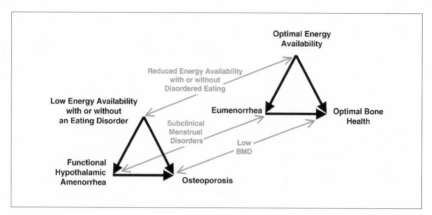

Female athlete triad. Courtesy of Female Athlete Triad Coalition.

went on, several of her teammates became concerned as she began once again to struggle with her disease. She restricted her food intake and often ate in secret, engaging in the bulimic behaviors of binging and purging. She abused laxatives and over-exercised. Because she was not consuming enough calories to support the demands she placed on her body, she produced less estrogen, so her menses stopped. Overuse injuries, including stress fractures, limited her running. As her nutrition status further deteriorated, electrolyte imbalances caused heart palpitations, and a protein deficiency made her ankles swell.

It became evident she needed to stop running until her condition stabilized. Again she was referred to an inpatient eating disorder treatment center. Upon her return, we had her sign a contract stipulating that she agree to make use of our support services and follow all recommendations. However, soon after that, she broke the contract. She was ordered not to run and was barred from participating in team practices and competitions, but she continued running on her own. At this point we had no choice but to remove her from the track and field team. It was painful to watch her self-destruct, but I have learned that you can't help someone who does not want to help herself. It is my hope that one day she will.

I am pleased to report that full-on treatment can beat the Triad and literally save a life. One of our athletic department graduate assistants, a former collegiate basketball player, struggled with this condition. In her case, energy deficiency was the issue. The presenting problem was excessive, obsessive exercise on a stationary bicycle and an elliptical machine for three-plus hours a day, every day. Her supervisor noticed that she was growing thinner and thinner. Alarmed, he asked me for help. We knew we had to do an intervention.

We met with her and told her how concerned we both were with her workout habits, her not eating enough, her sudden drop in weight, and her low energy levels at work. She cried and cried. Between sobs, she said she felt trapped and that she had become a slave to exercise to cope with the stress in her life. She told us of her abiding fatigue and not knowing how she could manage one day to the next. She said she was numb. We cried with her and told her we loved her and would support her every step of the way to a new beginning. She went regularly to counseling, learned about good nutrition, and adopted long-term strategies for healthy eating and exercise. She worked hard and regained control of her body, her mind, and her spirit. Today she is a productive professional, healthy wife, happy mother of two, and a talented recreational athlete.

The best way to prevent the Female Athlete Triad is through educating parents, coaches, and athletes about what it is, how to recognize it, and how to take steps to treat it. Once the coach and parents are aware of the problems their athlete may face, they should support her throughout her training and competition, as well as during her everyday life. Utilizing available experts—nutritionists, counselors, athletic trainers, and physicians—they should remind her that eating is an important part of successful training and performance; she should be focusing on health and a positive body image, while recognizing that weight or composition are irrelevant.

It's up to the athlete to monitor and track her monthly menstrual cycle and consult a physician if she has menstrual irregularities, recurrent injuries and illnesses, or develops stress fractures. Talking with a sport nutritionist will help her design a recovery plan and an appropriate diet that is specific to her sport and her energy needs. She must seek counseling if her thoughts are constantly about body shape and size.

Males, too, can fall prey to similar negative impacts of sport driving them to achieve an ideal image: muscular bodies with "six pack" abs. Some male athletes are particularly susceptible to the pressures surrounding performance and societal trends promoting muscularity and leanness. With the way that the media and our society look at men, these pervasive images can create body dissatisfaction that can lead to an emerging phenomenon called body dysmorphic disorder, an obsessive-compulsive condition that involves distressing thoughts about perceived appearance flaws.

Although the eating disorders in men are similar to what women experience, men most often strive to build body mass, whereas women obsess about being thin. Male athletes with body dysmorphic disorder are typically involved in sports that stress size and strength, such as football, wrestling, or competitive bodybuilding. They often resort to excessive use of muscle-building nutritional supplements, strict exercise, diet regimens, and even anabolic steroids. Companies producing and selling these products prey on athletes' insecurities about their bodies. Many individuals take higher doses of these products than recommended, which may predispose them to a variety of health concerns such as renal failure, elevated heart rate, and high blood pressure. Additionally, a poor sense of self and dissatisfaction with body image can lead to substance abuse.

Societal pressure, media images, and certain industries' concern with bottom lines all make people feel insecure about their bodies, whether by telling females that they should be thinner or males that they should be more muscular. Parents, coaches, athletic trainers, performance and personal trainers, and strength and conditioning coaches need to eradicate the erroneous concept that how one looks defines or improves athletic ability or promises success.

Day 24: Prattville, AL, to Columbus, GA, 105 miles

Hey Y'all,

Now on Eastern Standard Time; we're getting closer.

Today's start was very somber. Mike, our ride leader, announced that he was leaving the ride because his mother had developed a blood clot in her brain, and they were keeping her on life support until he arrived. He was not sure if he would see us in Savannah, so we all said our goodbyes. It was an emotional time for all of us.

Going over the route sheet this morning, the Alabama Boys saw that we had to take Auburn Road and asked if they could find an alternate route. The weather was fantastic, mid-sixties in the morning, with highs in the mid-seventies, sunny, no rain, and no humidity, light winds out of the northwest. We are very spoiled right now.

We had to cross the Alabama River via the Alabama River Parkway, which is a toll road, and that was a first, riding my bike through a toll booth (75 cents, please). We all sped past the gate and the staff paid, counting us as we went through—one, two . . . twenty-three, twenty-four.

Mike and Barbara's grandchildren attend the Emerald Mountain Christian School, and one grandchild is in the third grade. As a project, the class

Carrying our bikes over a bridge being repaired in Phenix City, Alabama.

is following our tour for their learning sections on map-reading, letter-writing, and geography. We have been sending them postcards from each overnight town (mine was sent from Fort Smith, Arkansas), and they have been writing us letters that we read each morning. So, today was a jersey day, and we made a trip to the school on the way out of town. What a blast! They were all outside the school to greet us. We mingled, had a presentation, introduced the international riders (Will and Klaus from Germany, Rachel from Britain, Johannes from Norway, and Stan from Kenya), and had cake. Talk about happy campers (the kids, too)!

Just as I was getting ready to get on the road again, another flat tire. So, a quick change and off again. Through the town of Milstead and into Tuskegee, home of Tuskegee University, the Tuskegee Airmen, and the Tuskegee Syphilis Study, one of the most infamous biomedical studies in U.S. history. The people were very friendly, everyone waving, cheering, and asking us questions. The university campus is very pretty and much bigger than I expected. After Tuskegee (I like saying the word as well as typing it), we were out in the middle of nowhere.

We had our lunch stop next to a big red barn and did not see signs of civilization until the town of Phenix City just before the state line. At one point, we had to do some trekking because a bridge was under construction.

We carried our bicycles over the torn-up section. We lucked out, because the supervisor was gone; otherwise, we would have had to take a couple of miles' detour. The matter-of-fact workers just looked the other way.

Again we had to experience more chip and seal roads than anyone wanted to; however, fewer hills, only 2,300 feet of climbing. See, parts of Alabama are flat.

Our state line marker was the bridge over the Chattahoochee River into Columbus. Unfortunately, the historic district of Columbus is all under construction right now; however, that did not deter me from finding my daily hot tea in a little coffee shop called The City Cafe.

After a nice hot shower, it was time to experience some local fare, so we found some good ol' southern-style cooking at Ruth Ann's Family Restaurant. What a feast: mac 'n' cheese, collard greens, fried okra, fried squash, mashed potatoes, carrot and raisin salad, rice, corn, peas, sweet potato casserole, pinto beans, and of course, corn bread. Oh, and homemade (by Ruth Ann herself) cherry pie. A meal fit for cross-country riders. Ummm, ummm good!

And we get to get up and do it again tomorrow—how fun!

Jenny

Chapter 21

A Case Study

My experience in working with many different sports for more than two decades has taught me two basic truths: (1) each athlete's case is unique and (2) shared themes arise across cases. The following case study is a typical story of a soccer athlete, but it could have been any other sport. I have seen this scenario played out time and time again. Over the years, my colleagues and peers have had countless discussions about athletes whose experiences are strikingly similar. The case is real; only the names are changed. As you read Michelle's story, consider the yearly 5.5 million injuries to youth in sports. And the numbers continue to climb.

The Case

Jack and Nancy were living their dream in a Chicago suburb with their two small children, Michelle and Tammy. Jack had been a three-letter athlete in high school, playing football, basketball, and baseball. Nancy played on her high school tennis team, was a cheerleader, and was president of the pep club. The teamwork, camaraderie, and hard work in school gave both of them many skills that helped pave the way to successful careers. After a brief business career, Nancy turned her attention to raising the girls. Michelle, age four, was high energy, athletic, and fun-loving. Tammy was two years younger and developing into a quiet, thoughtful, and kind child.

One day when Michelle saw some kids having fun playing soccer in a television commercial, she asked her mom if she could play soccer, too. Nancy was thrilled that she showed interest in a sport that offered physical activity and interaction with other kids. That afternoon they went to the local toy store and bought a soccer ball. For the next week Michelle carried her ball everywhere, kicked it around the yard every day, and even slept with it. By the end of the week, when her interest waned as it does with most four-year-olds, Nancy asked her if she would like to go to a soccer game. Michelle liked that idea, so they went to a local girls' high school soccer game. Because Nancy remembered how sports had influenced her life, she was eager to steer her daughter toward sports. She talked with a number of other mothers in the stands and discovered that many of their children began their soccer careers through the American Youth Soccer Organization (AYSO). The organization could provide an opportunity for Michelle to play to see if she really liked it. Nancy thought that fresh air, exercise, and playing with other girls would be good for her daughter.

When she called Jack to tell him about the day's events, he was especially pleased, having aspirations for his little girl to be an athlete. At registration they met parent volunteers who filled them in about the philosophy of the program and assured them that Michelle was just the right age to participate. (The under-five age group is one of the fastest growing groups in the United States.[48]) Gathered around a display of pictures of the teams playing, all the moms agreed that the children looked especially cute in their matching jerseys and shorts. Shin guards were required for protection, and even though shoes did not have to be official soccer cleats, all the kids had them. The children played happily together while their parents completed the paperwork. On the way home, Michelle chattered about the children she had met and the fun she would have. Her mom was thrilled and planned a trip to the sporting goods store to buy the necessary equipment. Nancy knew Michelle would quickly grow out of the cleats they bought, but she wanted to make sure she fit in with the other girls. Besides, she looked so darling in them.

The next Saturday Michelle and her mom reported to the soccer field in a neighborhood park. Michelle was reluctant to get out of the car because there were so many kids there and she was shy. "You said you wanted to play soccer, and we need to follow through. This will be fun," her mother said. At the check-in table a smiling volunteer directed them to the under-five kids' area. Another volunteer with a clipboard asked Michelle her name and then sent her to a corner of the field to meet her coach. Nancy joined the parents on the sideline. Michelle was assigned to Coach Shannon's group of five. Sitting in a circle, each girl said her name and her favorite food. Then Coach Shannon demonstrated dribbling the ball around cones. By the end of the drill Michelle was interacting freely with the other children.

The soccer season was fun for Michelle and her mom. The team practiced twice a week and competed on Saturdays. Social time after practice led to favorite new friends. Nancy provided the consistent support—transportation, team refreshments, encouragement of additional practice, and cheering. She called Jack from practice and boasted about how their daughter was more coordinated than any of the other children. Jack came to see Michelle's games, armed with the video camera. Every Monday morning he bragged to his coworkers about her natural talents and how she was doing. The team celebrated the end of the season three months later with a pizza party where each child received a participation trophy and posed for the team photo. Both mementos were proudly put on display in the den. Nancy and Jack were delighted that Michelle had become more outgoing and confident—ready for kindergarten and a whole new set of friends.

Michelle was excited to go to school. At the first parent-teacher meeting her teacher, Ms. Lane, reported that she was energetic, outgoing, very talkative, and popular with the other children but had a short attention span. She said that Michelle's favorite activity was outside recess when she played soccer. A month later Nancy and Jack received a note from Ms. Lane requesting another conference. She expressed concern that Michelle had not settled down and continued to be over-active and distracting to other children. Nancy suggested that soccer might be a healthy outlet. Her teacher supported the idea, so Nancy re-enrolled Michelle for the spring and summer AYSO sessions.

All during elementary school, soccer continued to be Michelle's primary activity. She loved being with her teammates and was developing skills and a passion for the sport. Her parents talked about steering her to other activities, but Jack pushed for Michelle to stay with soccer because she was developing into a talented player with a future.

She played year-round with multiple teams: a local club, traveling club, and school. The trophy shelf was a point of pride, laden with team photos, trophies, and awards. In third grade she was selected Most Improved Player by her club team. Accolades continued through each new season, and in middle school, Michelle was named MVP for her school and club teams. Even though other sports were available through school and her community, she and her parents saw no reason to try different ones. In fact, her soccer schedule did not allow any time for other activities. Nancy drove to practices and games six days a week. Fast-food drive-through restaurants became a daily ritual. Michelle made the local Olympic Development Program team, and luckily for Nancy, practice was only an hour's drive each way. For some parents it was as much as two-and-a-half hours one-way.

Family vacations were scheduled around soccer activities. When Jack and Nancy sat down to look at expenses, they were shocked to see how

A Case Study

much of the family budget was spent on team registration fees, travel, tournaments, and camps at big name college soccer schools. Although Michelle's younger sister, Tammy, never played soccer, she was always taken to practices and games. The family could not afford after-school care for her, so Tammy spent the time reading books on the sideline or watching a video in the van while Michelle practiced and played. Nancy and Jack believed the costs and sacrifices were worth it, especially if their daughter could get a full scholarship to college. Family dinner-table conversations often focused on soccer. At Jack's office, Michelle's accomplishments were a regular part of office discussions.

Now that Michelle was in high school, her athletic talents really shone. Captain of her club team and a top performer for her high school team, she thrived as a leader and in her friendships with her teammates. Her online social networking page revolved around soccer, with photos, stories, and motivational sayings. Her success gave her the lift she needed to work hard in school to maintain acceptable grades. She struggled to earn a B or C, but she was consistently the leading scorer on the field. The summer after her freshman year, at age fifteen, Michelle's world changed. During the third game of a weekend tournament, she made a move with the ball, and when she planted her left foot, her body went one way and her knee the other. She heard and felt the infamous "pop." Clutching her knee in pain, she fell down. Jack threw down the video camera and ran to her. He and Michelle's coach carried her off the field; the first-aid volunteers put ice on her knee; and her worried parents took her to the emergency room. Following up with an orthopedic specialist, they learned that Michelle had torn her ACL. Soccer would take a backseat to reconstructive surgery and many months of tough rehabilitation.

The family now found that physical therapy sessions and doctor appointments redefined their lives. Nancy preferred to be a soccer mom and feared her dream was fading. Throughout this process, Michelle missed the game, her teammates, and everything that meant success to her. She defined herself as a soccer player, and trophies, photos, and her family's commitment to her sport reinforced that image. Without her sport, Michelle was bored and easily distracted from her studies. When her average B-C grades began to suffer, her parents grew more concerned about her emotional well-being and future opportunities for college. Conversations at the dinner table now focused on her rehab and grades, with her parents feeling more and more frustrated as Michelle continued to withdraw. Without the outlet that soccer provided, she had difficulty turning her attention to schoolwork.

A Case Study

What kept her going through the pain, long hours of rehab, and separation from life as she knew it was her determination to return to her sport and the happiness and success it brought her.

After nine months, the doctor cleared Michelle to play, and she joined her high school team in April. Back on the field, Michelle soon realized that her knee could not withstand the rigorous schedule, and she had to sit out some practices, but sitting out during the games was not an option in her mind. Through sheer grit, she fought through pain to play. Her first full year back was a roller coaster of pain and swelling in her knee. Not one to complain, she did not want to be taken out of practices or games. The team really needed her, so she iced in silence and pushed on through. Despite her nagging knee, Michelle still made the all-district and all-regional teams. As high scorer, she carried the team to the state semifinals, losing to the eventual state champions 1–0.

By the beginning of Michelle's junior year, when she was seventeen, college recruiters were in full force. Home visits, letters, and phone calls from coaches were a daily part of her schedule. Jack loved to boast at the office about Michelle's recruiting. She wanted to be part of a well-established soccer program with a winning tradition. She was eager to make a decision by the end of her junior year, so that her senior year would be carefree. Travel costs added to the mounting expenses, but choosing the right college could mean a full scholarship. Nancy, Jack, and her club coach had been particularly strategic in selecting summer camps at colleges where coaches might remember her at recruitment time.

Michelle and her parents visited one local college, three in-state, and two out-of-state. At each school they talked with the coach, visited facilities, went on a campus tour, and spent some time with student-athletes. Admissions staff reviewed academic opportunities, student services, and costs. Michelle received several offers. A local school offered her a full athletic scholarship, as did another in-state school. An out-of-state school that routinely contended for the national championship offered her a partial scholarship with possible increases as she developed as a contributing player on the team. Her parents hoped that Michelle would select one of the schools that offered her a full scholarship and was close to home. However, they agreed to support her decision, and Jack understood her desire to win championships. Michelle favored the out-of-state college, even though she would have only a partial scholarship. She knew that she could improve at this big-name soccer school, with a coach who had connections to the USA national team and teammates who had the drive to win.

A Case Study

Spring term ended with Michelle's high school team winning the state championship and Michelle earning all-district, all-region, and all-state accolades. Confident that she would be capable of turning the partial scholarship into a full-ride by the end of her freshman year, Michelle made a verbal commitment to the out-of-state college. An official campus visit in the fall confirmed her decision. The college paid her travel expenses. This time even the campus tour held more meaning, as Michelle lingered in the state-of-the art soccer facilities and talked with the team in the locker room. She couldn't wait to be a part of this stellar group. Nancy and Jack were so proud that their daughter would be a member of a team at a school with a winning history. They had already shared the news of her college acceptance with many friends, family, and coworkers on their social networking page.

Michelle completed her senior year just as she had planned—free of the pressure from college recruiters—celebrating a state championship with MVP honors. Her knee was holding up as long as she iced after each workout. Having added another set of trophies to the family shelf, Michelle left home early to attend summer school and taste college life. She enrolled in six hours of classes to get a head start on her degree. The athletic department and her academic counselor helped her to determine her academic needs, advisor, and tutors. Michelle battled an urge to call home after a day of complete pre-participation physicals that left her reeling. She had never undergone such a comprehensive assessment of her body, with particular focus on her previous knee injury. She had put that injury behind her and could not understand why it was such a point of interest.

Even though official practice could not take place until fall semester, Michelle participated voluntarily with her new teammates, played pick-up soccer games, and attended regular weight training and conditioning workouts directed by the strength and conditioning coach. Formal weight training had never been a part of her soccer development. The physical impact of the grueling workouts was a rude awakening to a new set of performance, conditioning, and fitness expectations. Her whole body was sore. Michelle often felt weak, fatigued, and dizzy during workouts because the hot temperatures and high humidity were unlike the midwestern summers she was used to. She liked her teammates, though, and was making friends. The other freshmen were struggling as well, so she wasn't alone.

Summer semester merged right into the fall soccer season with two practices each day. Michelle's teammates came from other states and even other countries, and each had been the best on her respective team. She was no longer the top performer; in fact, she was even struggling to pass the required fitness tests. On a particularly hot and humid day of practice, she had successfully completed all but two tests when she began to shake and feel dizzy. The athletic trainer intervened when she saw Michelle running in a crooked line and stumbling. She was helped to the shade, cooled with iced towels, given a sports drink, and taken to the team physician where she received IV fluids. Held out from the next practice, Michelle was observed for further complications and educated on the importance of fueling her body with appropriate foods and fluids.

Eventually she was cleared to practice and became a participating member of the team; her schedule fell into a rhythm of practices, strength training, team meetings, film sessions, travel, soccer matches, rehab sessions, classes, study hall, and tutors. Her full-time academic schedule required study hall and class attendance when not traveling. She had time to do little else but sleep.

Her first media day was taken up with action photos and headshots for the media guide, live footage for highlight videos, and one-on-one interviews with the local press showcasing the team and the upcoming season. She was a soccer player! She belonged!

Michelle saw success on the field; however, like most freshmen, she was homesick and yearned for her family. Her parents acquired a satellite television package to see as many of Michelle's games as possible. Jack felt closer to his daughter and her soccer life by following team stats, the athletic department website, and fan blogs. As the fall semester continued, Michelle worked hard. Her dedication paid off. By the middle of the season, she had grown stronger and faster. She started for the remainder of the games, helped the team win the conference championship and go deep into the NCAA tournament, losing in the semi-finals at the College Cup. At the end-of-the-season banquet before winter holidays, she was named "Most Improved Player."

Motivated by her own accomplishments, the team's success, and the coach's promise to increase her scholarship for the next year, Michelle attacked spring semester with fierce determination. Practice was brutal, with workouts designed to challenge the team to higher performance levels. The players pushed themselves to prove worthy as starters. During a rainy practice, Michelle slide-tackled the ball, but she didn't get up. The athletic trainer ran onto the field as she clutched her left knee in pain crying, "Not again! No, not again!" The athletic trainer and teammates helped her off the field and took her to the training room. Upon examination, the athletic trainer reassured Michelle that her ACL was fine; however, she was concerned about her meniscus. She iced her knee, put her on crutches, and called the team physician who told Michelle to come right over. The physician assured her that the knee was stable but scheduled an MRI scan to assess other damage. The MRI showed that she had torn her medial meniscus and had articular bone surface damage. She was scheduled for surgery the next week. Devastated by this news, her parents rushed to see her. Relieved that the ACL was okay, Jack was confident that his daughter would return to soccer soon and stronger than ever.

When the day of surgery arrived, her parents paced nervously in the waiting room, anxious to learn results. After an arthroscopic procedure that lasted an hour, the surgeon emerged to tell them the news. The damage was much more extensive than the MRI had revealed. A large osteochrondral defect—a pothole—on the thighbone was discovered, so another surgery would be needed to repair the damage. Michelle said that she would do whatever it took to get back to soccer, even posting this promise on her web page. She worked very hard that month, strengthening her leg, maintaining her fitness level on a stationary bike, cheering her teammates on during their spring workouts, and spending more time with tutors since she was not playing.

Her parents returned to be at her side for the second surgery. After several hours in the operating room, the surgeon reported that the resurfacing of her bone was a success. She would be on crutches for three to four months and go through rehab for an entire year. Her fall season was not an option, and she would redshirt. Summer, fall, and winter were consumed by academics and rehabilitation.

Spring arrived, and the sports medicine staff released her to begin soccer activities. She was required to wear a brace designed to relieve stress to the inside of the knee while walking around campus and during cardiovascular conditioning. She began modified, time-controlled drills and worked her way into full practices. As she lengthened her practice time, struggles with her knee increased. She suffered from swelling, from pain that woke her at night, and walked with a noticeable limp. The sports medicine staff put her back on crutches and restricted her activity. Michelle began to worry that she would never return to her previous level of play. Her parents made regular calls, encouraging her to be positive. Her dad encouraged her to try just a little longer before giving up. As her sophomore season ended, Michelle had many discussions with her doctors, athletic trainers, coaches, and parents. The pain and swelling were constant, despite daily rehab, anti-inflammatory medication, and the brace. Michelle came to the realization that her knee could not withstand the rigors of soccer. Ultimately, she was given a medical leave from the sport. She would retain her scholarship by working 10 hours each week for the athletics department and continue her rehab, but she would never play soccer at the Division I level again. Jack and Nancy had never imagined that their daughter's career would end this way.

Michelle's final two years of college were difficult. The identity she had as a soccer player was gone. During her junior year, the team reached the NCAA College Cup finals but lost in overtime. Even though she was excited for the team's success, she was deflated by the thoughts that her play could have made the difference in the championship game.

Michelle struggled. Now that she could no longer play soccer, who was she? Her parents were supportive, but she knew they were disappointed. All their years of sacrifice had ended without the rewards they had envisioned. All those years given to soccer—and now with nothing to show for them. Not a day passed without her wanting to play. Michelle simply couldn't move on.

* * *

Whose dream was it? What would an expert say about Michelle's story?

This case scenario is all too familiar, according to Kristen Martin, coordinator of Team ENHANCE. "Some children are encouraged to participate in sports because their parents want them to be athletes. What begins with a child's genuine interest can take a misguided direction," says Martin. "Parents can have a tendency to latch onto the idea that sport is their child's ticket to fame and fortune."

Martin, who is a licensed clinical social worker and former collegiate swimmer, observes further that youth sports often are positioned as a child's central focus, instead of something fun to do. Michelle's mother wasn't very encouraging when four-year-old Michelle was nervous about her first practice. Instead, her mother gave her a mini-lecture on commitment and follow-through that would mean little to a four year old.

No doubt about it, Michelle's first season was a success. She had fun, made new friends, and grew more confident. That is what parents need to focus on. Her father, however, seemed to take more pride in bragging about her natural talents. Although the child's success is fun for the parents, their expectations that it continue send the wrong message, because a child believes she must persist to please her parents.

Soccer and other extracurricular activities are wonderful ways to help an active child release energy. I believe, however, that parents need to help their children explore different pursuits to foster balance, so they are not set on just one path. Michelle relied on soccer to make herself happy. Her parents reinforced her sole focus by displaying her awards and continually talking about her success. She defined herself as an athlete and lost sight of the person she was becoming. When she was injured, her life was all about getting back to soccer, instead of about taking care of her body and herself. She struggled emotionally and grieved disappointing her parents. Her sister appears to have been lost in Michelle's whirlwind, as well. Kristen Martin concludes that, "Michelle could not recognize that the many qualities that made her a star athlete would also make her a success in other endeavors; instead, she was lost without the external reinforcers that were her parents' approval."

Eventually, all athletic careers end, and life goes on. Parents and coaches can be so focused on an athlete's talent that they fail to help her discover her many other qualities. Encouraging children to pay attention to new interests and traits fosters a strong sense of self-worth and a recognition that their future can be filled with the joy and excitement they experienced playing their sport. Having worked with thousands of athletes, I have learned that, in the pursuit of excellence, we are most successful, reap the greatest rewards, and gain lasting satisfaction by holistically balancing our mind, body, and spirit.

Day 25: Columbus, GA, to Perry, GA, 97 miles

Hey Y'all,

The fatigue is starting to kick in, or make that sink in. It was a short day today and everyone needed it. To make things even better, the weather was fantastic. Seventies to start and up to the low eighties, with plenty of sunshine and low humidity. Nice smooth roads for most of the day. Then the best part yet: tail winds! By the afternoon, they were up to 20 mph.

Going over the route sheet this morning, we were told to have a picture ID with us, because we would be riding through Fort Benning. San Francisco Joe yelled out, "So we shouldn't wear a target on our jersey?"

One of the main rules of the ride is that you do not lean your bike against any of the vans. Well, the staff wanted to show Mike they had lost control of the group so they staged a rules break.

Now on to the ride. We left the hotel on the Columbus bike path, very nice, peaceful and empty. It took us through Fort Benning. When the guards saw the large colorful group coming, they did not worry about our IDs. That was probably a good thing; several in this group might have been detained.

We rode through the town of Buena Vista, Georgia, home to Josh Gibson, the "Black Babe Ruth," who hit 962 home runs in a seventeen-year career and had a lifetime batting average of 373 in the Negro Leagues. Never chosen by the Major Leagues, he died at thirty-five of a stroke, some say due to depression and alcohol abuse. He was the second Negro League player inducted into the Baseball Hall of Fame.

Sharing the road with logging trucks, we rode through Ellaville, a pretty little town. When we stopped there to help the local economy with a snack purchase, the people were very interested in what we were doing. They could not believe we were riding to Savannah, and when we told them we were coming from California, you could see the gossip chain starting.

We clipped a portion of Oglethorpe on the way through to Montezuma (good thing lunch was after Montezuma, so no revenge). After lunch it was a quick ride through the back roads of the Mennonite community—beautiful farms, homes, B&Bs, pecan (or as the locals say, PEE-can) orchards, corn, soybeans, timber, and Christmas tree farms—into the town of Perry. Tonight is our T-shirt swap, and no, my City Cafe T-shirt is not an option. They will have to fight over a Lady Vol souvenir.

And we get to get up and do it again tomorrow—how fun!

Jenny

Rules violation.

Chapter 22

SCORE

Good health requires exercise. Actually a simple thing to do, exercise does not need special equipment, a gym, or a coach—only the will to move. Each of us can enjoy regular physical activity anywhere, anytime. It is never too late to include it in your life, and what a wonderful gift it is to give to a child!

Today the highest number of children playing competitive sports is in the middle school years. However, these years also see the highest dropout rate from sports, because many kids don't believe they can compete at the next level. The alternatives to competitive sports are limited or nonexistent. What fill the gap are video games, hundreds of television choices, and surfing the Internet, all requiring minimal physical activity.

Sports play a rich role in our history and culture. Competition can be fun and bring out the best in us. However, when we look only at the win/loss column and disregard the experience before the final whistle, we miss what is really important. Winning does not necessarily signify fun, but when an activity is fun, everyone wins. That is the good news.

Are we pushing the limits of human performance? If we don't have a sense of balance about sports, we could be impairing our physical, emotional, and mental well-being. Former Division I collegiate swimmer Bryttany Curran presents a striking example of self-fulfillment. When asked if she is a swimmer, her response has always been, "I am a person who swims. I'm a person who loves Jesus. I'm person who plays the violin. I'm a person who loves music. I'm a person made up of many things."

Will we reach a pressure point where the body, mind, and spirit will break in the inexorable quest to shatter records? U.S. swimmer Tiffany Cohen won the gold medal at the 1984 Olympic Games, just missing the world record by one hundredth of a second. Despite winning the gold, she told me she was devastated when the TV commentators repeatedly emphasized her failure to break the world record. I was shocked at their reaction to her perceived failure. She won the gold medal, for heaven's sake! Watching that dim-witted and destructive broadcast tape, which was shown over and over, distressed me, as I thought about the pain she went through.

Sport psychologist and former collegiate diver Dr. Lauren Loberg believes that internal pressures can plague athletes. "Elite athletes never reach their goals. Perfectionism is what makes you good but also what hurts you." In a perfect world, everyone would have a dream that would stretch the individual beyond the perceived limits. I believe having a dream is crucial for growth and motivation. What is yet even more essential is the journey we take to reach that dream. It is the journey's bits and pieces, the stops and starts, the accomplishments along the way and lessons learned that build our character, give us intentional direction, and sweeten the victory. We lose our balance when the goal overshadows the process.

Few athletes have a sense of accomplishment that carries them forever. As time passes, so does the celebration of national champions. Even an Olympic gold medalist is on the top of the world for only a short time. We look at our champions and rarely think about all the losses and failures they had before they won. Considering the years of work and preparation required to be a top performer, the athlete had better love the sport apart from wins to endure the physical, mental, and emotional effort the activity requires. If winning, fame, and fortune are the only motivators, then the athlete has lost all perspective on the journey. How much more fulfilling their efforts will be if they recognize and enjoy the many benefits along the way. Athletes need to find meaning beyond sports. Performance specialist Loren Seagrave acknowledges the difficulty some athletes experience when they walk away from their sports and do not have other goals. "The adulation of the crowd, fan recognition, and the trappings that accompany success for the athlete can be addictive," he said.

Candace Parker, WNBA Rookie of the Year and U.S. Olympic gold medalist, has a good perspective on fame. "You learn to listen to those people in your close circle. Everybody else is just an opinion. Good or bad, you can't read too much into what they say because like the weather, they could change tomorrow," says Candace. "Basketball has taken me places and allowed me to meet so many different people. One day all of this will be gone. What do you have to show for it? If you're lucky, you will find personal satisfaction, a sense of pride and confidence, and lasting relationships."

Kara Lawson, WNBA professional and sports broadcaster for ESPN, agrees that the life of a professional athlete and broadcaster is challenging. "It is very difficult. By nature I am a planner, and every detail of my day is planned out. When I am playing basketball, I still have my hand in different things with ESPN. When I am full-time with the station, I am still training every day. During this time of my life I want to play basketball, while at the same time I need to prepare for the day when I won't be playing."

I am not surprised that Kara is an ESPN sports analyst. I remember the many times in the athletic training room when she did play-by-play commentary on sporting events on the television. We would turn down the volume and listen to her take on the game.

Like Kara, I believe in formulating a plan to embrace a new dream and set a new goal for Life Phase B. While honoring the accomplishments of Life Phase A and respecting the lessons learned, gather your resources and chart your plan for what's next. How do we start thinking about these goals and integrating our past experiences with our future healthy prospects? I have alluded to the SCORE model a few times, and I think this is a great formula to move on to your next stage in life. As you prepare to embark on a fresh voyage, look to the SCORE to make a smooth evolution. Ready? Let's go!

Kara Lawson in the studio. Courtesy of ESPN.

SCORE

S C O R E Model

S—SELF

Discovering your inner resource, developing self-esteem, creating motivation to become a valued member of the team.

C—CONFIDENCE

Building faith in your own abilities by understanding and trusting yourself. This is the route to trusting others.

O—OPPORTUNITY

A growing sense of self and confidence leads to clarity in recognizing, embracing, and taking advantage of the things that life brings.

R—REWARD

Sport provides tangible rewards, but some of the greatest are intangible, and so it is in life.

E—EXCITEMENT

Celebrating rewards sparks excitement and further energizes the next endeavor.

S—Self

Soul search. Evaluate. You have rich resources within you—your imagination and your dreams. Where have you been? Where are you now? Where do you want to go? And the big question: how do you want to get there? Envision your goal. Self needs to be the driver. The self is mind, body, and spirit interrelated. At times one may be more prominent, but all three are always present on some level. The concept of self is not selfishness but rather being self-motivated; developing self-esteem; creating a positive self-image; and establishing a self-identity. You are your motivator, and the support you elicit from others smooths the path to your goal. "There is no I in team," is a common saying, but I would argue that I's make up the team. If an individual is lost, the team is less effective. Each member brings strengths and unique contributions that are critical to the team's success. Once the Self is established, the CORE sets the foundation for the journey to reach the goal.

C—Confidence

Confidence means full faith in your own powers. In order to build confidence, we must understand and trust ourselves. Through experience, knowledge, risk-taking, and reflection, we develop a full connection with our mind, body, and spirit—our self. You cannot control what other people think or say, but you can control your reaction and how you feel. Once you trust your senses and instincts and learn to discern the positive from the negative, you can trust others. Confidence leads to self-assurance, decisiveness, and self-reliance as you pursue your goal.

The journey is not always smooth. Multitalented Bryttany Curran heeds her father's advice. "My dad says, 'Get outside your box.' The more you do it, the more comfortable you are with being uncomfortable. People ask me if I ever get nervous. That never goes away. It doesn't matter how much time I put in the pool or on the stage, it will always be uncomfortable, but I

Bryttany Curran displaying one of her many talents. Courtesy of Bryttany Curran.

get more used to the feeling," explains Bryttany. "Accepting this has built my confidence to explore other things like musical theatre, orchestra, and leadership."

When I was learning to ride my bike without training wheels, I developed an early sense of confidence. I have vivid memories of Dad running alongside me and then suddenly being aware that he was no longer holding onto my seat. "I'm on my own!"

Tamika Catchings. Courtesy of Michael Patton.

SCORE

O—Opportunity

A propitious juncture of circumstances can occur at any moment. When we are flexible and open to all things new and different as we experience and explore, opportunities present themselves. Recognize and seize them, and you can maneuver around roadblocks on the way to your goal.

Tamika Catchings, Olympic gold medalist, cites one crossroad as particularly significant in her personal and professional journey. When the Indiana Fever of the WNBA selected her as the first draft pick, she was unable to play because she was rehabbing her ACL that she had torn a few months earlier. "I was in Indiana, but I couldn't play, practice, or do anything. What I could do was get involved in the community. I was a part of every community event the Fever had. My mom and dad had always helped us to realize how fortunate we were and that we should give back. Eventually I started my own foundation so I could help people."

Even when I was a kid, my bike presented me with new prospects. It gave me the freedom to venture out to other neighborhoods, parks, and the mall. Weather permitting, I rode to school. With this newly found independence, I was able to explore and take advantage of every opportunity.

R—Reward

Reward yields satisfaction. Whether external or internal, the most meaningful ones are intangible. Medals, ribbons, trophies, plaques, and championship rings are material symbols awarded for goals met. However, the truly gratifying rewards are internal—the sense of joy, of stretching beyond perceived limits, of trying new ventures, of completing a step, of knowing you've done your best, of learning. The journey is the ultimate reward. In her sophomore year, when she didn't qualify for the NCAA meet, Bryttany Curran used the time to think about what it means to be great. "Being great is knowing that you poured everything that you have into the smallest of moments," she says.

Kara Lawson acknowledges the deep satisfaction of her Olympic experience. "My journey to being an Olympian is probably very different from that of the other players on that team. They have a God-given ability, and their talent level is so high. I wasn't in that core group. I had to go through two-and-a-half years of the training sessions, not knowing after each one if I would be called back. It was an emotional rollercoaster, but my love of the game carried me through. All the people who supported me over the years made it possible for me stand on the Olympic stage."

SCORE

E—Excitement

Excitement sets the goal in motion. Excitement is energy—the fire that motivates and gets the wheels rolling. It is amorphous and ephemeral. It can take the form of nervous energy before the adventure begins. Frequently, it arrives spontaneously on the journey and celebrates the outcome. Excitement is contagious and touches mind, body, and spirit. Its euphoric effect helps overcome pain and fatigue, both physical and mental. New roads can lead to the thrill of conquering the unknown.

Tracy Bonner makes sure there is excitement in her daily life. As an athlete, she cites the exuberance of the moment when she had to be perfect on the diving board to secure first place, the top medal, or the spot on the world team. "I feel that excitement in any form is an integral part of success. It is proven to be a factor in my reaching the goals I set for myself." She grew up in a place she likes to call, "Happyville," working hard every day in the diving well, on the dance floor, in the gym, and in class. After performing in the sold-out theatrical extravaganza Cirque du Soleil "O" show in Las Vegas ten times a week for seven years, Tracy was ready for a career change. She became a law enforcement officer. As a recruit, Tracy was the first person to complete the physical fitness portion with a 100th-percentile ranking, based on her age and gender, since the academy revamped its standards. "The initial idea of becoming an officer was exciting because of the unknowns and the attendant responsibilities in the oath to serve and protect. I am happy to go to work and don the vest, the heavy tool belt, and hit the street every day not knowing what it is that the next ten hours of my life might entail. There is one thing for sure—it will be exciting."

The SCORE formula is simple and clear but can be elusive in a society that measures success by net worth. With the CORE components of confidence, opportunity, reward, and excitement, our Self will engage in practices that expand and open us up to countless possibilities. Balance keeps us on our metaphorical bikes and moving forward.

When I was a child, our household rules limited television time, and there were no personal computers or cell phones. Because I spent more time playing outside with my friends, my need for exercise and physical activity is ingrained in me. Exercise feels good, and when I am riding my bike, distance and speed are not always important. However, other times I want a challenge. I set a goal and enjoy seeing what I am capable of doing. Regardless of my purpose in riding, I am moving and having fun.

Psychiatrist Dr. Kenneth Jobson reminds us that "the ones who wrap their sport and leisure properly in a balanced life have a richer life." What if we can rediscover play in our lives? What if it is possible to strike a balance that diminishes everyday stress and increases the sheer joy in living? The solution lies within each of us. I invite you to join me on the team of the willing.

Day 26: Perry, GA, to Vidalia, GA, 103 miles

Hi Y'all,

Vidalia, Georgia—all those onions—no tears, please!

Good things happen to good people, and this group must be good people because we had fantastic conditions again! Temperatures in the low sixties in the morning, getting up to the low eighties with relatively low humidity. Sunny, not a lot of climbing today (2,500 feet) and tail winds up to 15 mph—life is good.

Really a mellow, pleasant day. I think everyone is trying to soak in as much of these last few days as possible. Even some of the Big Dogs slowed down and rode with us mere mortals.

We rode through the towns of Grovania, Hawkinsville, which has a charming downtown area, and Antioch. We passed an active fire tower

Wares for sale in Eastman, Georgia.

(moderate fire conditions today). Just before the town of Eastman, we saw a sign in front of a house advertising aprons, bonnets, and quilts for sale. Dresses hung on the front porch.

Forest groves and corn were the scenery of the day. We bypassed Alamo—no one really wanted to go back to Texas, anyway—and went on to Glenwood.

Both of our rest stops were in the middle of fields, the first by a small church—open only on Sunday, so no rest room available—and the lunch stop by a farm and farm house. The house could have been taken right out of the movie *Fried Green Tomatoes*. An elderly couple who lived near the farm drove up on their John Deere tractor. I guess they are regulars, because they knew Barb and Karen and were very excited to see us. They sat around telling stories, asking each of us where we were from and about our ride. Lunchtime entertainment with very nice people. The international riders were thrilled to have a Kodak moment on the John Deere, because, to them, John Deere is such a quintessential American icon. The gentleman even loaned them his straw hat to capture the historic moment.

We were making such good time today that we decided to stop at Dairy Queen in Mount Vernon. Ice cream was a favorite of many on this trip, and they have indoor plumbing for a stall tactic. You see, getting to the hotel early has no advantage, because the luggage truck is the support truck. And it gets there when it gets there. So sitting around in your odoriferous cycling clothes in your room is no fun.

On to our next destination: Vidalia, Georgia, "The Sweet Onion City," complete with onions and everything! And just as we turned onto the main drag of Vidalia towards the hotel, the luggage truck passed us. Timing is everything! And it was only 2 p.m., a nice early day.

Tomorrow is the last day so we spent a lot of time at the RAP session going over logistics, the trip to the beach, and everything that will happen afterward. It will be a jersey day, so we will descend on Tybee Island in our America by Bicycle red, white, and blue.

And we get to get up and do it again tomorrow—how fun!

Jenny

SCORE

Chapter 23

On the Road

Even when the open road is yours for the taking, sometimes the unexpected will slow you down. When barriers arise, it's time to stop and look back at the beginning of your journey and be cheered by how far you have come. Psychiatrist Dr. Kenneth Jobson says that "recreation is one of the gifts our species has, and in this 're-creation' we discover the fullness of the life that we deserve." Cycling is the recreation that leads me to my life's fullness. On Day 27, May 20, 2006, I achieved my dream of winning a national championship when I completed my 2,905-mile journey across America on my bicycle—from Costa Mesa, California, to Savannah, Georgia. There were no big headlines or lead stories in the media about my triumph. I have no trophy, medal, ring, or crown. But when I think of that day, my heart expands, and I rejoice, and all I can say is, "WOW! Well done. I'm proud of you, Jenny."

If you are looking to discover the "fullness of the life that you deserve" as an athlete, I'd like to share with you what worked for me.

STEP 1. Create your vision. Before my wheels turned, I needed to see where I was headed. Why was this adventure so important to me? What did it mean to me, and how would I feel throughout the journey and then at the end when I reached my goal? I have worked diligently to be the best athletic trainer I can be. To arrive at the top of my profession, I studied, passed tests, learned on my own, devoted my time, and focused my energy. I have worked with athletic champions at every level. I have been fascinated and challenged to discover the best ways to help and inspire our athletes to be at the top of their game, set realistic goals, and pursue their dreams. Every day I watch young women triumph over adversity and achieve incredible feats. Because of them, I have seven national championship rings. They prevail over injury, score personal bests, set new records, and win championships. It came to me that it was time for me to do the same for myself personally. But what could that be?

I knew I would have to choose a goal that involved doing something I like, because when things get hard, you had better enjoy the process and be doing it for the right reasons. I wanted a physical challenge not many have mastered. For many people, running a marathon would come to mind. Why in the world would anyone want to do that? I don't run unless someone is chasing me. Running hurts. I know this because at one time I thought I was a runner. I trained faithfully, ran at a respectable pace, and finished strong in a half-marathon. That was enough to convince me that running was going to be a part of my life. I set my sights on running a marathon and began to train. I also began to get sick—really sick. I reached a level of fatigue so severe that a walk around my subdivision required me to stop and rest. Running was breaking me down. I knew I couldn't do a marathon. So I erased that goal from my bucket list. I needed to find something else.

All my life I have taken care of others. I have always been drawn to teaching, to helping others to set their goals, and to motivating them along the way. It was time to do this for myself. I found inspiration where I wasn't looking. My dear friend and hiking buddy Tom had a dream of hiking the entire Appalachian Trail (AT), starting at the southern-most point and walking northward to the end. The trail is 2,100 miles long and generally takes a veteran hiker six months to complete. Considering his academic teaching schedule, Tom took on the challenge over three summers. I helped him prepare for his AT hike by joining him on a seventy-mile training hike through the Great Smoky Mountains in thirty-five hours; doing another forty-two miles in twenty-four hours; and doing shorter day hikes of ten to twelve miles.

Once he achieved his initial goal, Tom decided to repeat the feat as a thru-hiker, doing the full 2,100 miles in one trip. It was not to be; he was diagnosed with pancreatic cancer. So he set a new goal. He would ride his motorcycle across the country, promoting pancreatic cancer awareness, research, and treatment. Even though his original plan had changed, he took on a new quest to challenge himself. The new pathway led to self-discovery and adventure that he could not have imagined. Thrilled and inspired by Tom's dream, I could clearly see my own goal: cycle across America and achieve my own national championship.

I love cycling. In fact, I could be the biking poster child. I'm no fool. I picked a sport where I sit down, and if I stop pedaling, the bike can keep on moving, I can eat and drink at will, and I create my own breeze. Cycling is a great way to see the country, and you see it differently on a bicycle. When going by car, you are rocking out to the radio, traveling on interstate highways, and bypassing towns and people and beautiful vistas along the way. After an Internet search, I registered with America by Bicycle, a great organization that sponsors long-distance bicycle trips. Since this would be the longest ride I had ever done, why not make it a doozy?!

STEP 2. Prepare. I ran into challenges immediately. Anticipating a whole new routine for my life was scary. The thought of putting my own needs first was disturbing. Though this felt awkward and even selfish, I had to do it. I had to be physically ready, and that would take a major time commitment to training—miles and miles to ride. I needed to organize my training schedule and learn to protect it. I work in a service-oriented culture that counts on my willingness to help others. Now I had to set different priorities and learn to say, "Another time." I wanted this ride to be fun. I never doubted my physical ability, but the question was how much would it hurt? If I did not train, it would hurt more and therefore be a whole lot less enjoyable. I imagined that in the beginning I would be elated to meet new people on the ride. I was excited to prove my ability to myself and knew that every day would bring new scenery, different terrain, diverse weather conditions, and new adventures. I believed that it would be satisfying to finish each day, and look back to see how far I had come, confronting the small adversities and the big challenges. The strategy of breaking up each long distance day into smaller sections worked for me. In fact, this parallels the way I approach my job each day. Using a familiar strategy played right into my comfort level. And most of all, I planned on having lots of fun.

As I learned how to ask for help in meeting the high expectations and performance standards of my profession and to make time for my personal goals, I began to experience a new sense of balance in my life.

My next task was to outline the prospects. What was this brand new adventure going to be like? I was nervous. I worried that I wasn't preparing enough. What if I wasn't strong enough? What if I couldn't finish the long miles, day in and day out? Since most of the time I trained riding solo, I could not gauge my progress and compare my abilities to those of others. Don't get me wrong—I enjoyed my training rides—my bike, my surroundings, my thoughts, and just me. In fact, as I rode, I solved one or two of the world's problems; I just needed the world leaders to ask me for the solutions. I knew it would be more fun to ride with people and knew I would need others to help me reach this goal.

After drawing a mental picture of what the trip would be like, I considered how I would feel when it was over. It would be a great physical and mental triumph. I was certain to feel satisfied, fulfilled, and proud. I'd be thrilled to complete such an undertaking, but I knew I would be sad to see the end.

Joe Whitney, my sport psychologist, guided my preparation. The most difficult exercise he assigned was to write about my self-image. I think this was so hard to do because I am used to putting everyone else first and staying in the background. Following Joe's suggestion, I carried a note pad with me to scribble my thoughts and reflections which I eventually shared with friends and family who happily contributed their own impressions, encouraging discussions I might never have had. This process generated positive self-talk. It helped me to see myself and hear how others see me. I looked in the mirror and met my ego: driven; proud of who I am, what I do, what I accomplish; strong; confident, becoming more so with preparation; a risk-taker; disciplined; a goal completer; determined; a go-getter; courageous; shy. I would rather set myself apart from others through action, not words, and I always do my best.

My confidence grew, and I knew that I would succeed. Identifying my strengths and matching them to my expectations of this journey was affirming. The Olympic Training Center spends a lot of money, time, and energy on researching and applying mental readiness. When athletes reach the Olympics, the caliber of talent evens out, and the physical differences are small. The edge is mental—it separates the medalists from the participants. But the great news is this: you can use this edge even when you're not trying to win a medal.

The ride was scheduled to begin in mid-April. To be ready physically, I needed to ride through the winter when most people are either resting, cross-training, or hunkered down in front of the television with a bowl of popcorn. I trained daily by cycling twenty miles to work, and I would tack on a few extra miles every chance I could get. As the weather grew colder, I layered on wind resistant and waterproof clothing. One day it was so cold my water bottle froze. The hot shower was a savior on that day. When the weather was not conducive to road safety, I would get up at "O-dark-hundred" and ride in front of the television on my stationary trainer, a piece of equipment that transformed my road bike into a stationary one. Watching the Winter Olympics motivated me and helped to pass the time, and I found a new appreciation for the sport of curling.

When I was traveling with the Lady Volunteer basketball team, I had to leave my bike at home. Arriving at a hotel, I would find the fitness room and hope the available bikes had pedals. You might be surprised at the number of facilities where the bikes are broken, parts are missing, or there are no bikes at all. When this happened three times in a row, I was increasingly frustrated. Having not ridden for over a week, in a state of panic one night I called Joe. He calmed me down by saying, "When you can't train the body, train the mind." We ran through my mental exercises. He reminded me of my vision, what the ride meant to me, why I wanted to do it, what the ride would feel like, and my self-image. It worked. I was psyched, motivated, empowered, and ready to ride and ride and ride. I believe the mental preparation was as important, if not more important, than the physical preparation. My mind would have to convince my body to conquer the fatigue and wear and tear, to beat the mind games that many miles, weather, terrain and road conditions could play on you. Now, when my athletes come to me tired or frustrated that they can't play because they are hurt, I encourage them to train the mind when they can't train the body, just as Joe taught me.

During one of my training rides on a warm, sunny Saturday afternoon in November, as I was twelve miles into a seventy-mile ride, I was hit by a car, a challenge that I could easily have done without. I was making a left-hand turn on a country road when the car hit me from behind, throwing me from my bike. As I lay dazed and bleeding in the middle of the road, someone called an ambulance to take me to the hospital. On the way, my associate Chris called my cell phone. I told her I was on the way to the hospital, and she asked which athlete I was taking. I answered, "This time it's me."

At the hospital I was treated for a concussion; my road rash was dressed, and the physician evaluated me for other injuries. I was fortunate. My equipment—jersey, shorts, gloves, shoes, and helmet, which cracked in three places—did its job in reducing the severity of my injuries. My bike did not fare as well. Twisted and crumpled, it was nowhere close to riding condition. The next month was spent on a stationary bike as my body healed and my bike was being repaired. Conversations with the driver's insurance company were interesting. They could not believe a bike could cost that much. During my recovery, one of my athletes, whom I had rehabbed successfully from an ACL injury, asked me, "Do you think this is a sign from God that you should stop riding your bike?" My response was, "Was your ACL a sign you should stop playing ball?" She told me she would get back to me on that one.

Preparation for the ride also included taking care of professional concerns, work responsibilities, communication issues, and provisions for family needs. Practical issues had to be addressed; being away from work and home for a month can really disrupt one's routine. Realizing, understanding, and not feeling guilty about others having to add to their workloads to cover my responsibilities meant I had to relinquish my sense of control to reach a certain level of peace. And finally, I slowly began to recognize that I was entitled to this.

STEP 3. Let's Ride! As it turned out, my preparation made all the difference. The trip unfolded the way I had imagined. On April 24, 2006, I joined twenty-three other riders and four support staff in Costa Mesa, California, where we dipped our rear wheels into the Pacific Ocean for our official start on a 2,905-mile trip that would end twenty-seven days later at Tybee Island, near Savannah, Georgia. Our group consisted of twenty men and four women. Five of the riders were from other countries. Men greatly outnumber women in the cycling world, so the gender disparity did not surprise me, but it did reinforce my resolve to inspire more women to take to the pedals.

We were off! I could hardly contain myself. I have always been a watered-down tree hugger, but the trees were hugging me. We rode 122 miles that first day, and I knew I was living my dream. Just as I anticipated, each day held adventures and challenges, big and small. When the winds are tough, the terrain long and flat, and the scenery more of the same, a pace line comes in handy. Cyclists ride in a tight line one behind the other, wheels so close they almost touch, creating a drafting effect to conserve energy. The lead rider pulls the group for an agreed-upon number of miles or time, after which he drops off the front of the line by moving to the side, slowing down and allowing the other riders to pass, then jumping on the back of the train. The group works as a team, each person sharing the load and allowing for recovery. A pace line requires focus and communication among the riders. Well organized, it is poetry in motion. Even when the conditions are not ideal for a pace line, riding with other people provides more eyes on the sites you don't want to miss, a photographer to prove you were there, and someone to share every adventure.

We averaged daily distances of 115 miles. Some days we were finished in five to six hours, while other days lasted closer to eight hours, depending on distance, wind, terrain, and weather. The winds were your friend as tail winds, your enemy as head winds, or annoying as cross winds. According to natural wind patterns, riding west to east afforded the greatest probability of tail winds. One day when the winds were kind, I road one hundred miles in under five hours, achieving what cyclists call the sub–five hour century, an honor bestowed on the recreational cyclist. However, another day would bring wicked head winds gusting at 25–30 mph. Climbing up hill I would look back to see if I was pulling an over-stocked Conestoga wagon. Then, after topping the mountain crest and thinking I could relax and enjoy the prize—a nice downhill stretch—a curtain of wind would drape over me preventing my sailing down the other side.

We had climbing days of 11,000 feet. One of those days in Arizona contained a seven-mile trek up Mingus Mountain, elevation 7,023 feet. I really struggled! I thought that maybe it was because of the altitude or maybe because it was the third long climb of the day. Then I looked down and realized I had climbed six and a half miles in the wrong gear—a hard gear. Instead of spinning up the mountain, I was grinding up the mountain. After a few choice words, all I could do was laugh and acknowledge that I would probably have the dubious honor of making the "Duh of the Day" on the ride's website. Every new turn put another exclamation point on the beauty and diversity of our country. The breath-taking scenery medicated physical pain and supplied mental energy.

It was always a treat to enter a small town. We were happy to find refreshments and modern comfort facilities, but even more delightful were the people we met. Invariably we would draw a small crowd wherever we were. Someone would ask, "Hey, what y'all doin'?" Boasting a bit, we said that we were cycling from Costa Mesa, California, to Savannah, Georgia. They didn't seem impressed and even looked puzzled. So when we rephrased it and spoke in terms of the local area—that we were cycling today from Elk City to Chickasha, Oklahoma, the townsfolk would be taken aback and say, "Wow, that's far!" Usually they offered us alternate routes that seemed to them a much better option than our itinerary, but I figured they had not covered the route from the perspective of a cyclist, so we held fast to the directions of our trusty cue sheets. Everywhere people were wonderful, offering water, snacks, and other supplies that might give us comfort. Some even offered us rides in their pick-up trucks. I guess they didn't understand we were doing this by choice. Riders occasionally got lost. Someone would make a wrong turn and ride a few miles before realizing the mistake. An about-face, back-tracking to the point of the miscue, and on the way again. Mike, an accomplished cyclist and the guy in charge, would call these bonus miles and point out that the cost of the trip just went down for that rider.

We endured every kind of nasty weather—hail, rain, snow, wind, desert heat—and roads so rough we vibrated. My feet hurt, my butt hurt, my fillings hurt, everything hurt as I rode with determination to reach the next county with the hope that tax dollars had improved the roads for a stretch. Cycling on most interstates is illegal, but not when it is the only road that can get you from here to there. And out west in the desert the only access is interstate roads and railroad tracks. The semi-trucks were polite. They moved over as far as possible and passed with small, warning toots from

On the Road

their horns as we swerved periodically to avoid the rubber debris and wire shards blown from their radial tires. The shards were the main cause of flat tires, or as the Europeans say, "puncture." They were impossible to see before the damage and difficult to find in the changing process. We used tweezers to remove the wire from the tire. If you did not find the little culprit, you were sure to have another flat a mile down the road. I was fortunate— only four flats the entire trip. Some of my comrades were well into double figures! Mechanic extraordinaire Jim, whose motto was "a bike should be silent" (he made no claim about the riders), was always available to take care of mechanical needs; however, knowing how to change a flat tire was a prerequisite for the ride. Some of the exits on the interstate were more than twenty miles apart, so because you were able to deal with the tire, we would be well on our way again by the time Jim could turn the support vehicle around and get to us.

On the smaller highways, we occasionally encountered a few rude motorists who honked incessantly and even threw empty cans at us. I don't understand this behavior. We cyclists are very small, don't go really fast, and are trained to hold a line on the edge of the road. We are even easier to get around than a tractor, that familiar vehicle on the back roads of rural America. Maybe it is our bright NASCAR- style jerseys and bathroom-tissue-padded shorts that grab the attention—we do look pretty cute! Karen, the behind-the-scenes workhorse of the staff and a very talented rider, taught us to take the high road and wave at rude motorists, emphasizing all five fingers showing. She figured killing them with kindness was the safest approach.

Keeping a positive attitude carried me through some very trying times. One of the riders was a Gloomy Gus. He never smiled, everything was hard, and nothing was ever going his way. We tried everything to change his attitude for the better, telling jokes, stroking his ego, and encouraging him to look at the bright side, saying, "We're not at the office." Nothing worked. So we finally decided not to ride with him. After a couple of days of riding by himself, he got the message and changed his attitude. Whenever a little negative thought started nudging my brain or fatigue began to take over, I launched into my deliberate self-talk to keep my legs pumping and in rhythm. I counted pedal strokes to ensure cadence, loudly sang my personal theme song, "I Am Woman . . . Hear Me Roar," and assured myself, no matter what, that I'd rather be cycling.

I never thought that I would be a cheerleader, but my job motivating athletes through their rehab calls on me to be exactly that. During this ride I became my own cheerleader, turning every struggle into an opportunity, reminding myself why I was doing this, and assuring myself that I was prepared and would finish. Meditation also served me well through the difficult stretches, and I used little goals, such as reaching the next mile marker or topping the next hill, and small triumphs to reach the big ones. One triumph occurred when I experienced a "no-chain day," that rare occurrence of gliding down the road on a bike as if no chain is needed to move you along—an effortless feeling of ecstasy that others might equate to a runner's high.

My ride of a lifetime across America produced life lessons.

> I own my *Self.*
> *Confidence* produces success.
> Create *Opportunities* of a lifetime.
> *Reward* your efforts, large and small.
> Enjoy the *Excitement* you create.

127 miles

Missing 127 miles produces a life-altering lesson. One day a member of our cadre became very sick. Being an athletic trainer, I automatically respond to the medical needs of others. Unfortunately, this time it included catching the bug. I was one of several members of our team who fell ill with the same symptoms. At the hotel in Winslow, Arizona, I spent more time in the bathroom than in my bed. When the group packed up to head to Gallup, New Mexico, I could not ride my bike. I was dehydrated, weak, and running a fever. I knew I needed a hospital and IV fluids. So, I spent 127 miles in the van eating ice chips. I was so distraught when I realized that I could never claim that I cycled every single mile of this ride. After two bags of IV fluids, a shot, a bit of solid food, and a better night's rest, I got back on my bike the next day and was reassured by Barb, staff member and mother to all, that we had many miles ahead of us.

My thoughts were spiraling downward. "I never should have told everyone I was doing this. I am letting them down. I'm embarrassed. I have let myself down. I can't claim cycling from coast-to-coast. I failed." Well, I did not ride every mile. But I did make the journey, and I stopped to help without hesitation. My commitment to caring for others competed with my desire to reach my personal goal.

On the Road

Psychiatrist Dr. Kenneth Jobson describes those dilemmas in life when competing ideals present a metaphorical fork in the road, and we have to make a choice. "What a tough decision. You also have to say, though, for some this choice is going to be a peak experience in their life," says Jobson. "Who's to say that's not a good choice—to be able to say that there was a moment in my life that I can look back on and say I claim this excellence with all the bounty, benefit, and self-esteem that goes with it. Might that choice have taken away from other things during that time? Yes, but if it's contextualized in the right personality and the right support, we carry with us a sense of mastery that will make us more likely to achieve the full life that we deserve."

I look back on those miles off my bike as part of my journey and recognize the moment with the words of Dr. Jobson: "I claim this excellence with all the bounty and benefit that goes with it." I am still conflicted, but I know I could not have made a different choice. Am I bothered that my miles cycled are 127 miles short of the intended goal? Yes, of course. However, I am now hearing what I tell student-athletes almost on a daily basis. It is important to set goals, prepare in every way to achieve them, and then begin the journey. The unexpected obstacles along the way present unexpected opportunities that confirm our values and skills, and all that we are to act without even thinking. I realize that these 127 miles taught me that even when I had to abandon my bike, I was still on this journey and discovering myself.

Now it's time for you. Take a deep breath, confirm your resolve, take the day on, and champion your next great adventure. The journey is more important than the destination. Here and now it is the SCORE that counts!

Day 27: Vidalia, GA, to Savannah, GA, (Tybee Island) 129 miles

All I can say is WOW! A happy ending to a fairytale trip. Absolutely ideal conditions—low seventies when we started and hot in the nineties when we finished. Sunny, and our most humid day. Some of us southern folk did not have a problem; others from less humid areas were very thankful we only had one day of this. Very smooth roads. Tail winds AGAIN! Gentle at first and then building up to 15 mph. Only 980 feet of climbing spread over more than one hundred miles, so climbing was under 9 feet per mile, or, in other words, FLAT. The hills we came across were in the form of bridges and overpasses—love that sea level.

Epilogue

When I began writing this book I had a number of subjects in mind that I wanted to share with my readers who would be joining me on my journey. At times, I was hard-pressed to sort out what ought to be included that would contribute to healthy living for athletes of any affiliation or any age, especially for children. Initially, I decided that the major considerations were injury prevention, nutrition, age, and developmental readiness, along with the contextual fabric of Title IX history, education trends, the rapid expansion of sports, and social norms.

Now, looking back over the contents, I see that the public's sometimes fanatical attention to sports, the twists and turns taken during my investigations, and the many people I met along the way added to my understanding of what it takes to live healthfully. Working my way through this broadening process gave more substance, credibility, and strength to my emerging holistic philosophy.

The stories of the athletes, coaches, physicians, and parents that I included here, along with my years of experience, provide overwhelming evidence that we are in a health crisis. For certain, in terms of sports, we cannot afford to entrust our well-being to unexamined customs and established institutional structures. Many changes must be made. It is up to each one of us to begin making a difference. Come on board!

The rewards are lasting and far greater than those of a winning season, especially if that season is overshadowed by repetitive injury, emotional stress, and the suppression of self. Don't misunderstand—winning is fun. The real win, though, has lasting significance if it is achieved through balance, our own clear choices, self-generated discipline, and hard work. It's the exhilaration, satisfaction, and pride of that triumph that open future possibilities and propel us forward to the next goal.

I am encouraging you to remember that if you should physically, mentally, or spiritually hit a rough spot as you ride, run, jump, dance, stretch, cycle, swim, leap, hop, roll, kick, dribble, or dive through the breadth and depth of life experience, you are better equipped now to ice 'n' go! Journey on.

Notes

1. David Elkind, *The Hurried Child: Growing Up Too Fast Too Soon* (Reading, Mass.: Addison-Wesley Publishing Company, 1981).

2. Stuart Brown with Christopher Vaughan, *Play: How It Shapes the Brain, Opens the Imagination, and Invigorates the Soul* (New York: Avery, 2009), 5.

3. Ibid., 42.

4. Geraldine Sealey, "No Sweat When Gym Class Cut," ABC News, September 30, 2009.

5. Ibid.

6. Philip Sherwell, "New DNA Test Offers Parents Chance to Find Children's Sports Gene," *The Telegraph,* December 6, 2008.

7. Harvey Araton, "Building the Next McEnroe," *New York Times*, May 7, 2010.

8. Elkind, *Hurried Child*, 31.

9. Ibid., 32.

10. Tom Farrey, *Game On: The All-American Race to Make Champions of Our Children* (New York: ESPN Books, 2008), 95–97.

11. Quoted in Ibid., 98.

12. Quoted in Ibid., 172–73.

13. Dave Ramsey, "The High Cost of Kids' Sports," http://www.daveramsey.com/article/the-high-cost-of-kids-sports, April 12, 2010.

14. U.S. Department of Education, National Center for Education Statistics (NCES) Website. www.nces.ed.gov.

15. Michael Aubrecht, "Jackie Mitchell—The Pride of the Yankees," *Baseball Almanac* (November 2003), www.baseball-almanac.com/articles/aubrecht8.shtml.

16. R. Vivian Acosta and Linda Jean Carpenter, "Women in Intercollegiate Sport: A Longitudinal, National Study, Thirty-Five Year Update, 1977–2012," http://www.acostacarpenter.org/.

17. Ibid.

18. Marlene A. Dixon, Bonnie Tiell, Nancy Lough, Kristi Sweeney, Barbara Osborne, and Jennifer E. Bruening, "The Work/Life Interface in Intercollegiate Athletics: An Examination of Policies, Programs, and Institutional Climate," *Journal for the Study of Sports and Athletes in Education* 2 (Summer 2008): 137–60.

19. Acosta and Carpenter, "Women in Intercollegiate Sport."

20. Andrea Adelson, "Women See Slow Progress for Athletic Director Jobs," *Orlando Sentinel,* July 9, 2010.

21. Ibid.

22. NCAA Survey, 2008–2009, http://www.ncaapublications.com/p-4022-gender-equity-in-college-coaching-and-administration-perceive.

23. Jay Coakley, *Sport in Society: Issues & Controversies* (New York: McGraw-Hill, 2001), 207–8.

24. Griffin, Pat, and Helen Carroll, "The Positive Approach: Recognizing, Challenging and Eliminating Negative Recruiting Based On Sexual Orientation," March 2009, www.nclrights.org/site/DocServer/Final_Negative_Recruiting_FINAL.pdf.

25. *Training Rules*, Woman Vision Production, 2009.

26. Coakley, *Sport in Society*, 212.

27. "Transgender Man Kye Allums Playing NCAA Women's Basketball," *San Diego Voice & Viewpoint*, http://sdvoice.info/index1.htm.

28. Kendall Clark, "Defining White Privilege," http//academic.udayton,edu/race/whiteness05.htm.

29. University of Tennessee Athletic Department Graduation Rates, October 2011, http://www.govolsxtra.com/news/2011/oct/25/uts-graduation-success-rate-up-to-76-percent/?partner=RSS.

30. University of Tennessee Graduation Rates, 2011, http://senate.utk.edu/files/2011/08/retreat-2011-faculty-senate_final-presentation.pdf.

31. Quoted in Mark Schwarz, "Delle Donne Finds Happiness at Delaware," December 31, 2008, http://sports.espn.go.com/espn/otl/news/story?id=3790359.

32. Quoted in Ibid.

33. Ibid.

34. STOP Sports Injuries website, http://www.stopsportsinjuries.org/.

35. Ibid.

36. Lee Bowman, "Keeping Athletes Safe: Schools Face Shortage of Athletic Trainers," *Knoxville News Sentinel*, September 5, 2010, sec. D.

37. Gina Kolata, "Perks of Cross-Training May End Before Finish Line," *New York Times*, August 16, 2011.

38. Elizabeth Arendt and Randall Dick, "Knee Injury Patterns Among Men and Women in Collegiate Basketball and Soccer," *American Journal of Sports Medicine* 23 (December 1995): 694–701.

39. Letha Y. Griffin et al., "Noncontact Anterior Cruciate Ligament Injuries: Risk Factors and Prevention Strategies," *Journal of American Academy of Orthopedic Surgery* 8 (May/June 2000): 141–50; Letha Y. Griffin et al., "Understanding and Preventing Noncontact Anterior Cruciate Ligament Injuries: A Review of the Hunt Valley II Meeting, January 2005," *American Journal of Sports Medicine* 34 (September 2006): 1512–32; David E. Gwinn et al., "The Relative Incidence of Anterior Cruciate Ligament Injury in Men and Women at the United States Naval Academy," *American Journal of Sports Medicine* 28 (January 2000): 98–102; T. E. Hewett et al., "Plyometric Training in Female Athletes: Decreased Impact Forces and Increased Hamstring Torques," *American Journal of Sports Medicine* 24 (December 1996): 765–73; T. E. Hewett et al., "The Effect of Neuromuscular Training on the Incidence of Knee Injury in Female Athletes: A Prospective Study," *American Journal of Sports Medicine* 27 (November 1999): 699–706; and Laura J. Huston and Edward M. Wojtys, "Neuromuscular Performance Characteristics in Elite Female Athletes," *American Journal of Sports Medicine* 24 (July 1996): 427–36.

40. Edward M. Wojtys et al., "Association between the Menstrual Cycle and Anterior Cruciate Ligament Injuries in Female Athletes," *American Journal of Sports Medicine* 26 (September 1998): 614–19.

41. Edward M. Wojtys et al., "The Effect of the Menstrual Cycle on Anterior Cruciate Ligament Injuries in Women as Determined by Hormone Levels." *American Journal of Sports Medicine* 30 (March 2002): 182–88.

42. Griffin et al., "Noncontact Anterior Cruciate Ligament Injuries"; Barry P. Boden, Letha Y. Griffin, and William E. Garrett, Jr., "Etiology and Prevention of Noncontact ACL Injury," *Physician and Sportsmedicine* 28 (April 2000); and Griffin et al., "Understanding and Preventing Noncontact Anterior Cruciate Ligament Injuries."

43. A. Caraffa et al. "Prevention of Anterior Cruciate Ligament Injuries in Soccer: A Prospective Controlled Study of Proprioceptive Training," *Knee Surgery, Sports Traumatology, Arthroscopy* 4 (1996): 19–21; Julie Gilchrist et al., "A Randomized Controlled Trial to Prevent Noncontact Anterior Cruciate Ligament Injury in Female Collegiate Soccer Players," *American Journal of Sports Medicine* 36 (August 2008): 1476; T. E. Hewett, et. al. "Cincinnati Sportsmetrics: A Jump Training Program Proven to Prevent Knee Injury," VHS, Cincinnati Sportsmedicine Research and Education Foundation, 1998; Hewett et al., "Plyometric Training in Female Athletes, 765–73; Hewett et al., "The Effect of Neuromuscular Training on the Incidence of Knee Injury in Female Athletes," 699–706; and Bert R. Mandelbaum et al., "Effectiveness of a Neuromuscular and Proprioceptive Training Program in Preventing Anterior Cruciate Ligament Injuries in Female Athletes: 2-Year Follow-up," *American Journal of Sports Medicine* 33 (July 2005): 1003.

44. "WNBA, Sparks Will Miss Parker," *Knoxville News Sentinel*, June 20, 2010, sec. D.

45. Lynn Sweet, "Michelle Obama Childhood Obesity Action Plan; Events around the Nation," *Chicago Sun-Times*, May 11, 2010.

46. Kathy Burns, "Alert: Protein Drinks," *Consumer Reports* (July 2010): 24–27.

47. S. Byrne and N. Mclean, "Elite Athletes: Effects of the Pressure to Be Thin," *Journal of Science and Medicine in Sport* 5 (June 2002): 80–94.

48. American Youth Soccer Association, http://www.ayso.org/Search.aspx?k=fastest+growing+age+group&s=All+Sites.

Appendix A

Numbers of Participants by Gender in High School Varsity Sports, 1972–2007

Year	Males	Females	Males % change previous year	Females % change previous year	Males % change from 1972–73	Females % change from 1972–73
1972–73	3,770,621	817,073				
1973–74	4,070,125	1,300,169	7.94	59.13	7.94	59.13
1974–75						
1975–76	4,109,021	1,645,039	0.96	26.53	8.97	101.33
1976–77						
1977–78	4,367,442	2,083,040	6.29	26.63	15.83	254.94
1978–79	3,709,512	1,854,400	-15.06	-10.98	-1.62	126.96
1979–80	3,517,829	1,750,264	-5.17	-5.62	-6.7	114.21
1980–81	3,503,124	1,853,789	-0.42	5.91	-7.09	126.88
1981–82	3,409,081	1,810,671	-2.68	-2.33	-9.59	121.6
1982–83	3,355,558	1,779,972	-1.57	-1.7	-11.02	117.85
1983–84	3,303,599	1,747,346	-1.55	-1.83	-12.39	113.85
1984–85	3,354,284	1,757,884	1.53	0.6	-11.04	115.14

1985–86	3,344,275	1,807,121	-0.3	2.8	-11.31	121.17
1986–87	3,364,082	1,836,356	0.59	1.62	-10.78	124.75
1987–88	3,425,777	1,849,684	1.83	0.73	-9.15	126.38
1988–89	3,416,844	1,839,352	-0.26	-56	-9.38	125.11
1989–90	3,398,192	1,858,659	-0.55	1.05	-9.88	127.48
1990–91	3,406,355	1,892,316	0.24	1.81	-9.66	131.6
1991–92	429,853	1,940,801	0.69	2.56	-9.04	137.53
1992–93	3,416,389	1,997,489	-0.39	2.92	-939	144.47
1993–94	3,472,967	2,130,315	1.66	6.65	-7.89	160.73
1994–95	3,536,359	2,240,461	1.83	5.17	-6.21	174.21
1995–96	3,634,052	2,367,936	2.76	5.69	-3.62	189.81
1996–97	3,706,225	2,474,043	1.99	4.48	-1.71	202.79
1997–98	763,120	2,570,333	1.54	3.89	-0.2	214.58
1998–99	3,832,352	2,652,726	1.84	3.21	1.64	224.66
1999–2000	3,861,749	2,675,874	0.77	0.87	2.42	227.5
2000–01	3,921,069	2,784,154	1.54	4.05	3.99	240.75
2001–02	3,960,517	2,806,998	1.01	0.82	5.04	243.54
2002–03	3,988,738	2,856,358	0.71	1.76	5.78	249.58
2003–04	4,038,253	2,865,299	1.24	0.31	7.1	250.68
2004–05	4,110,319	2,908,390	1.78	1.5	9.01	255.95
2005–06	4,206,549	2,953,355	2.34	1.55	11.56	261.46
2006–07	4,321,103	3,021,807	2.72	2.32	14.6	269.83

(2007 High School Participation Study, Digest of Education Statistics: 2009)

Appendix B

Certified Athletic Trainers by Gender, 2001–2009			
Year	**Certified Male Members**	**Certified Female Members**	**Total**
2001	54%	46%	22,389
2002	54%	46%	23,304
2003	54%	46%	23,632
2004	53%	47%	24,899
2005	52%	48%	25,353
2006	52%	48%	24,819
2007	51.1%	48.9%	25,516
2008	50.5%	49.5%	26,054
2009	49.9%	50.1%	26,565

(National Athletic Trainers' Association)

Appendix C

Certified Athletic Trainers in Professional Team Sports by Gender, 2011		
Sport	**Male**	**Female**
National Football League	114	1
National Basketball Association	58	0
Women's National Basketball Association	6	6
Major League Baseball	69	2

(www.pfats.com, www.nbata.com, www.phats-sphem.com, team websites)

Selected Bibliography

Archival Documents

"A Comparison Based Upon HEW'S Title IX Guidelines of Men's and Women's Intercollegiate Athletic Programs at the University of Tennessee." 1980. Office of Institutional Research, University of Tennessee, Knoxville.

Acosta, R. Vivian, and Linda Jean Carpenter, "Women in Intercollegiate Sport: A Longitudinal, National Study, Thirty-Five Year Update, 1977–2012." http://www.acostacarpenter.org/.

Blaufarb, Marjorie, and consultants and staff of the American Alliance for Health, Physical Education, and Recreation. "Title IX and Physical Education: A Compliance Overview." 1976. U.S. Department of Health, Education, and Welfare, Office of Education, Washington, D.C.

College Athletic Trainers' Society. "2003 Salary and Benefits Survey." 2004. Josephine Lee, Georgia Institute of Technology Athletic Association, Atlanta, Georgia. http://www.collegeathletictrainer.org/symposiums/past.html.

"Gender Equity in College Coaching and Administration: Perceived Barriers Report, 2009." NCAA. http://www.ncaapublications.com/p-4022-gender-equity-in-college-coaching-and-administration-perceive.

Griffin, Pat, and Helen Carroll, "The Positive Approach: Recognizing, Challenging And Eliminating Negative Recruiting Based On Sexual Orientation," March 2009. www.nclrights.org/site/DocServer/Final_Negative_Recruiting_FINAL.pdf?

NCAA Sports Sponsorship and Participation Rates Report, 1981–82—2007–08. http://www.ncaapublications.com/p-3779-1981-822005-06-sports-sponsorship-and-participation-rates-report.aspx.

Articles in Newspapers and Periodicals

Ahillen, Steve. "Area Trainers Say Job is 'Rewarding'." *Knoxville News Sentinel,* September 5, 2010, sec. D.

Andrea Adelson. "Women See Slow Progress for Athletic Director Jobs." *Orlando Sentinel,* July 9, 2010.

Araton, Harvey. "Building the Next McEnroe." *New York Times,* May 8, 2010, sec. B.

Arendt, Elizabeth and Randall Dick. "Knee Injury Patterns Among Men and Women in Collegiate Basketball and Soccer: NCAA Data and Review of Literature." *American Journal of Sports Medicine* 23 (December 1995): 694–701.

Bowman, Lee. "Keeping Athletes Safe: Schools Face Shortage of Athletic Trainers." *Knoxville News Sentinel,* September 5, 2010, sec. D.

Burns, Kathy. "Alert: Protein Drinks." *Consumer Reports* (July 2010): 24–27.

Byrne, S., and N. Mclean, "Elite Athletes: Effects of the Pressure to Be Thin." *Journal of Sports Science and Medicine* 5 (June 2002):80–94.

Caraffa, A., G. Cerulli, M. Projetti, G. Aisa, and A. Rizzo. "Prevention of Anterior Cruciate Ligament Injuries in Soccer: A Prospective Controlled Study of Proprioceptive Training." *Knee Surgery, Sports Traumatology, Arthroscopy* 4 (1996): 19–21.

Dixon, Marlene A., Bonnie Tiell, Nancy Lough, Kristi Sweeney, Barbara Osborne, and Jennifer E. Bruening, "The Work/Life Interface in Intercollegiate Athletics: An Examination of Policies, Programs, and Institutional Climate." *Journal for the Study of Sports and Athletes in Education* 2 (Summer 2008): 137–60.

Dusek, T. "Influence of High Intensity Training on Menstrual Cycle Disorders in Athletes." *Croatian Medical Journal,* 42 (February 2001):79–82.

Faude, Oliver, Astrid Junge, Wilfried Kindermann, and Jiri Dvorak. "Injuries in Female Soccer Players: A Prospective Study in the German National League." *American Journal of Sports Medicine* 33 (November 2005): 1694–1700.

Frierson, John. "Hall Won't Play for Chattanooga." *Knoxville News Sentinel,* September 5, 2010, sec. D.

Gilchrist, Julie, Bert R. Mandelbaum, Heidi Melancon, George W. Ryan, Holly J. Silvers, Letha Y. Griffin, Diane S. Wanatabe, Randall W. Dick, and Jiri Dvorak. "A Randomized Controlled Trial to Prevent Noncontact Anterior Cruciate Ligament Injury in Female Collegiate Soccer Players." *American Journal of Sports Medicine* 36 (August 2008): 1476–83.

Griffin, Pat. *The Positive Approach: Recognizing, Challenging, and Eliminating Negative Recruiting Based on Actual or Perceived Sexual Orientation.* The National Center for Lesbian Rights Sports Project (January 2009): 2–3.

Griffin, Pat, and Helen J. Carroll. *Equal Opportunity for Transgender Student Athletes.* October 4, 2010. www.nclrights.org/site/DocServer/TransgenderStudentAthleteReport.pdf.

Griffin, Letha Y., Julie Agel, Marjorie J. Albohm, Elizabeth A. Arendt, Randall W. Dick, William E. Garrett, James G. Garrick, et al. "Noncontact Anterior Cruciate Ligament Injuries: Risk Factors and Prevention Strategies." *Journal of American Academy of Orthopedic Surgery* 8 (May/June 2000): 141–50.

———, Marjorie J. Albohm, Elizabeth A. Arendt, Roald Bahr, Bruce D. Beynnon, Marlene DeMaio, Randall W. Dick, et al. "Understanding and Preventing Noncontact Anterior Cruciate Ligament Injuries: A Review of the Hunt Valley II Meeting, January 2005." *American Journal of Sports Medicine* 34 (September 2006): 1512–32.

Gwinn, David E., John H. Wilckens, Edward R. McDevitt, Glen Ross, and Tzu-Cheg Kao. "The Relative Incidence of Anterior Cruciate Ligament Injury in Men and Women at the United States Naval Academy." *American Journal of Sports Medicine* 28 (January 2000): 98–102.

Hewett, T. E., Amanda L. Stroupe, Thomas A. Nance, and Frank R. Noyes. "Plyometric Training in Female Athletes: Decreased Impact Forces and Increased Hamstring Torques." *American Journal of Sports Medicine* 24 (December 1996): 765–73.

——, Thomas N. Lindenfeld, Jennifer V. Riccobene, and Frank R. Noyes. "The Effect of Neuromuscular Training on the Incidence of Knee Injury in Female Athletes: A Prospective Study." *American Journal of Sports Medicine* 27 (November 1999): 6699–706.

Huston, Laura J., and Edward M. Wojtys. "Neuromuscular Performance Characteristics in Elite Female Athletes." *American Journal of Sports Medicine* 24 (July 1996): 427–36.

Kolata, Gina. "Perks of Cross-Training May End Before Finish Line." *New York Times,* August 16, 2011.

Mandelbaum, Bert R., Holly J. Silvers, Diane S. Watanabe, John F. Knarr, Stephen D. Thomas, Letha Y. Griffin, Donald T. Kirkendall, and William Garrett, Jr. "Effective-ness of a Neuromuscular and Proprioceptive Training Program in Preventing An-terior Cruciate Ligament Injuries in Female Athletes: 2-Year Follow-up." *American Journal of Sports Medicine* 33 (July 2005): 1003–10.

Bell, Mihalik, S. W. Marshall, and K. M. Guskiewicz, "Measurement of Head Impacts in Collegiate Football Players: An Investigation of Positional and Event-Type Differ-ences." *Neurosurgery* 61(6) (December 2007): 1229--35.

Mountcastle, Sally B., Matthew Posner, John F. Kragh, Jr., and Dean C. Taylor. "Gender Differences in Anterior Cruciate Ligament Injury Vary With Activity." *American Journal of Sports Medicine* 35 (October 2007): 1635–42.

Paretsky, Sara. "How Sports Can Change a Girl's Life." *Parade,* April 25, 2010, 14.

Parker-Pope, Tara. "As Girls Become Women, Sports Pay Dividends." *New York Times,* February 16, 2010, sec. D.

Sundgot-Borgen, J., and M. K. Torstveit. "Prevalence of Eating Disorders in Elite Athletes Is Higher Than in the General Population." *Clinical Journal of Sports Medicine* 14 (January 2004):25–32.

Schwarz, Alan. "At 17, Baseball's Next Sure Thing." *New York Times,* May 16, 2010, SportsSunday.

Söderman, Kerstin, Håkan Alfredson, Tom Pietilä, and Suzanne Werner. "Risk Factors For Leg Injuries in Female Soccer Players: A Prospective Investigation during One Out-Door Season." *Knee Surgery, Sports Traumatology, Arthroscopy* 9 (2001): 313–21.

"WNBA , Sparks Will Miss Parker," *Knoxville News Sentinel,* 20 June 2010, sec. D, p. 7.

Wojtys, Edward M., Laura J. Huston, Melbourne D. Boynton, Kurt P. Spindler, and Thomas N. Lindenfeld. "The Effect of the Menstrual Cycle on Anterior Cruciate Ligament Injuries in Women as Determined by Hormone Levels." *American Journal of Sports Medicine* 30 (March 2002): 182–88.

——, Laura J. Huston, Thomas N. Lindenfeld, Timothy E. Hewett, Mary Lou V. H. Greenfield. "Association Between the Menstrual Cycle and Anterior Cruciate Liga-ment Injuries in Female Athletes." *American Journal of Sports Medicine* 26 (September 1998): 614–19.

Books

Bigelo, Bob, Tom Moroney, and Linda Hall. *Just Let the Kids Play: How to Stop Other Adults from Ruining Your Child's Fun and Success in Youth Sports.* Deerfield Beach, Fla.: Health Communications, Inc., 2001.

Blumenthal, Karen. *Let Me Play.* New York: Simon and Schuster, 2005.

Brown, Stuart, with Christopher Vaughan. *Play: How It Shapes the Brain, Opens the Imagination, and Invigorates the Soul.* New York: Penguin Group, 2009.

Bryan, Wayne, with Woody Woodburn. *Raising Your Child to Be a Champion in Athletics, Arts, and Academics.* New York: Kensington Publishing Corporation, 2004.

Brzycki, Matt. *A Practical Approach to Strength Training.* Chicago: Master's Press, 1998.

Burnett, Darrell J. *It's Just a Game! Youth, Sports & Self Esteem: A Guide for Parents.* New York: Authors Choice Press, 2001.

Carpenter, Linda Jean, and R. Vivian Acosta. *Title IX.* Champaign, Ill.: Human Kinetics, 2005.

Chastain, Brandi, with Gloria Averbuch. *It's Not About the Bra: Play Hard, Play Fair, and Put the Fun Back into Competitive Sports.* New York: HarperCollins, 2004.

Coakley, Jay. *Sport in Society: Issues & Controversies.* New York: McGraw-Hill, 2001.

Corwin, Donna G. *Pushed to the Edge: How to Stop the Child Competition Race So Everyone Wins.* New York: Berkley Books, 2003.

Crowley, Chris, and Henry S. Lodge. *Younger Next Year.* New York: Workman Publishing Company, Inc., 2007.

Diggs, Joetta Clark. *Joetta's 'P' Principles for Success: Life Lessons Learned from Track & Field.* Joetta Clark Diggs, 2009.

Elkind, David. *All Grown Up and No Place to Go: Teenagers in Crisis.* Cambridge, Mass.: Da Capo Press, 1998.

———. *The Hurried Child: Growing Up Too Fast Too Soon.* Cambridge, Mass.: Da Capo Press, 2001.

———. *Miseducation: Preschoolers at Risk.* New York: Alfred A. Knopf, 1989.

———. *The Power of Play: Learning What Comes Naturally.* Berkeley, Calif.: Perseus Books Group, 2007.

———. *Ties That Stress: The New Family Imbalance.* Cambridge, Mass.: Harvard University Press, 1995.

Farrey, Tom. *Game On: The All-American Race to Make Champions of Our Children.* New York: ESPN Books, 2008.

Fish, Joel, with Susan Magee. *101 Ways to Be a Terrific Sports Parent: Making Athletics a Positive Experience for Your Child.* New York: Simon and Schuster, 2003.

Ginsburg, Richard D., and Stephen Durant, with Amy Baltzell. *Whose Game Is It, Anyway?* New York: Houghton Mifflin Company, 2006.

Griffin, Pat. *Strong Women, Deep Closets: Lesbians and Homophobia in Sport.* Champaign, Ill.: Human Kinetics, 1998.

McMahon, Regan. *Revolution in the Bleachers: How Parents Can Take Back Family Life in a World Gone Crazy Over Youth Sports.* New York: Gotham Books, 2007.

Mueller, Frederick O., and Robert C. Cantu. *Football Fatalities and Catastrophic Injuries, 1931–2008.* Durham, N.C.: Carolina Academic Press, 2010.

Paley, Vivan Gussin. *A Child's Work: The Importance of Fantasy Play.* Chicago: University of Chicago Press, 2004.

Pipher, Mary. *Reviving Ophelia: Saving the Selves of Adolescent Girls.* New York: Ballantine Books, 1994.

Pollack, William. *Real Boys: Rescuing Our Sons from the Myths of Boyhood.* New York: Henry Holt and Company, 1998.

Porto, Brian L. *A New Season: Using Title IX to Reform College Sports.* Westport, Conn.: Praeger Publishers, 2003.

Rogers, Susan Fox, ed. *Sportsdykes: Stories from On and Off the Field.* New York: St. Martin's Press, 1994.

Schriver, Debby. *In the Footsteps of Champions: The University of Tennessee Lady Volunteers, the First Three Decades.* Knoxville: University of Tennessee Press, 2008.

Sey, Jennifer. *Chalked Up: Inside Elite Gymnastics' Merciless Coaching, Overzealous Parents, Eating Disorders, and Elusive Olympic Dreams.* New York: HarperCollins Publishers, 2008.

Simon, Rita J., ed. *Sporting Equality.* New Brunswick, N.J.: Transaction Publishers, 2006.

Smith, Ronald A. *Pay for Play: A History of Big-Time College Athletic Reform.* Champaign: University of Illinois Press, 2011.

Sokolove, Michael. *Warrior Girls.* New York: Simon and Schuster, 2008.

Starkes, Janet L., and K. Anders Ericsson, eds. *Expert Performance in Sports: Advances in Research on Sport Expertise.* Champaign, IL: Human Kinetics, 2003.

Suggs, Welch. *A Place on the Team: The Triumph and Tragedy of Title IX.* Princeton, N.J.: Princeton University Press, 2005.

Ware, Susan. *Title IX: A Brief History with Documents.* Boston, Mass.: Bedford/St. Martin's, 2007.

Interviews by Authors

Anonymous. Telephone interview, October 10, 2010.

Bayh, Birch. Telephone interview, tape recording. January 25, 2007.

Bloom, Jamie. Telephone interview. August 21, 2011.

Bonner, Tracy. Telephone interview. August 21, 2011.

Catchings, Tamika. Telephone interview, tape recording. July 12, 2010.

Clark Diggs, Joetta. Telephone interview, tape recording. April 28, 2010.

Clark, Kristine. Telephone interview, tape recording. May 19, 2010.

Coleman, P. Kay. Telephone interview, tape recording. April 8, 2010.

Collins, Michael. Telephone interview, tape recording. April 22, 2010.

Cronan, Joan. Tape recording. June 18, 2010.

Curran, Bryttany. Tape recording. April 9, 2010.

Gray, Josh. Telephone interview, tape recording. April 28, 2010.

Griffin, Patricia. Telephone interview, tape recording. May 26, 2010.

Hammond, Edward H. Telephone interview, tape recording. May 5, 2010.

Hofmann, Chris. Tape recording. July 11, 2010.

Howe, Lisa. Tape recording. November 14, 2011.

Howland, Kerry. Tape recording. May 20, 2010.

Izzo-Brown, Nikki. Telephone interview, tape recording. June 11, 2010.

Jennings, Debby. Tape recording. June 16, 2010.

Jobson, Kenneth. Tape recording. April 20, 2010.

Langenfeld, Andrew. Telephone interview, tape recording. September 27, 2010.

Lawson, Kara. Telephone interview, tape recording. April 30, 2010.

Loberg, Lauren. Tape recording. April 21, 2010.

Lopiano, Donna. Skype interview, tape recording. April 13, 2010.

Martin, Kristen. Tape recording. April 13, 2010.

Mason, Heather. Tape recording. May 28, 2010.

Mayhew, Anne. Tape recording. April 9, 2010.

McCray, Nikki. Telephone interview. February 27, 2012.

McDaniel, Meg. Telephone interview, tape recording. September 23, 2010.

McLean, Lindsy. Telephone interview, tape recording. September 21, 2010.

Moore, Steve. Telephone interview. September 27, 2010.

Morgan, Rebecca. Tape recording. April 29, 2010.

Moshak, Damian. Telephone interview. November 14, 2011.

Mueller, Frederick. Telephone interview, tape recording. November 18, 2010.

Palmer, Violet. Telephone interview, tape recording. April 20, 2010.

P., Lauren. Telephone interview, tape recording. November 14, 2011.

Parker, Candace. Skype interview, tape recording. April 25, 2010.

Rankin, Sue. Telephone interview, tape recording. May 28, 2010.

Ryan, Kate. June 14, 2010.

Seagraves, Loren. Telephone interview, tape recording. May 5, 2010.

Sisco, Stacey. Tape recording. June 14, 2010.

Summit, Pat. Tape recording. June 19, 2010.

Sweet, Judy. Tape recording. July 1, 2010.

Turner, Lee. Tape recording. October 21, 2010.

VanDerveer, Heidi. June 24, 2010.

Wobser, Jane. Telephone interview, tape recording. April 10, 2010.

Wobser, Jeff. Telephone interview, tape recording. April 10, 2010.

Youmans, William T. Tape recording. April 8, 2010.

Online Sources

Adelson, Andrea. "Women See Slow Progress for Athletic Director Jobs," *Orlando Sentinel*, July 9, 2010. articles.orlandosentinel.com/2010–07–09/sports/os-female-athletic-directors-0710–20100709_1_coaching-minority-bcs-schools.

Aubrecht, Michael, "Jackie Mitchell—The Pride of the Yankees," *Baseball Almanac*, November 2003, www.baseball-almanac.com/articles/aubrecht8.shtml.

American Bar Association Website. http://www.abanet.org/legaled/statistics/stats.html/.

American Institute of Stress Website. www.stress.org.

American Youth Soccer Association Website. http://www.ayso.org.

Association of American Medical Colleges Website. http://www.aamc.org/members/gwims/statistics/stats09/table1/pdf.

Bell, Mihalik, S.W. Marshall, and K. M. Guskiewicz. "Measurement of Head Impacts in Collegiate Football Players: An Investigation of Positional and Event-Type Differences." December 2007. U. S. National Library of Medicine, National Institutes of Health Website. http://www.ncbi.nlm.nih.gov/pubmed/18162902.

"Best Practices for Coaching Soccer in the United States." www.mayouthsoccer.org.

Canadian Association for the Advancement of Women and Sport and Physical Activity Website. http://www.caaws.ca/olympics/2006/history/olympic_games.cfm

Brown, Curt. "Participation in Youth Sports on the Decline." *South Coast Today,* May 22, 2011. http://www.southcoasttoday.com/apps/pbcs.dll/article?AID=/2011052.

Chen, Grace. "The Pros and Cons of Mandatory Gym Class in Public Schools." October 29, 2009. Public School Review Website. http:/www.publicschoolreview.com/articles/158.

Digest of Educational Statistics: 2009. http://nces.ed.gov/programs/digest/d09/.

Diversity across Higher Education Community. June 1, 2009. http://live,psu.edu/story/39988/nw69.

Executive Summary, 1981–82 to 2007–08 NCAA Sports Sponsorship and Participation Rates Report. NCAA Website. http://www.ncaa.org/.

Executive Summary, "The 2007 National School Climate Survey." GLSEN Website. www.glsen.org.

Female Athlete Triad Coalition. www.femaleathletetriad.org.

Forbes Website. http://www.forbes.com.

Grappendorf, Heidi, and Nancy Lough. "An Endangered Species: Characteristics and Perspectives from Female NCAA Division 1 Athletic Directors of Both Separate and Merged Athletic Departments." Spring 2006. www.thesmartjournal.com/endangered%20species.

Kilgore, Adam. "Nationals, Bryce Harper Reach a Deal." *Washington Post*, August 17, 2010. http://voices.washingtonpost.com/nationalsjournal/2010/08/nats_harper_reach_deal.html.

Hilgers, Laura. "Youth Sports Drawing More than Ever," July 5, 2006. http://www.cnn.com/2006/US/07/03/rise.kids.sports/index.html.

National Collegiate Athletic Association. "Probability of Going Pro." December 2, 2010. http:"www.ncaa.org/wps/wcm/connect/public/NCAA/Resources/Basketball +Re source+Probablility+of+Going+Pro?

Noffsinger, Jodi. "Phys. Ed Cuts May Leave Children's Health Behind." November 20, 2005. http://www.foxnews.com.

Parker-Pope, Tara. "As Children Grow, Activity Quickly Slows." *New York Times,* July 16, 2008. http://www.nytimes.com/2008/07/16/health/research/16exercise.

——— "Early Focus on One Sport Raises Alarms." *New York Times,* September 2, 2008. http://www.nytimes.com/2008/09/02/health/02well.html?_r 1.

"Percentage of Obese Adults in All 50 States," July 7, 2011. http://www.seattlepi.com/news/article/Percentage-of-obese-adults in all-50-states-1456089,php#ixzz1WAJbBTgD.

Petrecca, Laura. "Number of Female 'Fortune's 500 CEO's at Record High." *USA Today,* October 27, 2011. http://abcnews.go.com/Business/number-female-fortune-500-ceos-record-high/story?id=14822840#.UArSw3Djo7A.

Pickett, Brent. "Homosexuality." *Stanford Encyclopedia of Philosophy* (Spring 2011) http://plato.stanford.edu/archives/spr2011/entries/homosexuality/>.

Ramsey, Dave. "The High Cost of Kids' Sports." April 12, 2010. http://www.daveramsey.com/article/the-high-cost-of-kids-sports.

Rhode, Deborah L., and Christopher J. Walker. "Gender Equity in College Athletics: Women Coaches as a Case Study." March 26, 2008. http://www.ncaa.org/wps.portal/ncaahome+GE+in+College+Athletics+Coaches.

Schwarz, Mark. "Delle Donne Finds Happiness at Delaware." December 31, 2008. http://sports.espn.go.com/espn.

———. "Outside the Lines: For the Love of the Game." ESPN, December 31, 2008. http://sports.espn.go.com/espn/otl/news/story?id=3790359.livepage.apple.com.

Sealey, Geraldine. "No Sweat When Gym Class Cut." September 30, 2009. http://www.ihpra.org/ABCNEWS_com/NoSweatWhenGymClassCut.htm.

Sherwell, Philip. "New DNA Test Offers Parents Chance to Find Children's Sports Gene." Telegraph Media Group Limited, December 6, 2008. http://www.telegraph.co.uk/news/worldnews/northamerica/usa .

Show, Jon. "Basketball Still Tops in Youth Participation." August 17, 2009. *Sports Business Journal* 20. ttp:/h/www.sportsbusinessjournal.com/article/.

Sports Illustrated Website. http://sportsillustrated.cnn.com/.

Stockdale, Charles, and Douglas A. McIntyre. "The 10 industries that pay women the least." April 4, 2011. http://www.dailyfinance.com/2011/04/11/the-10-industries-that-pay-women-the-least/.

STOP Sports Injuries Website. http://www.stopsportsinjuries.org/.

Sweet, Lynn. "Michelle Obama Childhood Obesity Action Plan; Events Around the Nation." *Chicago Sun-Times,* May 11, 2010. http://blogs.suntimes.com/sweeet/2010/05/michelle_obama_unveils_childho.html.

The National Federation of State High School Associations Website. http://www.nfhs.org.

U.S. Department of Education, National Center for Education Statistics (NCES) Website. www.nces.ed.gov.

"Transgender Man Kye Allums Playing NCAA Women's Basketball," San Diego Voice & Viewpoint. http://sdvoice.info/index1.htm.

University of Tennessee Athletic Department Graduation Rates, October 2011. http://www.govolsxtra.com/news/2011/oct/25/uts-graduation-success-rate-up-to-76-percent/?partner=RSS.

University of Tennessee Graduation Rates, 2011. http://senate.utk.edu/files/2011/08/retreat-2011-faculty-senate final-presentation.pdf.

WNBA Fan Clubs Website. www.wnbafanclubs.com/.

Women in Sports Website. http://infoplease.com/spot/womeninsportstimeline.

Women's Parliamentary Radio Website. http://www.wpradio.co.uk/.

America at Work | America at School. http://memory.loc.gov/ammem/awlhtml/awlwork.

Video Recordings

Hewett, T. E., et al. *Cincinnati Sportsmetrics: A Jump Training Program Proven to Prevent Knee Injury.* Cincinnati Sportsmedicine Research & Education Foundation, 1998.

Training Rules. Woman Vision Production, 2009.